George R. Northgraves

Mistakes of Modern Infidels or Evidences of Christianity

Comprising a Complete Refutation of Colonel Ingersoll's so-called Mistakes of Moses and of Objections of Voltaire, Paine, and Others against Christianity

George R. Northgraves

Mistakes of Modern Infidels or Evidences of Christianity
Comprising a Complete Refutation of Colonel Ingersoll's so-called Mistakes of Moses and of Objections of Voltaire, Paine, and Others against Christianity

ISBN/EAN: 9783337259358

Printed in Europe, USA, Canada, Australia, Japan

Cover: Foto ©Lupo / pixelio.de

More available books at **www.hansebooks.com**

MISTAKES

OF

MODERN INFIDELS;

OR

EVIDENCES OF CHRISTIANITY,

COMPRISING A COMPLETE REFUTATION OF COLONEL INGERSOLL'S
SO-CALLED MISTAKES OF MOSES, AND OF OBJECTIONS
OF VOLTAIRE, PAINE, AND OTHERS
AGAINST CHRISTIANITY.

By REV. GEORGE R. NORTHGRAVES,

DIOCESE OF LONDON, ONT., CANADA.

God having spoken on divers occasions, and many ways, in times past, to the fathers by the prophets: last of all, in these days, hath spoken to us, by His Son. *St. Paul to the Hebrews*, 1, 1, 2.

LONDON, CANADA:
CATHOLIC RECORD OFFICE.
1885.

Entered according to Act of the Parliament of Canada in the year 1885,
By REV. GEORGE R. NORTHGRAVES,
In the Office of the Minister of Agriculture

DEDICATION.

TO THE

RIGHT REVEREND JOHN WALSH, D. D.,

BISHOP OF LONDON, ONT., CANADA,

THIS WORK IS RESPECTFULLY DEDICATED, BY PERMISSION, AS A TESTIMONY OF THE HIGH ESTEEM, AFFECTION AND VENERATION ENTERTAINED FOR HIM BY

THE AUTHOR.

LETTER OF APPROBATION

FROM THE RIGHT REVEREND JOHN WALSH, D.D.,

BISHOP OF LONDON, ONT., CANADA.

London, Canada, Dec. 29th, 1884.

Rev. G. R. Northgraves,

REVEREND AND DEAR SIR:

I am glad to know that you have prepared a work in reply to Ingersoll's "Mistakes of Moses," and that it is now ready for publication.

Judging by your known ability and ripe scholarship, I am satisfied that your work will be a thorough and triumphant refutation of the misleading sophisms and specious but superficial objections of the infidel school against the truth of the Christian Religion.

This Religion is the most priceless treasure which this fallen, sin-stained world possesses. It is indeed the light of the world and the salt of the earth—the light of revealed truth for the intellect, the healing salt of heavenly graces for the wounds and corruptions of the heart. It is our pillar of cloud by day, our pillar of fire by night protecting us from the enemies of our salvation and guiding our footsteps through the desert of life towards the promised land. There is no dark problem of life which it has not solved, there are no anxious questionings of the soul for which it has not the most satisfactory answers. Into every Gethsemane of human grief and agony it has entered as an angel of consolation. Veronica like, it has wiped the blood and tears and sweat from the face of suffering humanity. It has cared for the poor, it has fed the hungry, it has clothed the naked, it has visited and consoled the sick, it has sanctified and sublimated human sorrow, it has brought hope and comfort into the darkness of the dungeon, it has freed the slave, it has ennobled and dignified labor, in fine, it found the human race tattered and torn and bleeding by the way-side of the world and like the good Samaritan it has taken it up in its protecting arms, has poured wine and oil into its wounds and has restored it to health and strength.

Those therefore who attack the Christian Religion and strive to weaken its hold on the human intellect and heart are the worst enemies of man's highest interests—are in fact "*hostes humani generis.*"

Now what do the modern apostles of infidelity propose to substitute for the saving truths and the graces and blessings of the Christian Religion? They have no substitutes save doubt, negation, despair, no happiness here and no hopes of happiness hereafter. Can such husks of swine feed the hungry soul or satisfy the infinite longings and cravings of the human heart? Can such things make life tolerable or worth living? Can they reconcile the poor, the sick and the suffering to their hard lot? Can they content the toiling masses with the terrible hardships of their lives ; with the harsh social inequalities that surround them? Says one of the preachers of unbelief—Schopenhauer— "To take away belief in a Divine Providence is to incur one of the most serious and striking losses which are involved in a rejection of Christian and ecclesiastical teaching. Here is the system of things—one huge machine—with its jagged iron wheels ever going round amid a roaring din, its heavy hammers and giant-pistons which ring out a deafening crash as they come down; and man without help or protection looks upon himself and discovers that he is placed in the centre of all the wild commotion: he has no security, not for a single moment that the wheels in some unforeseen movement may not lay hold of him and tear him asunder—that some fall of a hammer may not smash him to atoms in its descent. The sensation of being abandoned, and at the mercy of something else—something which no prayer can reach—is terrible indeed!" Such is the world which the gospel of infidelity and despair would create around us—a world like to that of the abyss and its doomed inhabitants; but it is not God's world in which we live and labor and hope; it is not the world blessed and sanctified by Christianity which presents to us the Eternal God as our Father and Protector, Jesus Christ as our Redeemer and Saviour, which preaches us an Evangel of immortal hopes, which teaches us that this life is but the threshold of an immortal life, is but the passage to an eternal kingdom of happiness, where the poor shall be made rich, where the weak shall become strong, where the aged and decrepit shall renew their youth like the eagle, where the harsh inequalities and terrible hardships of our temporal state must for ever cease, where the man of toil shall rest from his labors, where in fine, "God shall wipe away all tears from their eyes and death shall be no more, nor mourning, nor crying, nor sorrow, shall be any more for the former things shall have passed away." (Apocalypse, xxi, 4.) In view of the momentous issues involved in the questions raised by the infidel school, in view of the nearest and dearest interests of individual man and of society attacked and imperilled by the agents of unbelief—a work like yours which exposes the sophisms of the aforesaid school, which confutes its errors which thoroughly refutes and pulverizes its objections and which triumphantly defends the outworks and the fortress of Christian truth and belief—such a work, I say, is eminently deserving of the favorable recognition and patronage of the public and is sure to receive hearty encouragement and warm welcome from all who love "the faith once delivered to the saints."

Wishing you every blessing,
I am, Reverend and dear Sir,
Very faithfully yours,
✠ JOHN WALSH,
Bishop of London.

CONTENTS.

	PAGE
Letter of Approbation from Rt. Rev. Bishop Walsh	5
Introduction	11

CHAPTER.
1. Liberty and License.— Free- Will.— Col. Ingersoll's Inconsistencies.................................... 13
2. Religious and Political Liberty. — Col. Ingersoll's Sneers at the Clergy.— Indifferentism in Religion.. 21
3. Punishment of Idolatry.—Everlasting Punishment... 30
4. Slavery.. 37
5. Existence of God.................................. 48
6. Refutation of Objections against God's Existence.... 56
7. Creation and Providence........................... 61
8. Necessity of Revelation.— Insufficiency of Unaided Reason.—Spirituality and Immortality of the Soul, 72
9. Necessity of Revelation.— Results of Unaided Reason. — Degrading Rites of Paganism.—Human Sacrifices.— Extermination of the Canaanites......... 78
10. Necessity of Revelation.— Results of Infidelity...... 91
11. Mysteries in Religion 94
12. Possibility of Revelation.— Immediate and Mediate Revelation.— Historical Certitude................ 100
13. Miracles.. 108
14. Prophecy... 115
15. The Fact of Revelation............................ 122
16. Authenticity and Integrity of the Pentateuch.— Septuagint Translation. — Antiquity of Written Language 124
17. Authenticity and Integrity of the Pentateuch.— Testimony of the Later Sacred Writers.............. 135
18. Authenticity and Integrity of the Pentateuch.— Testimony of the Later Scriptures.— Pagan Testimony, 145
19. Authenticity and Integrity of the Pentateuch.— Objections of Messrs. Paine and Ingersoll Refuted.... 150
20. Authenticity and Integrity of the Pentateuch.—Proof from Jewish Festivals........................... 161
21. Authenticity and Integrity of the Pentateuch.— Intrinsic Evidence of its Language................. 165
22. Authenticity and Integrity of the Pentateuch.— Intrinsic Evidence of its Language, continued....... 175
23. Authenticity and Integrity of the Pentateuch.—Testimony of History.— Events in Joseph's Life....... 181
24. Authenticity and Integrity of the Pentateuch.—The Testimony of History, continued................. 189
25. Authenticity and Integrity of the Pentateuch.— The Bondage in Egypt................................ 195

CHAPTER.	PAGE
26. Authenticity and Integrity of the Pentateuch.—The Ten Plagues of Egypt	201
27. The Ten Plagues of Egypt.—Refutation of Objections	211
28. Authenticity and Integrity of the Pentateuch.—Testimony of History, concluded.	221
29. Authenticity and Integrity of the Pentateuch.—The Testimony of Geography	228
30. Truth of the Pentateuch.—Proofs of the Sincerity of Moses	234
31. Truth of the Pentateuch.—Continued	240
32. The Truth of Genesis.—Moses not Deceived, nor a Deceiver.—His Sources of Information	246
33. The Truth of Genesis.—Testimony of Pagan Traditions	252
34. The New Testament.—Its Authenticity and Truth.—Christianity a Divine Religion	260
35. Objections Refuted.—Creation.—The Firmament.—Heaven	268
36. Objections Refuted.—The Creation	275
37. Objections Refuted.—The Creation of Plants and Animals.—The Sun Standing Still.—Chinese Astronomy	286
38. Objections Refuted.—Astronomy.—God not Responsible for the Sins and Errors of Men	294
39. Colonel Ingersoll's Anthropomorphism.—Antiquity of Man.—King Cephren's Date.—The Cave-Men,	299
40. Evolution.—Fabulous Chronology.—Antiquity of Man.—Savagery and Civilization	308
41. The Sabbath.—Account of Creation Consistent.—Origin of Man.—Christian Morality	317
42. The Garden of Eden.—Immortality of the Soul	329
43. The Fall of Man	336
44. The Deluge.—Its Possibility.—The Gathering of the Animals	341
45. Capacity of Noah's Ark.—Pagan Traditions of the Deluge.—Colonel Ingersoll's Blunders.—The Testimony of Geology	348
46. The Origin of Language.—Babel.—Evidences of One Original Tongue	358
47. Christian vs. Infidel Morality: Polygamy: Divorce: Free-Love	373
48. Increase of the Israelites in Egypt.—The Tribe of Dan.—The Number of First-Born Males	380
49. The Flight from Egypt.—The Manna.—Refutation of Miscellaneous Objections.—Religious Ceremonies	394
50. Miscellaneous Objections Refuted.—Ritual Laws.—Flocks and Herds in the Desert	405
51. Miscellaneous Objections Refuted.—Conclusion	415

INTRODUCTION.

THE works of many noted skeptics have of late years attracted greatly the attention of the public in America, especially those of Thomas Paine and Col. Robert G. Ingersoll. Many answers to their arguments have also been published, some of which are very able, and others rather feeble. Especially has the latter writer been already severely handled by such able polemics as Judge Black, and more lately by Rev. Father Lambert and others: still, as far as I am aware, there has not been made as yet any attempt at a complete answer to his book "Some Mistakes of Moses," published in Washington, 1879, which, over his own signature, he declares to be "the only correct edition" of this work. I have long been of opinion that the public are, at present, in need of a hand-book which will answer the most mischievous of modern skeptics' objections against the TRUTH and INSPIRATION of Holy Scripture, and will at the same time furnish a reliable synopsis of the arguments whereby these attributes of Scripture can be maintained. Believers in Christianity who become familiar with such a book will be "ready always to give an answer to every man that asketh a reason of the hope that is in them." Yes, and they will be able to carry the war into the enemy's country, by showing the inconsistencies of Infidelity, and the weakness and dishonesty of the arguments by which Infidels uphold their cause.

It could not be expected that, within the limits of a small book like this, all the proofs of the Truth of the Bible should be compressed. Nevertheless, I hope and believe that enough will be found to confirm the faith of many readers, and to answer at least *all* that Colonel Ingersoll has advanced to impugn it, in the book to which I intend chiefly to devote my attention, his "Some Mistakes of Moses." At the same time, while answering Colonel Ingersoll, many of the difficulties put forth by Paine and Voltaire will be refuted. In fact the gallant Colonel has not been at all scrupulous about using the artillery of those who preceded him in the work of attacking Revelation; for most of his arguments have been taken bodily from old authors, and have been before now ably answered, some of them sixteen hundred years ago.

There are some who are of opinion that such attacks on Religion ought to be treated as unworthy of notice. The writer of this work prefers to coincide with the opinions of those illustrious writers who, in the third and fourth centuries of the Christian Era, thought it useful to answer the objections of Celsus, Porphyry, and Julian, the Apostate. When Infidel objections against Religion are widely circulated, as they are to-day, many souls may be lost through partaking of the poison, unless they have access to the antidote. Besides, it strengthens the faith of sincere Christians to find that the objections so pertinaciously raised by enemies of Religion are capable of being satisfactorily refuted.

MISTAKES OF MODERN INFIDELS.

CHAPTER I.

LIBERTY AND LICENSE.—FREE-WILL.—COLONEL INGERSOLL'S INCONSISTENCIES.

COL. INGERSOLL so mixes up the subjects which he treats, that I find it almost impossible to follow him chapter by chapter without weakening the chain of reasoning which I propose to adopt. As the Colonel is a resolute advocate of Liberty, I presume he will not complain if I take the liberty of answering him systematically, though I may have to bring together portions of his work which are scores of pages apart.

The main object of Mr. Ingersoll's attack on Moses is professedly to proclaim liberty to Men, liberty to his Country, to the Clergy, to the Schools, even to the Politicians. This theme occupies the first four chapters of his work, and in a free country such as both he and I live in, it is certainly a plausible pretext to present before an audience which must be predisposed to listen to anything said in favor of that boon which they have so long and so satisfactorily enjoyed, particularly when its praises are uttered in the choice language which the Colonel knows so well how to employ.

But may not the term *liberty* or *freedom* be used as a cloak for *license*, or immunity from law? It has often been so used; and thus when the talented and intrepid

Madame Roland was led to the scaffold in the name of Liberty, it is well known how she apostrophized the Statue of the Goddess of Liberty, near which the scaffold was erected:

"O Liberty! what crimes are committed in thy name."

We must therefore carefully distinguish between that desirable liberty which is the birthright of man, and that license, that freedom from lawful authority, which opens the door to the commission of crime.

Liberty is of various kinds. The first of which I shall speak is that liberty of the human soul which is called Free-will. There are two ways in which we may conceive that we would not possess Free-will: 1st, if the acts of our will were determined by some extrinsic force: 2ndly, if the acts of the will were caused by an inevitable intrinsic force, or necessity.

It is conceded by all that the act of our will is not controlled by an extrinsic force. The members of our body may be acted upon by such a force so that the inclination of our will be not obeyed by them, but the inclination of the will is intrinsic to it and no outside power can control it.

Fatalists, however, maintain that our will is subject to an intrinsic determination which it necessarily obeys. Materialists who maintain that man is merely a material organization, and that the acts of the human mind are the necessary results of our organization, actually destroy Free-will though they proclaim it in words.

Free-will consists in the faculty of choosing. By this faculty we can choose between action and inaction, between one act and another, between good and evil. If we possessed not this faculty it would be vain to enact laws: it would be impossible to obey them. It would be useless to exhort or command us, for we would have no power to give our consent. We would be equally undeserving of praise or censure, rewards or punishment. These consequences of Fatalism and Materialism are repudiated by all mankind: for every one feels in himself his freedom of will, and knows when he exercises it. We are fully conscious that certain acts which we have done are the result of our choice, and if the result has been beneficial we resolve to act again in the same way. If the result has not been according to our desire, we propose to act differently in future.

Every human being possesses the inward consciousness of Free-will. We know by our inward consciousness that we exist, think, judge, feel, love, hate, will, rejoice, and grieve. By the same inward consciousness we know that by some power existing in us, and coming from us, we can and do reflect and meditate, acquire knowledge and even move our body. If this testimony of our interior sense be false or doubtful, there can be no certitude whatever. This principle within us possesses, therefore, a true activity and is the cause, not the mere occasion or instrument of our acts. The existence of this principle is the foundation of moral order, and the principle itself we denominate the human soul. It is this principle which is free. Christianity bases on this freedom of our soul, her whole moral code. It is the foundation of merit and demerit. Without it, there could not be either free thought, a free press, free men or free women, which Col. Ingersoll declares to be so desirable. Yet with strange inconsistency the Colonel endeavors to excite horror and indignation against God for having bequeathed this liberty to man! He arraigns Almighty God for having conferred upon His creatures that liberty concerning which he himself says "until the clergy are free they cannot be intellectually honest." (P. 24.)

God made man capable of knowing and serving Him on earth, or of repudiating and disobeying Him. By exercising this freedom, some have become like angels in virtue, others have plunged into demoniacal vices. Yet this freedom, this power of doing evil is a means by which the merits and rewards of the virtuous are augmented.

"He that could have transgressed, and hath not transgressed, could do evil things and hath not done them. Therefore are his goods established in the Lord." Ecclus. xxxi, 10, 11.

It is undoubtedly an impenetrable mystery, why a God who is infinitely good should tolerate the existence of moral evil, sin, whereas we know that His infinite power could prevent it; but we may well conceive that as the elimination of the liberty we possess from the human soul would deprive man of an important means of merit, that it is better that, for the sake of those who will make good use of it, God should give us that liberty, even though He knows that many will abuse it, and that He in His justice will punish such abuse.

Hence Col. Ingersoll's interrogatories from page 140 to 143 are as absurd as they are irreverent. I cull from them the following:

"Of course God knew when he made man, that he would afterwards regret it. He knew that the people would grow worse and worse, until destruction would be the only remedy. He knew that he would have to kill all except Noah and his family...... Why did he fill the world with his own children, knowing that he would have to destroy them?.... It is hard to see why God did not civilize these people. He certainly had the power to use, and the wisdom to devise the proper means. What right has a God to fill the world with fiends? Can there be goodness in this? Why should he make experiments that he knows must fail? Is there any wisdom in this?"

I may add that Mr. Ingersoll grossly misrepresents the case when he asserts that God filled the world with fiends. God made man sinless, and for a noble purpose, for an end more sublime than all his other creatures, angels excepted, and he gave to man, even after the original fall, all the graces needed to enable him to persevere in virtue. Man's own perversity was the cause of his fall.

Such is the Christian theory, which Col. Ingersoll should have refuted if he desired to overthrow Christianity; but instead of this he sets up a man of straw of his own manufacture, and he amuses himself by pulling it to pieces.

The next conundrum which he puts forward so pompously (page 142), is therefore for himself to answer:

"What right has a man to charge an infinite being with wickedness and folly?"

Surely he who does this is guilty himself of wickedness and folly, blasphemy and presumption. I leave to a discerning public to decide whether Mr. Ingersoll has not left himself open to the charge. The Christian does not.

We have seen, as a specimen of the Colonel's inconsistencies, that he regards liberty as the basis of honesty, yet he arraigns our Creator for having imparted it to man. A third position which he takes is irreconcilable with either of the others. He maintains that God did not create the world. The universe is the result of the operation of natural causes.

"The statement that in the beginning God created the heaven and the earth, I cannot accept. It is contrary to my reason, and I cannot believe it. . . . . . . To conceive of matter without force, or of force without matter, or of a time when neither existed, or of a being who existed for an eternity without either, and who out of nothing created both, is to me utterly impossible." (P. 60.)

It is therefore clear that the Colonel believes only in the existence of matter, which is the only principle of force. Our souls, therefore, if we have souls, are merely organized matter, according to him.

This is stated in another form on page 86, where he puts the doctrine of Evolution among the demonstrated results of scientific investigation. On page 88 he is somewhat more moderate, as the same doctrine is merely put forward as the more probable opinion. On page 57, however, he endeavors to prove Creation absurd, and on page 85 he declares that life was evolved from monad up to man during millions of ages.

What are these monads? They are supposed to be the ultimate atoms, the primary constituents of matter. Following up the Colonel's theory, by their agglomeration, man must have been evolved. But have these monads the faculty of choice? Have they Free-will? A mountain of granite has also been formed from monads, and the ultimate constituents of a steam-engine are monads also. Does Colonel Ingersoll claim intellectual freedom for these? The truth is, the materialist entirely destroys the freedom of the soul, for freedom cannot be a faculty of any aggregation of material monads.

With his inconsistencies in his treatise on liberty, the Colonel appears somewhat as Junius is described by Byron in his "Vision of Judgment." I make a slight alteration to suit the application:

"The moment that you had pronounced him one,
    Presto! his face is changed, and he was another;
And when that change was hardly well put on,
    It varied till I don't think his own mother
(If that he had a mother) would her son
    Have known, he shifted so from one to t' other;
Till guessing from a pleasure grew a task
At this great lecture-making "Iron Mask."

I've an hypothesis—'tis quite my own;
    I never let it out till now for fear
Of doing people harm. . . .
    It is—my gentle public, lend thine ear!
'Tis that what *Ingersoll* we are wont to call
Was *really, truly*, nobody at all.

It is evident from the reasons we have given that the soul of man possesses Free-will. This doctrine is inculcated by Christianity. It is also taught by Moses, as will be seen by reading the 30th chapter of Deuteronomy, and especially by the 19th verse: "I have set before you life and death, blessing and cursing; therefore choose life that both you and your seed may live." In regard to human liberty, then, Moses is right, and so is Christianity. Col. INGERSOLL and other materialists ARE MISTAKEN.

While treating of the co-existence of moral evil

with God's infinite power and wisdom, I have said this is an impenetrable mystery; nevertheless I have given a reason why it may be better so. Col. Ingersoll rejects all mystery:

"I do insist that a statement that cannot possibly be comprehended by any human being, and that *appears* utterly impossible, repugnant to every fact of experience, and contrary to everything that we really know, must be rejected by every honest man." (P. 57.)

This statement is very loose. I will prove hereafter, when treating of mysteries in religion, that we may reasonably expect mysteries when we contemplate the truths which relate to God. For the present I need only show the fallacy of the Colonel's reasoning as applied to the case under consideration. The existence of sin is a fact. The existence of God is not denied squarely by Colonel Ingersoll. The co-existence of the two, therefore, is admitted as possible. It is neither "repugnant to experience," nor to "everything we really know." It may *appear* to be impossible when the apparent incongruity is first presented to our mind, but, as I have already shown, the incongruity is but *apparent*, not *real.*

Were you to inform a wealthy lady in a ball-room that the magnificent jewels that encircle her neck and wrists, and by their brilliancy astound the beholders, are merely charcoal or lamp-black, she would be indignant at the assertion, unless she were somewhat acquainted with chemistry. Indeed, unless she were very well versed in that science, she would, even then, know only by the authority of others that you had spoken the truth. Here, then, what appears utterly impossible is the truth. Moreover, though scientists have discovered that these substances, with properties so opposite, are identical, no one has yet been able to comprehend how the same atoms or monads which compose the latter substances can be so arranged as to produce a diamond.

Here we have a fact which "cannot possibly be comprehended by any human being," at least in the present condition of science, and which, in all probability never will be understood. Yet such a fact "must be rejected by every honest man," according to Colonel Ingersoll.

It is evident that there are even in Nature truths above human understanding. It is therefore bad reasoning to assert that a doctrine must be rejected because it is incomprehensible. Indeed, we need only oppose to this position of Mr. Ingersoll his own confession:

"I do not pretend to tell how all these things really are." (P. 57.)

He is speaking here of the existence of the universe. The existence of the universe is, however, a fact. He therefore acknowledges that mysteries are to be believed, in the same breath with which he repudiates them all.

CHAPTER II.

RELIGIOUS AND POLITICAL LIBERTY.—COLONEL INGERSOLL'S SNEERS AT THE CLERGY.—INDIFFERENTISM IN RELIGION.

WE have next to consider the nature of the Intellectual liberty which Mr. Ingersoll claims. He declares he wishes "to free the orthodox clergy."

(P. 16.) From what? From the obligation of teaching what they believe God has taught.

"They are not employed to give their thoughts, but simply to repeat the ideas of others." (P. 17.)

For the purpose of throwing ridicule upon the belief that we are bound to adhere to revealed doctrines he misrepresents them thus:

"The wicked get all their good things in this life, and the good all their evil, ... no matter how absurd these things may appear to the carnal mind they must be preached and they must be believed. If they were reasonable there would be no virtue in believing," etc. (P. 18.)

The clergy must "attack all modern thought, point out the dangers of science," . . . . must "show that virtue rests on ignorance and faith, while vice impudently feeds and fattens upon fact and demonstration." (P. 22.)

"The scheme of salvation is absurd. . . . . If the people were a little more ignorant, astrology would flourish — if a little more enlightened, religion would perish." (P. 25.)

The clergy must show "the wickedness of philosophy, ... the immorality of science." (P. 19.)

As to the assertion, "they are expected to point out the dangers of freedom, the safety of implicit obedience" (p. 19), much depends upon what is meant by freedom, and to whom implicit obedience is to be paid. If by freedom we are to understand immunity from all law, certainly freedom is dangerous; yet this is precisely the freedom which the Colonel demands throughout his book. If by implicit obedience is meant obedience to the Supreme Ruler of the Universe, such obedience is certainly safe, and is a duty resting on mankind.

The misrepresentations of Christian doctrines are not confirmed by any proofs. They rest on Mr. Ingersoll's mere assertion. They therefore require no refutation. I deny that Christianity teaches what is contrary to reason. I deny that Christianity teaches that virtue rests on ignorance or that science is immoral. On the contrary, we are called upon by the great Apostle of the Gentiles (Rom. xii, 1,) to present to God our "reasonable service." The service of God is reasonable, because he is the Creator, the Master, the Father of all. "The son honoreth the father and the servant his master; if then I be a father, where is my honor? and if I be a master, where is my fear? saith the Lord of Hosts." (Mal. i, 6.)

I find then that Col. Ingersoll in his book, and indeed in many of his lectures, maintains:

1. That whether God exists or not, it is of no importance to us to pay him homage: and that even in the hypothesis that God has revealed our duties in the Bible or otherwise, we are not bound to accept his revelation.

2. That neither God nor man has a right to punish those who believe or teach error. (Pp. 32 to 34, 258.)

3. That slavery is essentially wicked, as tolerated in Scripture. (P. 245.)

4. That Christianity has been the great persecutor against those who freely expressed their opinions. The persecuting spirit of Infidelity will be seen from the 10th chapter of this work.

To the consideration of the rest of these teachings I will devote the remainder of this chapter.

Mr. Ingersoll says:

"A belief in one God is claimed to be a dogma of almost infinite importance, ... for my part I think it infinitely more important to believe in man. Theology is a superstition, Humanity a religion." (P. 244.)

"Certainly all cannot be right; and as it would require a life-time to investigate the claims of these various systems, it is hardly fair to damn a man forever simply because he happens to believe the wrong one." (P. 39.)

"All worship is necessarily based upon the belief that some being exists who can, if he will, change the natural order of events." (P. 49.)

All kinds of worship "are the offspring of error." (P. 49.)

Running through the above extracts we find the following errors:

First, that God cannot change the natural order of events: that is to say, that miracles are impossible.

Secondly, that want of faith in God ought not to entail everlasting punishment.

Thirdly, that worship is not due to God.

Fourthly, that Religion is a matter of little or no importance.

Other errors there are in these passages; but they need not be pointed out here as they will be dealt with in their proper place. Even I will here only deal with the last two errors which I have pointed out. The other two will be treated respectively in chapters 13 and 3.

And here I will stay a moment to hurl back a sneer which the brave soldier thinks proper to fling at Christianity in this connection. He says:

"Nearly all these religions are intensely selfish.

.... In the olden time these theological people who quartered themselves upon the honest and industrious, were called soothsayers, seers, charmers, prophets, enchanters, sorcerers, wizards, astrologers and impostors, but now they are known as clergymen." (P. 40.)

Whether Christianity or Ingersollism be the selfish religion, we may judge from the second extract given above. He here puts forward as a plea for indifference to religion, the suggestion that there really will be no punishment for neglect: "It is hardly fair to damn a man forever simply because he happens to believe the wrong" religion. There is here no thought of self, forsooth! It reminds me of a couple of horse thieves in the West who were sent by their gang to a certain farmer's enclosure to ply their vocation. On their return, when questioned why they had no horses, they answered that conscientious scruples had prevented them for carrying out their design. When their comrades indignantly demanded what conscience had to do with them, the unsuccessful hunters said : " Oh ! we received information that a detachment of the vigilance committee were expecting such a raid and were ready to hang us on the nearest tree, so we thought it more honorable to leave the horses to their owner, under the circumstances." This is Colonel Ingersoll's idea of unselfishness.

The sneer at the Christian clergy needs no reply. The writer of this is a Priest of the Catholic Church, and believes that *She* alone presents truly the doctrines of Christianity. He cannot therefore claim to speak for the clergy of other denominations. However, I doubt if among those who professedly propagate Christianity, there is any class who have sunk so low as the Infidel High-Priests, the New-York propagandists of Infidelity, whose bare-faced propagandism also of immorality, obliged the United States government to step in to arrest their proceedings. Neither is it seemly on the part of Colonel Ingersoll to accuse the "theological people" of mercenary motives, as if this humanitarian gentleman, for so it seems he would wish to be styled, "quartered" not himself upon many honest and industrious people when he delivered his lectures, whether at the rate of $25,000 per annum, or 50 cents a head for admission.

But is the character of the clergy, as Colonel Ingersoll has painted it, correct? He describes them as charmers, impostors, etc., who have taken to their office for sake of lucre. I do not deny that there have been sad cases of depravity among the priesthood, that from time to time there have been great scandals, the consequences of which have been deplorable. But does this show universal corruption? Are we to judge *all* by the wickedness of comparatively few, especially as we know that the abuses were always condemned by the Supreme authority of the Church? Is there nothing to admire in the noble fortitude and zeal of hundreds of thousands of holy priests who were martyred for the truth during the first three centuries of the Christian era? Is there to be only censure for the clergy of the 11th century to whom, chiefly, was due the peaceful revolution known as the "Truce of God," by means of which the barbarous character of war was permanently changed so as to be waged thereafter, more in accordance with the laws of humanity and religion? Was it for the sake of lucre that in the 13th century the friars taught patience to the oppressed serfs of Europe by their own example of voluntary poverty? Is it for earthly gain that at this day so many of the clergy, animated by missionary zeal, devote themselves to carry the knowledge of the gospel to China, Japan, India, Algeria, Patagonia, and the Indians of North America? Were the hospitals and orphan asylums and schools, instituted and supported mainly by the unremitting efforts of the clergy in Colonel Ingersoll's own city of Peoria, as well as in other cities of this continent, the work of mere sorcerers, enchanters and impostors seeking only for self-aggrandizement? On the title-page of his book, Mr. Ingersoll claims to be a benefactor of the world on the plea that he is destroying weeds, thistles, etc. He acknowledges that he is sowing no grain. Well, I think the people of America of good sense would prefer such thistles as many of the clergy have sown and would let their professing benefactor go to Heligoland or anywhere he likes, providing they will never hear from him again.

It is a fact well-known, and I believe it is true of the Protestant as well as of the Catholic clergy, that they are not, as a body, working for lucre's sake. If this were so, they made a great mistake in becoming clergymen, for usually the clergy receive very small pay for the amount of work they do, in comparison with professional men or even tradesmen. Yet as a class they are superior both in learning and morals, probably to any other class in the community. Wicked or scandalous conduct on the part of clergymen, attracts great notice, and is talked of by everyone, precisely because such conduct is rare, while similar conduct by people in other professions is passed over without notice or comment. Mr. Ingersoll's insinuations are as slanderous as they are malicious.

Let us now consider Colonel Ingersoll's position that Religion is of no importance: that we can afford to be indifferent whether religion be true or false.

In the first place it is a question of truth, eternal truth. Col. Ingersoll himself says:

"Let us dedicate them (our schools) to the science of eternal truth. Let us tell every teacher to ascertain all the facts he can—to give us light, to follow Nature, no matter where she leads," etc. (P. 28.)

The discovery of Truth, then, is a matter of vast importance. In this the Christian perfectly agrees with Mr. Ingersoll, who very eloquently expatiates on the grandeur of this subject. I do not deny, I acknowledge that the Colonel is really a fluent speaker and writer, and in some respects a very able man. He is not, however, a reasoner, at least in his theological writings. He may be more skilful as a lawyer.

The Colonel, then, frequently sounds the praises of science as the means whereby human happiness is to be attained, because science teaches truth. But indifference to Religion is indifference to truth. It therefore betokens weakness of intellect, mental imbecility. Why does the Colonel recommend it? But more: Indifference to Religion exposes man to God's anger. It is an insult offered to God, and surely God will punish it, as surely as He is just. God must be the essence of Truth, Infinite Truth. If we refuse his Revelation, or if we are indifferent to it, we virtually accuse God of falsehood. God, from His very nature, cannot be equally pleased with those who accept and those who reject His teaching. Now, religion teaches that He rewards those who believe and put into practice His teaching, while He punishes those who disregard it. The stake is great. Truth, Duty and Interest, the great motives which govern human actions, combine in adjuring us not to be indifferent in so important a matter as our eternal welfare. Indifference in Religion is, therefore, both a crime and a folly. The intellectual freedom, then, which Colonel Ingersoll claims, and which he explains to mean Indifference to Religion and Revelation, is both unsafe, unphilosophical and criminal. Intellectual freedom in matters which do not concern morality, that is to say our moral relations to God, our neighbors and ourselves, is quite legitimate: but let not intellectual freedom become license, immunity from the laws of God and man, for then neither God nor man can tolerate it.

There is, at least, good reason to suppose that God has made a Revelation to man, wherein He discloses the manner in which He wishes to be honored. A vast portion of mankind asserts that this is the case. Then it is evidently our duty and interest to discover this, instead of inventing a new religion, such as Mr. Ingersoll's religion of "Humanity." The Revelation of God, when known, will no doubt tell us more about the right religion of Humanity, than all the cleverest human Religion-Makers can tell.

But the Colonel objects: it is too much trouble to investigate the claims of this Revelation. I answer, first, be the trouble what it may, there is no more important matter to occupy our attention. We labor all our lives to secure worldly comfort. Why not devote some part of our time to the securing of everlasting happiness? Secondly. The trouble is not so great, perhaps, as the Colonel represents it to be. When the inquiry is made with the proper disposition of submission to the divine law, there is no doubt God Himself will facilitate the matter. "Seek ye the Lord, while He may be found; call upon Him while He is NEAR." (Is. lv., 6.) If it be possible that you fail *after taking* the proper trouble, be sure God will not hold you guilty for your failure.

CHAPTER III.

PUNISHMENT OF IDOLATRY.—EVERLASTING PUNISHMENT.

The next position which we have to consider is whether God or man has a right to punish believers in or teachers of error. Col. Ingersoll reproaches God thus:

"This God was not willing that the Jews should think and investigate for themselves. For heresy the penalty was death .... Intellectual liberty was unknown .... He demanded worship on pain of sword and fire; acting as spy, inquisitor, judge and executioner." (P. 257.)

This is repeated under so many forms that it becomes nauseous and it would be shocking to repeat it as the changes are rung on it. I have already shown that the intellectual liberty here claimed is the right to disobey and dishonor God, and that God cannot tolerate it. The right of God to punish even internal acts of our soul which are sinful, being contrary to His law, cannot be denied, as He is the Supreme Master of the Universe. He has given to us indeed Free-will, but under the injunction that we shall use it in subjection to His laws. If we disobey we must be liable to punishment. The reasonableness of this has been already proved. Indeed Mr. Ingersoll himself has acknowledged that laws are necessary, and that men have the right to impose them.

"Laws spring from the instinct of self-preservation . . . . It is impossible for human beings to exist together without certain rules of conduct, certain ideas of the proper or improper, of the right and wrong, growing out of the relation. ' Certain rules must be made and must be enforced. This implies` law trial and punishment." (P. 235.)

Surely it is a subversion of order to give man a right of controlling his fellow man by law and fear of punishment, yet to refuse it to God. On the Colonel's own principle that we must reject what is incomprehensible, and evidently absurd, every honest man should reject his conclusions. Indeed man cannot have such a right, unless it comes to him from God, for on the hypothesis that there is a God, the whole government of the Universe must be under His control and we have a perfect right in answering Mr. Ingersoll to assume God's existence, for he pretends that his arguments on this subject are valid on this assumption. He professes with this assumption to prove Christianity absurd.

But the Colonel lays special stress upon the fact that God punishes everlastingly. If it is reconcilable with God's goodness, that He punish at all, there is no inconsistency with His goodness that punishment be everlasting. The matter depends altogether on the enormity of the sin. Now since sin consists in disobeying and turning away from God who is the Infinite Good, its enormity being proportioned to its object, deserves everlasting punishment; and such punishment must be inflicted, unless it be either freely pardoned or sufficiently atoned for. Now God cannot be obliged to pardon freely, from the very fact that such pardon is a free act; nor can man sufficiently atone for his sin in the next life, since he is no longer in the state of probation, and he is therefore incapable of atoning. There is, therefore, in the doctrine of everlasting punishment, nothing against reason.

We may now pass to the question whether man may punish his fellow man for believing and teaching error. Certainly from himself as man, no one can derive any right whatsoever over his fellow man: for as men merely, they are equal in the possession of a common humanity, and as individuals they are independent of each other, as long as there is no encroachment made on each other's rights. But if it can be shown that God has at any time delegated to men authority to punish, it cannot be doubted that such men must possess this authority. Thus it is that legislators claim the right to punish not only such acts as murder and theft, but also the dissemination of political opinions supposed to sap the basis of the constitution of a country. An effort to weaken the allegiance of subjects to the government of the country would, especially in critical periods, as in time of war, even be punished with death. High treason is amenable to a similar penalty.

To come now to the particular cases spoken of by Mr. Ingersoll, Christian States, or States called Christian have frequently made laws to punish those who have persistently promulgated by overt acts, doctrines opposed to those generally received: especially when those overt acts have been subversive of public morals and detrimental to the public welfare. With these laws we have no concern here as they have no connection with our subject. We have to deal with the laws God established among the Jews.

Under the old law it was enacted that Idolaters among the Israelites should be slain, and also those who enticed others to Idolatry. (Deut. xiii.) Hereupon Col. Ingersoll draws a harrowing picture:

"If my wife, the mother of my children had said to me, 'I am tired of Jehovah, he is always asking for blood; he is never weary of killing; he is always telling of his might and strength; always telling what he has done for the Jews; always asking for sacrifices; for doves and lambs—blood, nothing but blood. Let us worship the sun. Jehovah is too revengeful, too malignant, too exacting. Let us worship the sun. The sun has clothed the world in beauty; it has covered the earth with flowers; by its divine light I first saw your face and my beautiful babe.' If I had obeyed the command of God, I would have killed her. . . . . . . For my part I would never kill my wife, even if commanded to do so by the real God of this universe." (P. 258.)

It is true, the death sentence is a severe one; still the world has not yet found it advisable to abolish it from the penal code. There are a few, comparatively very few, advocates for the total abolition of capital punishment. The great bulk of mankind still believe that it is advisable to retain such punishments on the statute books, in order to control evil-doers the more effectually. I do not propose to discuss which of these opinions is to be preferred. It is sufficient that the common sense of mankind agrees that there are cases when capital punishment may be inflicted; nay, that there are occasions when it is expedient to inflict it. Now we must remember that the Mosaic legislation was intended for men who had Free-will and passions; men prone to all the temptations, and having all the tendency to evil, to which men are subjected to-day. Even considering the state of slavery from which they had just emerged, the gross immorality, idolatry, and barbarism into which their Egyptian masters were sunken, and which to a great extent must have corrupted many of the Israelites on account of the intercommunication of the two nations, stern laws were more needed for the restraint of the people than they would be to-day among a people who have been progressing in refinement and civilization for centuries under the elevating influence of the Christian religion. Yes, I say the Christian religion, for to Christianity we owe the emergence of our ancestors from barbarism.

It may be said, "this might justify the infliction of the death penalty upon murderers and thieves, but not upon idolaters, whose only fault was against religion." The nature of the Jewish law must be borne in mind. The form of government of the Jews was a theocracy. God was their king. Moses was their governor and judge. Their form of government differed from that of all other nations, for " what nation is there upon earth as thy people Israel, whom God went to redeem for a people to himself, and to make him a name, and to do for them great and terrible things?" (2 Kings, vii., 23. Prot. Bible, 2 Samuel.) God expressly declares that he himself occupied the kingly office, and when in the old age of Samuel, the people desired a king, God said "they have not rejected thee, but me, that I should not reign over them." (1 Kings viii., 7. Prot. Bible, 1 Sam.)

From all this, it follows that those who were guilty of Idolatry, were not only false to God, but also to their actual king and country. They were guilty of High-Treason as well as Idolatry. The necessity of having a stern law against this crime is evident from the frequency with which the people actually fell into Idolatry both before and after the law was promulgated. After all, the law was not always carried out strictly. Idolatry was frequently punished with death: sometimes the nation was allowed by God to be subdued by their enemies on account of it, but always, on their repentance, God showed mercy to them, and manifested his mercy by restoring them to even temporal prosperity. He exercised the pardoning prerogative of the Sovereign. Thus even when they had served "Baalim and Astaroth and the gods of Syria and of Sidon and of Moab and of the children of Ammon and of the Philistines," when they "cast away the strange gods . . . . He was touched with their miseries" and raised up Jephtha for their deliverance. (Judges x.) Thus was His stern justice tempered with the most tender mercy. And after all, during the whole period which lapsed between the promulgation of the law and the appointment of King Saul, three hundred and thirty-nine years, we do not read that ever Colonel Ingersoll's harrowing picture had its original a fact. We do not find proof, that any Israelite was required to make his "dimpled babe," (Col. Ingersoll has a peculiar affection for babes that are dimpled,) motherless, by his own hand. In fact it does not seem that this was really required by the law, except under very extraordinary circumstances. The nearest relative, even the husband or the father was required to inform the proper authorities upon, not the tempter, but the enticer, that is the persisting tempter to Idolatry, and if necessary to cast the first stone after he or she had been legally condemned to execution. The public good was placed before private affection. It was one of the cases which will occur from time to time, that he who is bound to see the law enforced, may have to enforce it, even when the duty is disagreeable.

We read in Roman History that after the expulsion of Tarquin the Proud, Junius Brutus the Consul was required to try a number of young men, who had formed a conspiracy for the tyrant's restoration, amongst whom were his own two sons. Few situations could be more affecting and difficult than that of father and judge. Justice impelled him to condemn, nature, to spare the children he loved.

Being brought to trial before him, they were condemned to be beheaded in his presence, while he looked on with unaltered countenance. It has been beautifully said: "he ceased to be a father that he might execute the duties of the consul, and chose to live bereft of his children rather than to neglect the public punishment of crime."

As Col. Ingersoll has informed us that under similar circumstances he would not have fulfilled the public duty, perhaps he people of Illinois acted wisely in not accepting his proffered services in the Supreme Magistracy of their State.

Among the Jews, the extreme case of which we are

speaking, could not have occurred very frequently; but when it did occur, I presume it had to be met with courage.

CHAPTER IV.
SLAVERY.

We now come to the question of Slavery as permitted under the Old Law.

The following passages will show the law of slavery as it existed under the Mosaic dispensation.

"If thy brother, constrained by poverty sell himself to thee, thou shalt not oppress him with the service of bond-servants; but he shall be as a hireling and a sojourner: he shall work with thee until the year of the jubilee. And afterwards he shall go out with his children, and shall return to his kindred and to the possession of his fathers. For they are my servants, and I brought them out of the land of Egypt; let them not be sold as bondmen."

"Let your bondmen and your bondwomen be of the nations that are round about you. And of the strangers that sojourn among you, or that were born of them in your land, these you shall have for servants: and by right of inheritance shall leave them to your posterity, and shall possess them forever. But oppress not your brethren the children of Israel by might."

"If the hand of a stranger or a sojourner grow strong among you, and thy brother being impoverished sell himself to him or to any of his race, after the sale he may be redeemed." Any of his brethren shall redeem him. . . . . . But if he himself be able also he shall redeem himself." (Lev. xxv, 39, 49.)

It is then provided that such servitude shall end with the year of jubilee; but if the redemption take place before that year, the master shall be re-imbursed according to the period of redemption.

A further passage regards the bondage of Jews:

"If thou buy a Hebrew servant six years shall he serve thee; in the seventh he shall go out free for nothing. With what raiment he came in, with the like," let him go out. (Ex. xxi, 2, 3.)

The conditions under which a married man may be manumitted are then detailed. If his wife entered the service with him she is manumitted with him. If the wife was already in perpetual bondage, she and the children remain with the master. If the servant desire to remain in bondage with his family, his bondage shall be made perpetual and his ear shall be bored with an awl as a mark thereof.

Fathers cannot sell their daughters into bondage, but can dispose of their service, and their treatment with proper respect is provided for.

Several crimes are then enumerated which shall be punished with death. Among them:

"He that shall steal a man, and sell him, being convicted of the guilt, shall be put to death."

"He that striketh his bondman or bondwoman with a rod, and they die under his hands, shall be guilty of the crime. But if the party remain alive a day or two, he shall not be subject to the punishment, because it is his money." (Exod. xxi.)

From the above extracts it will be seen how different was slavery among the Jews from that which prevailed in all nations, not enlightened by Revelation from God. The Christian view of slavery is the development of the Jewish view, with due regard to the different circumstances of the human race at the time of Moses, and during the Christian era. Under Christianity, St. Paul tells u

"Be not held again under the yoke of bondage." (Gal. v, 1.)

The yoke of bondage here referred to is the yoke of Paganism or Infidelity. Even Judaism is a yoke of bondage in comparison with Christianity. The Infidel theory of Free thought is really a slavery to our passions.

"You have not received the spirit of bondage again in fear; but you have received the spirit of adoption of sons." (Rom. viii, 15.)

God's love manifested in the mysteries of Christ's life on earth gives a true freedom which makes us indeed servants and children of God, but delivers us from the slavery of sin and enables us to resist the temptations which from within and without ourselves, entice us to sin.

"There is neither Jew nor Greek: there is neither bond nor free, ... for you are all one in Christ Jesus." (Gal. iii, 28.)

"But Christ is all in all." (Coll. iii, 11.)

All distinctions of nationality and condition in life are merged in the character of God's children. Christians must regard each other as equal, as members of Christ's mystical body. They must love one another.

"There shall be lying teachers among you, ... for speaking swelling words of vanity, they allure (you) in desires of the flesh, of riotousness, promising (you) liberty, when they themselves are slaves of corruption: for by whom a man is overcome of the same also he is the slave. . . . . . The dog is returned to his own vomit; and the sow that was washed to her wallowing in the mire." (2 Peter ii, 1, 18 to 22.)

That is to say, under pretence of liberty, Freethinkers will entice you to libertinism. They are slaves of corruption, for they acknowledge no control but that of their own desires, hence bereft of God's grace they devote themselves to corruption and are its slaves, as the sow wallowing in the mire, etc.

"Wast thou called, being a bondman? care not for it: but if thou mayest be made free, use it rather. For he that is called in the Lord being a bondman is the freeman of the Lord. Likewise he that is called being free, is the bondman of Christ." (1 Cor. vii, 21, 22.)

That is: be not troubled if you are in a state of servitude. Even the slave who becomes a Christian is made the Lord's freeman: freed from moral slavery. The freeman on becoming a Christian is Christ's bondman, bound to obey his law.

Servants, bondmen if you will, are therefore exhorted (Eph. vi.) to obey their masters with fear and trembling, that is with due respect . . . . with a good will doing service."

This exhortation is given that they may profit by the position they are in to acquire the grace of God by their patience. In all this there is no justification for the inhuman treatment of slaves, such as takes place in most slave-holding countries; but we may infer that there are circumstances in which *slaveholding* is justifiable, while *slave-trading* or the abduction of freemen into slavery is as unjust as any other species of robbery. Slave-holding may possibly be lawful, for example, when a man, condemned to death accepts slavery as a lesser evil, or when a man sells his liberty for some benefit which he could not otherwise obtain. Hence the Apostle, while not justifying the slavery which existed so generally at that time does not make a general condemnation against it. He contents himself with commanding masters to deal kindly with their slaves.

"Masters . . . forbear threatenings. Knowing that the Lord both of them (slaves and servants) and of you is in heaven; and there is no respect of persons with Him." (Eph. vi., 9.)

"Masters, do to your servants that which is just and equal: knowing that you also have a master in heaven." (Coll. iv., 1.)

Hence also when the slave Onesimus, having robbed his master Philemon, was converted to Christianity, the same Apostle sent him back.

"Not now as a servant, but . . . . a most dear brother." (Philemon, verse 16.)

"Trusting in thy obedience, I have written to thee; knowing that thou wilt also do more than I say." (21.)

In the face of all this Col. Ingersoll says:

"The New Testament is more decidedly in favor of human slavery than the old." (P. 249.)

If this be so then the Old Testament slavery must be a very moderate one. We have seen that the New Testament rather regulates the manner in which slaves should be treated, than justifies the tenure by which slaves were held, or the laws by which they were governed. It is true, the Abolition party in the United States would go much further, and to their prejudices Col. Ingersoll appeals against Christianity. In one respect the above extracts of the

New Testament are not necessarily opposed to the views of moderate Abolitionists, for it nowhere speaks of slavery as an expedient institution. At all events, modified by the rules laid down by the Apostles, slavery becomes humane, and is little more than a lengthened term of service.

It is now to be remarked that Col. Ingersoll, in vilifying the form of slavery laid down in the Old Testament, makes no effort to prove slavery evil, under all circumstances. We are to take this for granted on his word. He says:

"Do you believe that the loving Father of us all, turned the *dimpled* arms of babes into manacles of iron?" etc. (P. 247.)

"For my part I never will, I never can worship a God who upholds the institution of slavery." (P. 249)

And he falsifies the law by endeavoring to make it appear that the stealing of men, babes, and women was permitted; also their whipping without cause.

"Were the stealers and whippers of babes and women the justified children of God?" (P. 248.)

We have seen above that the man-stealer was condemned to death (Ex. xxi, 16,) and that he who whipped a slave to death was held guilty of murder. (See also Deut. xxiv, 7.) If, however, he survived a day or two, the presumption was that the death was accidental rather than intentional, and as *manslaughter* is not now punished as *murder*, neither was the master held guilty of murder in this case. The slave was called his master's money, because he was really money's worth to him. (Ex. xxi, 21.)

From Deuteronomy xxiii, 15, it will be seen that a slave fleeing from his master on account of ill usage was not to be delivered back to him, and he to whom the slave fled was commanded not to oppress him. This does not look like the brutal slave system which obtained in other countries, and which even flourished in modern times. Against the brutal slavery which reduces man to the level of the beast, I believe every true Christian would protest. For such slavery as this there is no warrant in Holy Scripture.

On reading carefully the passages from Exodus and Leviticus, above quoted, it will be seen that the bondage of the Hebrew was expressly declared to be only that of the hireling, or one employed for wages, except when he sold his labor to his master, in which case his bondage, similar in kind, was extended till the year of jubilee. Then, if by his own act the servant desired to bind himself for life, he could do so. The piercing of the ear was no very barbarous act. Our ladies who, every day, undergo the same operation for the sake of adorning themselves with ear-rings, do not consider that they undergo exceedingly ill usage.

The fact is simply this: the Hebrew slaves were mostly either insolvent debtors who sold their labor so as to pay their debts, or thieves who had no other means of making restitution.

But it is said that the strangers, the heathens in Jewish bondage, were cruelly treated. Mr. Ingersoll says:

'The heathen are not spoken of as human beings. Their rights are never mentioned. They were the rightful food of the sword, and their bodies were made for stripes and chains." (P. 248.)

In Chapter 9, I will have occasion to speak of the Jewish warfare against the heathen. At present we have to deal with the question of slavery. Colonel

Ingersoll misstates the case when he says that the heathen had no rights; for it is clear from the words of the law above quoted that heathen slaves were treated just as Hebrews in bondage, with the single exception that their bondage might be perpetual, unless they became Hebrews by adoption.

God, the Supreme Master of all, the possessor of all goods, the controller of all our destinies, gave to the Hebrews this extended power of dominion over the stranger nations, as a penalty which he had the undoubted right to inflict on account of their crimes.

Let us now compare the slavery which existed among heathen nations with that permitted among the Jews. Cotemporaneously with the promulgation of the Mosaic law there was slavery in Egypt, and the monuments which are extant to this day attest the cruelty with which slaves were treated. The treatment of the Israelites, who were in fact guests and immigrants by invitation, unjustly enslaved, is a specimen of heathen slavery. Pharaoh "set over them masters of the works to afflict them with burdens."

"And the Egyptians hated the children of Israel and afflicted them and mocked them."

"And they made their life bitter with hard works." (Exod. i.)

At last the order was given by Pharaoh that all the male children of the Israelites should be cast into the river, that they might not increase too fast.

Truly the slavery usual among heathen nations was an intolerable tyranny. As it existed among the Greeks, Romans, and other nations, it was no better than we have described. The slave-trade was a regular business, authorized by the laws. There was no restriction on the master's power to put his slaves to death, and they were regularly butchered without mercy, or put into the arena to fight with each other or with wild beasts for the amusement of the public. Other cruelties need not be enumerated, as they are well known to all. The Hebrew law restrained the master, the Pagan laws placed him under no restraint whatsoever.

Christianity could not abolish slavery all at once, but even before its establishment as the religion of the state, its influence was felt as a civilizer, and the condition of the slaves was ameliorated. The doctrine of St. Paul could not but bear fruit. Under the influence of that doctrine the Christian could not regard his bondsman as a slave, but as "a dear brother." (Philemon, 16.)

When the church became free, her efforts were at once directed towards rendering the condition of the slaves tolerable, and freeing them by degrees. Slaveholders who put their slaves to death without a warrant from the judge were excommunicated.

Thus as early as A. D. 305, the Council of Elvira decreed many years of penance against a mistress who should beat her bondmaid so that she should die within three days. If it were proved that the death were intentional, the penance lasted seven years, if accidental, the period was shorter.

St. Ambrose, Bishop of Milan, in 385, declared it to be a "most noble act of generosity to redeem captives, to rescue men from death, women from danger to their virtue, to restore children to their parents, parents to their children and citizens to their country." He therefore ordered the sacred vessels of his church to be broken and sold for the purpose of delivering slaves. In 585 the Council of Matisco decreed that the property of the church should be applied either to the relief of the poor or the redemption of slaves, and in 625 a similar law was made by the Council of Rheims, and in 844 by the Council of Verona. The Council of Lyons in 566 declared excommunicated those who would reduce freemen to slavery.

There are many other decrees of councils both of these and later dates, all aiming at the gradual extinction of slavery. I need only add here the reasons given by the illustrious Pope Gregory I., when he freed some slaves held by the church authorities to show that it was the desire of the Catholic Church always, not only to ameliorate the condition of slaves, but also to free them as soon as it could be done without subverting the existing relations of society. Pope Gregory I. says:

"Our Redeemer, the Creator of all things assumed human flesh, that by the grace of His Divinity, the bonds which held us in slavery might be broken, and that we might be restored to our first liberty: It is therefore right that men, created and brought forth by nature free from the beginning, but reduced to slavery by the laws of nations, should be restored to that liberty to which they were by nature born."

It is thus seen that to the gradual triumph of Christian principles is due the progress made in recognizing the human rights of slaves, and in liberating them. The bragging infidels of to-day would know nothing of these natural rights of man if they had not been previously instructed in them by Christianity, for until Christianity laid down these principles, nothing was known of them. Even the great philosophers did not discover them by the use of their powerful intellects. . Homer tells us in the Odyssey, B. 17, that slaves possess from Jupiter only half the mind. Plato approves of this doctrine (Dialog. 8 on laws), and Aristotle expressly undertakes to prove by a lengthy argument that "some men are born for liberty, as others are for slavery; a slavery which is not only useful to the slaves themselves, but moreover just." (Polit., ch. 3.)

As a consequence of all this, we may here remark that the slavery permitted under the old law, mitigated as it was in comparison with the slavery common in heathen countries, was not intended to be the the normal condition of foreigners. The Mosaic law was the preparation of man for Christ's advent. If, therefore, slavery was permitted at all, it was because the existing state of society required that to some extent the surrounding nations should be held under the influence of fear, as they themselves by fear endeavored to extend their sway into the countries which surrounded them.

Before leaving the important subject of Liberty, it it may be well to give a summary of the propositions which I have proved, and which I am satisfied, cannot be refuted. I have proved:

1. That man possesses Free-will, which is the foundation of all liberty.

2. That God acted wisely in endowing us with Free-will.

3. That Col. Ingersoll's materialism destroys Free-will and therefore all liberty, though he inconsistently claims at the same time liberty of thought.

4. That his attack upon God, for having made us free to choose between good and evil, is in reality an attack upon all freedom.

5. That the existence of Free-will justifies the punishment of the wicked.

6. That Col. Ingersoll is wrong in making God the cause of evil.

7. That intellectual liberty is, indeed, given to man, but that it must be controlled by the laws and teaching of God.

8. That it is no valid objection to a doctrine that man cannot understand it.

9. That Col. Ingersoll has in many things misrepresented the teachings of Christianity.

10. That Indifferentism to Religion is both criminal and foolish.

11. That the Mosaic laws against unbelief and Idolatry were just, especially as Judaism was a Theocracy.

12. That Col. Ingersoll maligns the Clergy.

13. That Christianity is not the persecuting system which Col. Ingersoll represents it to be.

14. That Christianity, by its influence, ameliorated the condition of slaves and gradually emancipated them.

15. That the mitigated slavery permitted under the Mosaic law was strictly just, though it was not intended to be the normal condition of men, arising as it did from the peculiar circumstances of the period.

CHAPTER V.

EXISTENCE OF GOD.

NOTHING is so absurd as not to have been maintained, nothing so evident as not to have been denied by some who call themselves philosophers. Hume denied the existence of spirits, Berkeley denied that of bodies, while Pyrrho professed to doubt everything, even his own existence. The very fact of doubting our own existence proves that we exist; for he who exists not cannot doubt. Our own existence is therefore a truth so firmly rooted in our consciousness that in reality we cannot doubt it.

Moreover we are conscious of the existence of affections which are produced in us by beings not ourselves, beings over which we exercise no control. Hence we are certain, not only of our own existence, but also of the existence of other beings, some of which are like ourselves, others unlike us.

Now it is not my intention to enter upon a lengthy proof of the existence of one God. This has been done by many very able writers, and the arguments by which this truth is established can be readily ascertained by consulting their works. Besides, there are very few who deny it, and those who do, undoubtedly deny it because they wish to live free from responsibility to a higher Power. They deny it, because they wish there were no God to whom they would have to render an account. Hence the Prophet David says:

"The fool hath said in his heart, there is no God." (Ps. xiii, 1; Prot. Bible, Ps. xiv.)

He hath said so in his heart, his affections, his will, not in his understanding.

Thomas Paine fully admits in his "Age of Reason" that he believes in God, and that reason conclusively leads to this belief. Col. Ingersoll does not positively deny the existence of God, nor positively affirm it, though in some of his works he endeavors to weaken the force of the reasoning by which this truth is established. In the book now before me, he professes only to attack the God of the Bible.

On page 136 he adds:

"When I speak of God, I mean the being described by Moses: the Jehovah of the Jews. There may be for aught I know, somewhere in the unknown shoreless vast, some being whose dreams are constellations, and within whose thought the infinite exists. About this being, if such a one exists, I have nothing to say." (P. 136.)

I propose, therefore, in this work merely to indicate some of the plainest proofs that there is a God, a personal being, a pure spirit, infinite in perfection.

I have already pointed out that we are conscious of our own being, and of other beings, like and unlike ourselves. From this truth we institute the following:

METAPHYSICAL PROOF.

1. Some being exists. This being must be either created or uncreated. If it be uncreated, there exists an uncreated being.

If it be created, there must also exist an uncreated being; for a created being could not have created itself, it must therefore have been created by another being, which also must have been created by some other unless it were itself uncreated. Thus we must either reach an uncreated being, or we must say there is an infinite created series without a Creator, which is an absurdity.

It follows then that there is an uncreated being existing, not from any exterior cause, but by necessity of its nature: that is there exists "a necessary being, dependent on none, though all things existing depend upon it." This being is God.

We may therefore, for the purposes of this chapter, define God to be "The Supreme and Self-Existing Being upon whom the universe depends."

Atheists endeavor to weaken the force of this reasoning by asserting that in the eternity of the past there must have been an infinite series of causes. Colonel Ingersoll practically makes the same assertion:

"It appears reasonable to me, that force has existed from eternity. Force cannot, as it appears to me, exist apart from matter. Force in its nature is forever active, and without matter it could not act, and so I think matter must have existed forever. To conceive of matter without force, or of force without matter, or of a time when neither existed, or of a being who existed from eternity without either and who, out of nothing created both, is to me, utterly impossible." (P. 60.)

"It has been demonstrated that force is eternal." (P. 77.)

"If anything can be found without a pedigree of natural antecedents, it will be then time enough to talk about the fiat of creation. There must have been a time when plants and animals did not exist upon this globe. The question, and only question is whether they were naturally produced." (P. 88.)

All this supposes the existence of a number of progenitors actually infinite, made up of units. Now before the addition of the last unit, it must have been infinite or finite. If it were infinite it could not be increased: but it is in fact increased by the addition of the last unit: it is therefore finite. The addition of unity to a finite number cannot make it infinite: therefore the existence of a number actually infinite is absurd.

2. Colonel Ingersoll likewise supposes the universe to be eternal, at least in its monads. The eternity of these monads is an absurdity. The monads must be beings not existing by necessity of their nature, otherwise each of them would be infinite, as necessary existence cannot be limited, and the necessity which causes them to exist would make each monad in itself a God, infinite in force and in all perfection. Now if the monads are a reality, they are finite beings, changeable, being acted upon by extrinsic forces which govern them. Therefore they must be contingent, and therefore entirely dependent on the really eternal necessary being, God.

3. If the universe, or the monads which compose the universe, were eternal, acted upon by blind forces, intrinsic to them, it is a mathematical consequence, that the state of things at present existing, would have been reached millions of years ago, or equally millions of millions of years ago, and it would at the same time be existing, yet not existing to-day. Thus the theory of the eternity of matter cannot be reconciled with its present condition. Matter must therefore have been created with time, and it cannot be eternal.

4. If one of the series, being contingent, requires its cause, it is absurd to say that an infinite series suffices as its own cause. Contingency or dependency pertains to the essence of its being, and the infinite collection of contingent beings must equally depend upon a first or necessary being as its cause.

PHYSICAL PROOF.

The existence of a supreme intelligent being ruling all things, is proved by the admirable order existing in the universe.

Proof. The being who adopts sure and fitting means to attain ends which are evidently designed, is intelligent.

But the Supreme Cause from whom the universe proceeds has adopted such means :

Therefore the Supreme Cause from whom the universe proceeds, is Intelligent.

The evidences of the adoption of fitting means to attain the ends designed by the Supreme Cause of the universe, are to be seen everywhere in nature, in the anatomy of man, in the construction of every organ of sense, the eye, the ear, etc., in the whole organization of the human body. It would occupy too much space to enumerate in detail here the facts which evidence design. They are acknowledged by all, and may be found in works which explain the construction of the human body, and even the bodies of animals, even the most insignificant of which in every part of their frame, give testimony to the wonderful Intelligence which must have been at work in their creation. The same is to be said of plants and trees, the grass which clothes the earth, the grain which grows in the fields.

If a beautiful palace, a dwelling-house, a watch, a steam-engine, a well-written book, evidence genius and intellect in those who have produced them, how much more do the works of God bear witness to His Supreme Intelligence! The most noble works of art are miserable abortions in comparison with the wonderful works of God.

When further we bear in mind that this earth with all that it contains, is but a speck in the universe, and that throughout the universe these wonders are repeated, we may exclaim:

"The heavens show forth the glory of God, and the firmament declareth the work of His hands." (Ps. xviii., 1, Prot. Bible Ps. xix.)

This physical proof of the existence of God cannot, perhaps, be more appropriately closed than by quoting the words of Thomas Paine, the Voltaire of America.

"Everything we behold carries in itself the internal evidence that it did not make itself. Every man is an evidence to himself that he did not make himself, neither could his father make himself, nor his grandfather, nor any of his race, neither could any tree, plant or animal make itself; and it is the conviction arising from this evidence that carries us on, as it were, by necessity, to the belief of a first cause, eternally existing, of a nature totally different from any material existence we know of, and by the power of which all things exist; and this first cause, Man calls God."

"Canst thou by searching find out God? Yes; because in the first place I know I did not make myself, and yet I have existence, and by searching into the nature of other things I find that no other thing could make itself; and yet millions of other things exist: therefore it is that I know by positive conclusion resulting from this search, that there is a power superior to all things, and that power is God." **Age of Reason.**

MORAL PROOF.

The universal consent of mankind in recognizing the existence of a God is an irrefragable proof of His existence.

It is true that some travellers have at times stated that certain small barbarous tribes have acknowledged no God, but in these cases they have usually spoken doubtfully: "It is said, the report is," etc. Their testimony in most of these cases has been contradicted by other travellers who were more intimate with the habits of the tribes in question. The opinion has also sometimes arisen from the fact that these tribes had no public worship, but on inquiry it has been discovered that there were private forms of worship, fetishes, etc.

It cannot be denied, then, if we except two or three tribes, of whom doubt exists, that the entire human race has always recognized the existence of a Deity. The fact is attested by historians and travellers of every country, and of all ages. The ancient philosophers, Plato, Socrates, Cicero and others have refuted atheism on these grounds, and atheists themselves acknowledge that it is a fact. Hence, all nations have words in their language to denote a Supreme Being.

The whole human race cannot be supposed to err in a matter of morals, unless there be an adequate cause for such error, and as the belief is universal the cause of error, if error there be, should be universal also. The existence of the belief is explicable if we suppose that God had revealed Himself to primeval man, and that the belief had been handed down by tradition through succeeding generations, but any assigned causes which might explain the introduction of such belief by the gradual influence of human passions, inclinations, desires or love of gain are totally inadequate, because such causes are necessarily local and personal to individuals. In fact, the passions and inclinations of men would lead them to reject the notion of a Supreme Authority to whom they should be subject, and at whose behest they would be obliged to sacrifice their natural inclinations. The belief in a Supreme Being must therefore be deeply rooted both in the reason and conscience of the whole human race, and must have originated in the certain knowledge of primeval man that a Deity exists.

CHAPTER VI.

REFUTATION OF OBJECTIONS AGAINST GOD'S EXISTENCE.

1. To evade the force of the proofs of God's existence, atheists have invented many theories. Pantheism is one of them. This system is subtle, but under pretense of acknowledging God, it in reality rejects Him. Pantheism makes God consist of all existing beings: that is to say, all existing beings are one subtance, which is infinite, and is God. If this theory be true, the mechanic who has produced a piece of machinery is identical with his work. Try to persuade him of this. Use the Pantheists' argument, and you will say to the mechanic, "the cause must contain the essence and attributes of the effect, otherwise it could not produce it." The most ignorant might answer, "I have not in me all the material

attributes of my work, but I have the power of producing that and other works like it." Thus the whole theory of Spinosa and the Pantheists falls to the ground. The attributes of the work are not materially in the workman, but they are in him either eminently or virtually: that is either in a greater degree or in the power of production. Thus also God must possess all the perfections of His creatures.

According to the Pantheists, all beings are but one substance: thus we may say John is Peter: I am Newton, and Newton is Leibnitz. Thus all the disputes of these great men, are the disputes of the universal infinite substance with himself.

This system would be merely ridiculous, were it not that it takes away God's personality, and makes God the author of all impiety, takes from us all responsibility for our actions, inasmuch as our acts all become the necessary manifestations of God's attributes.

We have proved that God is a real being, uncreated, necessary and self-existent. The necessity of existence implies absence of limit. God is therefore infinite in all perfection. He is One, Eternal, Unchangeable, Free, Independent, Omnipotent, Spiritual, Immense, All-Wise, Holy, True, Good, All-Happy, Just and Provident over His works. With these qualities He must be a Personal Being. This is implied especially in His attributes of Freedom, Independence, Spirituality, Wisdom, etc. We have proved His Intelligence: Intelligence implies Personality.

2. It is objected by modern infidels, against the physical proof of God's existence, that God also should have a cause or designer, if the argument be valid. Col. Ingersoll also, maintains the same, though

not in the work at present under consideration. This argument is thus stated:

    Whatever affords evidences of design must have a designer,
    But God affords evidences of design,
    Therefore God must have a designer.

Now in answer to this, I must point out the difference between a contingent and a self-existent being. It is quite true that a contingent being must have a designer, but a self-existent being, a being which exists by the intrinsic necessity of its nature cannot have a designer. The existence of a contingent being, such as are all beings which affect our senses, necessarily implies that there must be a cause, and ultimately a Great First Cause, but this First Cause is the necessary being, which is Infinitely Perfect, Eternal, Self-Existing, and therefore not depending on any extrinsic cause or designer. God does not afford evidence of being designed: but all Creatures do.

3. We have seen that Col. Ingersoll professes to have nothing to say about God: (P. 136:) that is to say he does not mean either to assert or deny His existence. However he maintains that such a God requires no worship.

"He has written no books, inspired no barbarians, required no worship, and has prepared no hell in which to burn the honest seeker after truth." (P. 136.)

He further maintains that all worship is the result of an erroneous belief, and he gives such an account of the origin of the belief in God as to make it evident that he desires to destroy this belief. Thus he says:

"And as all phenomena are, by savage and barbaric man accounted for as the action of intelligent beings for the accomplishment of certain objects, and as these beings were supposed to have the power to assist or injure man, certain things were supposed necessary for man to do in order to gain the assistance, and avoid the anger of these gods." (P. 48.)

"All worship is necessarily based upon the belief that some being exists who can, if he will, change the natural order of events. The savage prays to a stone that he calls a God, while the Christian prays to a god that he calls a spirit, and the prayers of both are equally useful. The savage and the Christian put behind the Universe an intelligent cause, and this cause whether represented by one God or many, has been, in all ages, the object of all worship. To carry a fetish, to utter a prayer, to count beads, to abstain from food, to sacrifice a lamb, a child or an enemy, are simply different ways by which the accomplishment of the same object is sought, and all are the offspring of the same error." (P. 49.)

"The error" is that "there is a being who can, if he will, change the natural order of events." This is a denial of God's Omnipotence, and therefore of God Himself, for His Infinite power is inseparable from His existence. The worship of God is said to spring from this belief.

It is evident from this, that Colonel Ingersoll blasphemes that which he knows not. Ignorance in ordinary matters may be deplorable, but it is not criminal when our duties are not concerned. When, however, ignorance exists in regard to a duty, it becomes culpable, unless it is excused by the fact that it cannot be dispelled: but when a man acknowledges his ignorance of duty, and yet speaks injuriously of that which he knows not, his culpability is increased, and when his Maker is the subject of his gross and indecent jokes, his Maker to whom he must owe his being and all that he possesses, all that he enjoys, his ingratitude becomes blasphemy. It is difficult to believe that in such a case as that of Mr. Ingersoll, the ignorance can be invincible and excusable. I hope indeed that a merciful God will lead him to better courses, but I cannot help thinking that his present ignorance of God is inexcusable.

The Colonel, while maintaining that the worship of God is derived from error, suggests that the belief in His existence is an error too, arising from the human inclination to attribute effects to a cause. This continent is flooded with Infidel literature, which endeavors to account for the universal prevalence of the supposed error by the influence of an interested priesthood and by ignorance of the laws of nature.

In answer to all this I can say without fear or hesitation, none of these causes, nor all of them together can account for the fact which themselves acknowledge as such. Priestly influence might succeed in some places. It could not succeed in all: and usually it would be the effect, not the cause of the belief. At all events, even where it might exist, it would last only for a time. It cannot explain a universal fact. Ignorance was not universal, and even if it were it would be diminished as men became more skilful and learned. The advantages which some might derive from the propagation of the belief, would be counterbalanced by the advantages which others would derive from its rejection, so that it is absolutely impossible that such should be the origin of universal belief in God. The belief is founded deep in the reason and nature of man. This is the only solution which can be given for its universality. This proves that it must have its origin in our creation, and that it comes from the Creator Himself. This is the view which the great philosophers of ancient times took of this subject. Plutarch says:

"If you traverse the earth, you may find cities without walls, literature, kings, palaces, riches and money: cities without colleges and theatres, but a city without temples and gods, without prayers, oaths, oracles, and sacrifices to obtain the favor of the gods, and which does not endeavor to avert evil by religious forms, no one ever saw." Hence this great thinker was of one mind with Plato and Aristotle that the belief in God originated in a primeval revelation made by God to man. Kant, while denying the conclusiveness of all other proofs of God's existence, acknowledged that on this ground alone, the universality of the belief, it ought to be recognized as demonstrated.

Colonel Ingersoll's remarks on the non-necessity of worship will be treated in Chapter 49.

CHAPTER VII.

CREATION AND PROVIDENCE.

We already proved in Chapter 5, that the universe was created by God. Of course, atheists endeavor to account for its existence without Divine intervention.

Epicurus, Democritus and others held that atoms of matter floating in infinite space coming in contact with each other by chance or law formed by degrees the world and all its surroundings, including sun, moon, planets and stars. Democritus wrote about the year 440 or 430 B. C. He did not attribute to chance, but to law, the formation of the universe, and he made the gods themselves subject to this law. The gods were also aggregates of atoms, only mightier than men. Plato refuted this atomic system, and held that all things must depend on one God, the Fountain of all force, the Creator of the order which exists in the universe. The material, however, he erroneously believed to be eternal. Epicurus maintained substantially the theory of Democritus, but he added that the Gods, as happy and imperishable beings, could take no interest in the affairs of men. Hence he believed that men should act on earth without any reference to God or the gods.

Thomas Paine and Colonel Ingersoll both seem to have adopted the views of Epicurus: Mr. Paine adopted it in part only; but Colonel Ingersoll seems to have swallowed it *holus-bolus*.

We have already quoted (Chapter 5,) several passages in which he maintains that force and matter are eternal, and that all beings have their eternal pedigree of natural antecedents. He thus accounts for the existence of man.

"Modern science tells that man has been evolved through countless epochs, from the lower forms." (P. 95.)

"The Moner is said to be the simplest form of animal life that has yet been found. It has been described as an organism without organs. It is a kind of structureless structure, etc. By taking this Moner as the commencement of animal life, or rather as the first animal, it is easy to follow the development of the organic structure through all the forms of life to man himself." (P. 96.)

Let us see how this atomic system will stand the test of reason.

It is related of the renowned philosopher, Father Kircher, that he was intimate with a certain philosopher who believed in this atomic theory of the production of the world by law and not by divine power, and their discussions on the subject were frequent but fruitless.

On one occasion Father Kircher had made the purchase of a magnificent globe of the heavens, and was examining it when his friend entered his study. The first object which met the visitor's eye was the globe, and he greatly admired it. He asked Father Kircher who was the manufacturer, for he was desirous of having made a similar globe for his own use. Father Kircher answered:

"It was not manufactured. It was made by the concurrence of atoms."

"But," replied his friend, "atoms never concur to make a beautiful piece of mechanism like this. Cease joking and tell me seriously who was the maker, as I would wish to have one made like it."

"Seriously," said Father Kircher, "it had no maker. It is so beautiful because the atoms aggregated according to the law of nature."

His friend could not but see that Father Kircher was aiming at his favorite theory; still he said:

"I know that you are making yourself merry at the expense of the atomic theory; but after all we have no experience of atoms coming together to form a beautiful piece of workmanship like this, perfectly turned, the stars and constellations so well delineated and the brass work so complete."

"Well," replied Father Kircher, "if you cannot conceive of a piece of work like this made without a skilful mechanic, how can you so pertinaciously maintain that the universe, of which this is but a poor and inadequate representation was made by the action of blind forces and laws? Are there not more wonders in the single blade of grass than in this globe?"

The transformation of the butterfly from the egg to the caterpillar form, and from the caterpillar to the butterfly, its varied organic structure in each case, and its ability to propagate its own species, the adaptation of the leaves on which it feeds to the time when the caterpillar appears are wonders inimitable by human art. Must not all this be the work of an intelligent cause?

Whatever may have been the effect of this appeal on Father Kircher's friend, surely it should have produced conviction. A celebrated divine aptly asked:

"What is more foolish than the assertion that the world was made by chance or blind force, whereas all the skill of art could not produce an oyster?"

In fine, the disposition of the various parts of the universe, and of the atomic elements which compose it, is such that all take their own office, and such a connexion is found between them that they seek a common end, to which they are brought without disturbance.

This might be illustrated by innumerable examples. The law of gravitation keeps in their places the sun and stars, causes the earth and planets, both primary and secondary, to revolve in their wonderful orbits without confusion, and so admirably is this law balanced, that another law would result, in a comparatively short time, in the complete subversion of the whole system. This fact alone implies the operation of an Intelligent Cause, not only for the production of the material, but also for the existence of the law itself.

We do not, and need not, deny the existence of ultimate indivisible atoms of matter. Many observed facts appear to demonstrate their existence. But each elementary substance is proved to have its own peculiar atoms with special qualities, and these qualities are such that from one such substance another cannot be formed, as far as we are aware; while the atoms of these different substances combine to form the vast variety of compounds which are found in existence, and which are also evidently calculated to meet the end which an Intelligent Designer had in view. The atoms themselves must be the work of the same Intelligent First Cause.

In the details of Creation the same common end is found. We cannot point to any object which has not properties contributing to the safety or comfort of the earth's occupants. Instances of this may be found in works on Chemistry, Natural Philosophy, etc. All this denotes that the First Cause has arranged all things intelligently and with an end in view.

The same is to be said of plants and animals. Their organization is complete for the purpose of their growth from a seed or embryo. The materials necessary for their life are within their reach. They possess the means of gathering what is necessary for their subsistence, and, moreover, they produce the very germs which, after they are dead, people the earth with the same kinds of beings as before. We judge that a watch or a locomotive must have had a maker. It could not have been formed by the concurrence of atoms by chance or law. What would we think of a watch or a locomotive which, by an arrangement of saws and files and hammers and lathes, automatically produced germs which, placed in the ground, or in the bark of a tree, produced new watches or locomotives without number? Surely we would not attribute such a machine to chance agglomeration of atoms, or to any law of blind material forces. Yet this is exactly what occurs in the reproduction of plants and animals.

Chance is said to occur when some obstacle prevents a cause from obtaining its natural effect, or which turns an object from its natural course. The order of nature is regular, and cannot arise from any but an Intelligent Cause. The theories of such materialists as Democritus, Epicurus, Spinosa and Colonel Ingersoll are therefore absurd. Not only was the Universe fashioned by God, but the matter of which it is formed was created. This will be further elucidated in Chapter 35, when we treat of the Mosaic account of Creation.

Paine, speaking of certain parts of the Bible in which God is represented as taking part in human affairs, says:

"When we contemplate the immensity of that being who directs and governs the incomprehensible WHOLE, of which the utmost ken of human sight can discover but a part, we ought to feel shame at calling such stories the word of God." (Age of Reason.)

Colonel Ingersoll likewise maintains that it is beneath God's dignity, if there is a God, to interfere in the affairs of men. We have seen already that he maintains that God is not to be worshipped. So also whenever miracles are related in the Bible, he refutes only by ridiculing them.

Thus he attacks the miracle by which the sun stood still in the heavens at the command of Joshua, x, 13, and he ridicules the miracles of Moses:

"It is impossible to conceive of a more absurd story than this about the stopping of the sun and moon." (P. 75.)

"It seems hardly reasonable that God, if there is one, would either stop the globe, change the constitution of the atmosphere or the nature of light, simply to afford Joshua an opportunity to kill people on that day, when he could just as easily have waited until the next morning. It certainly cannot be very gratifying to God for us to believe such childish things." (P. 76.)

A like difficulty is made of the statement (4 Kings xx. Prot. Bible, 2 Kings,) that the shadow went back ten degrees "in the dial of Ahaz." (P. 79.)

This he calls "a useless display of power." Similarly he objects to the history of the creation of Eve, the temptation and fall of our first Parents, the flood, the confusion of tongues, the ten plagues of Egypt, the passage through the Red Sea, the miraculous events by which God's power and goodness were manifested to the Jews while they wandered in the deserts of Sinai.

In chapter 13 we will prove the reasonableness of Miracles. At present we have only to deal with the objection that such miracles as Messrs. Paine and

Ingersoll are pleased to consider unworthy of God are therefore unworthy of credence. The Jews were specially living under God's protection. Under His direct leadership they were brought out of Egypt with a strong hand. They were punished for their disobediences, but still God did not abandon them. They were punished by being condemned to wander in the desert for forty years. What wonder is it that during that time they should receive many marks of God's special Providence and care for them? Many things of small import to a man who can gather 400 or 500 dollars a night by lecturing against Moses, were of the utmost importance to a nation, just escaped from slavery, and wandering in an inhospitable land. It was just the occasion for God to manifest his power, and he showed his tender care by such miracles as bringing water from the rock of Horeb when they were thirsty, sending manna and quails to be their food, and taking care that even their clothing should not wear out. Be it remembered that the chief argument brought against these facts is that they were unworthy of God, and that He might have provided for them otherwise. Surely He might; but because Col. Ingersoll could travel from his home to Washington by the Baltimore and Ohio Railroad, is that a reason why he could not pass through Pennsylvania? Col. Ingersoll maintains that the five books of Moses were not written till "hundreds of years after Moses was dust and ashes." Well, be it so for the present. Will the Colonel explain how the impostor who then palmed them on the public as the work of Moses could presume to insert in them the following law?

"Six years thou shalt sow thy ground, and shalt gather the corn thereof. But the seventh year thou shalt let it alone and suffer it to rest, that the poor of thy people may eat, and whatsoever shall be left, let the beasts of the field eat it: so shalt thou do with thy vineyard and thy olive yard." Ex. xxiii, 11, and Lev. xxv, 4.

In the last mentioned chapter the fiftieth year is also appointed a year of rest and jubilee, and it is added:

"But if you say, what shall we eat the seventh year, if we sow not nor gather our fruits? I will give you my blessing the sixth year and it shall YIELD THE FRUITS OF THREE YEARS. And the eighth year you shall sow and shall eat of the old fruits until the ninth year." (20 to 22.)

Such a law was never thought of in any other nation: but by the Jews the law was accepted and acted upon. Here then was the promise of a standing miracle every seven years, and surely if the promise had not been fulfilled the evidence of the forgery would have been patent to all. The observance of the Sabbatical year is frequently attested by Josephus; Ant. xi, 8; xiv, 10. Tacitus also mentions this fact (Hist. v, 1,) which he attributes to idleness, being ignorant of the true cause.

Who will, in the face of such a law, presume to say that the Jewish nation was not under the special patronage of the Most High, the Ruler of the Universe? Who will presume to call in doubt the fact that they lived amidst miracles?

Let us now examine philosophically this theory that God cannot interfere with man, especially when the matter on which He is supposed to intervene, appears to such men as Messrs. Paine and Ingersoll to be beneath His notice.

We have proved already God's Immensity and Omnipotence, and Mr. Paine acknowledges it. Must we not then admit that God knows as much about our acts in detail as He does about the more important fact of our existence or of the existence and motions of the solar system?

He declares that God *governs* and directs the incomprehensible whole. How can this be if He rule not also its most minute parts? At what stage of incubation do human acts begin to be worthy of God's notice?

The truth is, God knows *all* things, the small equally with the great. He can do all things, and He is equally great, whether "stretching out the heavens like a pavilion, or bringing forth the blade of grass for cattle." He is equally wonderful whether measuring out its clothing to the sparrow, or ordering the sun and moon to cause the seasons and tides, and the succession of day and night. The philosophy of Messrs. Paine and Ingersoll was exploded when Plato 1900 years ago refuted Democritus and Epicurus, even before the birth of the last named. It would seem that the philosophers of the skeptical school think that God has no time to spare to think of matters which affect His creation. What must be their idea of Infinite knowledge?

The historical portions of the Bible, such as the history of Samson, ridiculed by Mr. Paine, the histories of Abraham, Moses, Joshua, and other portions of Holy Scripture ridiculed by Col. Ingersoll, far from being useless or absurd, are full of illustrations of the life of Christ on earth, of mystic allegories which pious readers have discovered in them, and of evidences of God's Providence in detail. They are therefore calculated to make men both wiser and better; and indeed the lesson they inculcate would be sufficiently valuable if we learned from them nothing more than that God's Providence watches over mankind in all our actions.

That the Providence of God watches over His Creation is clear from the following considerations.

A created being cannot preserve itself, on the withdrawal of its efficient cause, unless it can preserve by its own nature the perfection which has been communicated to it. But the creature cannot preserve itself by its own nature, for then there would be in the creature the quality of self-existence which belongs only to the Creator or First Cause. The continued action of the Creator is therefore necessary for the continued existence of the creature: just as the moon, shining by the light of the sun, ceases to shine when the rays of the sun are intercepted by the intervention of the earth during a total eclipse of the moon. It follows that if God were to withdraw His conserving action from any creature, its existence would be at an end. It follows also that annihilation of being is possible only to God, the fountain of existence; for as He alone can create, and He alone can preserve by the continued act of creation, which conservation implies, He alone can annihilate by ceasing to conserve. Thus we infer that God's Providence over creation is **constant.**

CHAPTER VIII.

NECESSITY OF REVELATION.—INSUFFICIENCY OF UNAIDED REASON.—SPIRITUALITY AND IMMORTALITY OF THE SOUL.

God being such as we have described him in chapters 5 and 6, it ought to be unnecessary to enquire, do we need more light concerning Him, than Reason affords? Or is Revelation useful or necessary that we may know how we are to worship Him, or as, Col. Ingersoll asserts, is there no need to worship Him at all?

Even with all the help afforded by Revelation, a reasonable man would naturally say, "on such a subject we cannot have too much light." So thought Cicero, Plato, Socrates, etc., but so Col. Ingersoll does not think. He is wiser than these great reasoners. His thoughts are final decrees, his conceptions are infallible and uncontrovertible. Thus:

"For me it is impossible to believe the story of the deluge." (P. 164.)

This is conclusive!

"Ignorance (of Christians) believes, Intelligence (of the Colonel) examines." (P. 161.)

"My own opinion is that General Joshua knew no more about the motions of the earth than he did about mercy and justice." (P. 74.)

"I cannot believe these things. (P. 238.)

"A book that is abhorrent to MY head and heart cannot be accepted as a Revelation from God." (P. 238.)

Let us now see what he says of the necessity of Revelation.

"It is not easy to account for an infinite God making people so low in the scale of intellect as to require a revelation. (P. 41.)

On this point Thos. Paine agrees with Mr. Ingersoll; but Paine gives a semblance of argument for his position which the latter does not. He says:

"It is *only* by the use of reason that man can discover God. Take away that reason, and he would be incapable of understanding anything. How then is it that these people (Christians) reject reason?" Age of Reason. (P. 26.) N. Y. edition.

"It is *only* in the Creation that all our ideas and conceptions of a word of God can unite . . . . And this word of God reveals to man all that is necessary for man to know of God." *ibid.*

In fact, Deists all agree that we are to believe only in "Natural Religion."

It is proper to remark here that both Mr. Paine and Col. Ingersoll (P. 53,) misrepresent Christians in stating that we "reject reason." Revelation presupposes Reason. Beasts have no Revelation, because they have no reason; but reason has its proper use. Reason judges truth which lies within its scope, but beyond the field of truth which reason can reach, there lies a vast expanse which unaided reason can never know. Here then is a field in which, even according to Mr. Paine's admission, Revelation has ample scope; for he virtually admits, that a proper sphere of Revelation is that body of Truth which we did not know before, for he says:

"The person to whom a Revelation is made did not know it before." Age of Reason.

Mr. Paine acknowledges the Immortality of the soul, or at least declares his conviction of its probability and says that it is his hope. Col. Ingersoll, Tyndall and D. M. Bennet do not pronounce for or against it.

The truth or falsity of this doctrine is to us, after God's existence, the most important doctrine of Religion, since on it depends what we must do for God, our neighbor and ourselves: also whether or not we are to expect a happy or miserable everlasting future. Yet Mr. Paine, with the aid of Reason, cannot assert that the doctrine is certain.

Does it not follow, then, that light is needed on this subject more than reason affords?

The prayer of the Russian poet to God for light is the dictate of Reason.

> "Thou art: directing, guiding all, thou art:
>   Direct my understanding, then, to thee.
> Control my spirit. Guide my wandering heart.
>   Though but an atom midst immensity,
> Still I am something fashioned by thy hand.
>   I hold a middle rank twixt heaven and earth;
> On the last verge of mortal being stand,
>   Close to the realms where angels have their birth,
> Just on the boundaries of the spirit land."

Reason whispers to us that there is within us a principle differing from our body and from all things material, for this principle judges, thinks, reasons, wills—incites to great and noble deeds. Bodies cannot do these things. That principle, then, differs from the body, and does not necessarily perish with the body.

But does reason alone assure us of Immortality? The doubts of Mr. Paine and other Deists answer "No." Many of the greatest thinkers of ancient and modern times have acknowledged that without a

Revelation from God, they must always be in doubt upon this subject.

Cicero says:

"No one would ever offer himself to die for his country, without great hope of immortality. . . . . I cannot explain how it is that there is in our minds a certain presentiment of future ages." (*Quæst. Tusculanæ.*)

"It is for a God to say which of these opinions is true. For us, we are not in a condition to determine even which is most probable."

Socrates says:

"The clear knowledge of these things is impossible in this life, or at least extremely difficult. The wise man ought therefore to hold what seems to him most probable, until he have a more sure light, or until the word of God Himself will serve as a guide."

Plato, Aristotle and Plutarch are of the same opinion and say that Immortality, Creation and the Providence of God are ancient traditions of the human race which deserve the greatest deference.

Thus these great Philosophers from Reason alone came to the conclusion that we need Revelation.

Many are of opinion that by Reason this truth is demonstrable, but even if this be the case, Reason would never have discovered the demonstration were it not guided by Revelation, and Mr. Paine would never have guessed its truth.

The Binomial Theorem of Newton, and Taylor's Theorem have been demonstrated in other ways than their first discoverers employed, and there is many a man who can now demonstrate them, who would never have discovered them.

Modern deists boast very loudly about "Natural

Religion" and Col. Ingersoll about the "Religion of Humanity," but they would know nothing of either the Religion of Nature or of that of Humanity if Christianity had not been beforehand to teach its principles to them. Its good features are borrowed from Christianity. Natural Religion or the so-called Religion of Humanity is like Æsop's jackdaw, dressed in peacock's feathers. Strip it of its feathers, it will be a jackdaw still. Yet Mr. Paine says, with his usual coarseness:

"Of all the systems of Religion that ever were invented, there is none more derogatory to the Almighty, more unedifying to man, more repugnant to reason and more contradictory in itself than this thing called Christianity." (Age of Reason, part 2.)

Mr. Ingersoll also reviles Christianity. In order to do so he misrepresents the clergy as sordid. We have already shown this. The doctrines of Christianity he represents as debasing, and he pretends that she inculcates ignorance, opposes the diffusion of knowledge, and encourages hypocrisy. These statements, mere false assertions without attempt at proof, are of no weight. I will, however, confront them with the admissions of well-known infidels. Voltaire says:

"It remains for us to consider the happy effects of this light of the Gospel, not only in increasing but in *producing* the happiness of mankind, and in being the consolation of the human race. Those who have combatted religion must at least acknowledge that it announces truths which will secure happiness to mankind. Her practice is established on kindness and beneficence. One God adored from heart and mouth, and all duties fulfilled, make of the world a temple and of all men brothers."

Frederick of Prussia says:

"If the Gospel contained only this precept: Do not to others what you would not wish them to do to you, we would be forced to acknowledge that these few words comprise all morality."

Christianity, not Deism, nor Atheism, has been able to substitute a reverence for morality for the barbarous manners of Paganism. Christianity alone has saved multitudes of children abandoned by unnatural parents, has built houses of refuge to succor travellers on the mountains of perpetual snow, has rescued captives by heroic acts of self-denial, has organized bands of angels of mercy to relieve sufferers in the pest-houses, and has illuminated man by instructing him in a morality which reason alone never could have discovered.

She alone has given courage to her disciples to lay down their lives by millions in testimony to the truth. She teaches fully and without uncertain sound our duties to God. She alone can give us tangible proof of God's intense love for mankind, manifested in our Redemption: she alone can give to the dying the consolation of a certain hope, pointing to our crucified Saviour as its pledge.

An oath is the foundation of jurisprudence. Christianity alone makes it sacred and inviolable. Marriage, elevated to be a sacred rite, raises woman to her proper sphere, while under Deism and Polytheism she is as degraded as in Utah and Turkey.

CHAPTER IX.

NECESSITY OF REVELATION.—RESULTS OF UNAIDED REASON.—DEGRADING RITES OF PAGANISM.—HUMAN SACRIFICES.—EXTERMINATION OF THE CANAANITES.

Let us now consider the necessity of Revelation from another standpoint. Let us look at the moral results of unaided Reason.

Man existed on earth, at all events, for four thousand years before Christ. Rationalists say that he must have existed hundreds of thousands of years. We may for our present purpose allow them all the time they ask. During this period what progress did reason make in inculcating religion and morality? Even Deists acknowledge that if we except the precept, "Remember that thou keep holy the Sabbath day," the ten commandments comprise a summary of the natural moral law. Let us see what knowledge of these important precepts had those countries which did not know the true God.

Col. Ingersoll wishes us to believe that the Pagans were better instructed in these matters than were Christians or Jews. He says:

"We read the Pagan sacred books with profit and delight. With myth and fable we are ever charmed, and find a pleasure in the endless repetition of the beautiful, poetic and absurd. We find in all these records of the past, philosophies and dreams, and efforts stained with tears, of great and tender souls, who tried to pierce the mystery of life and death, to answer the eternal questions of the Whence and Whither." (Preface, p. ix.)

"Thousands of years before Moses was born, the Egyptians had a code of laws. . . . . The Egyptian code was far better than the Mosaic." (P. 235.)

"Long before the Jewish savages assembled at the foot of Sinai, laws had been made and enforced, not only in Egypt and India, but by every tribe that ever existed." (P. 235.)

"The Bible is a book that 'necessarily excites the laughter of God's children.'" (P. 34.)

"The real oppressor, enslaver and corrupter of the people is the Bible." It "fills the world with bigotry, hypocrisy and fear." (P. 43.)

There is much more of the same kind.

Elsewhere he elevates the sacred books of the Hindoos above the Bible, and he states that these books are 4,000 years anterior in date to the Pentateuch.

In chapter 40 we will treat more in detail of the teachings and antiquity of the Hindoo sacred books. We shall now see what Reason and their Sacred books, together with their schools of Philosophy did for the heathen nations up to the time of Christ.

There were philosophical schools in India, Egypt, Chaldæa, Phœnicia, Greece and Rome. In all of these countries innumerable gods were worshipped. In them all, might held the place of right. Slavery was, as we have seen already in chapter 4, most barbarous. Their religious feasts were orgies of cruelty, impiety, jealousy, intemperance. And though Col. Ingersoll maintains (p. 126) that in process of time, man progressed in religion, as in everything else, it is clear to any one who is at all acquainted with the real history of the matter, that their beliefs degenerated as time moved on. Thus Père Cœurdoux, a French Jesuit, of whom Max Müller says "to this modest missionary," belongs the credit "of having anticipated some of the most important results of Comparative Philology by at least fifty years," says of the Veda:

"Since the Veda is in our hands, we have extracted from it texts which serve to convince them of those fundamental truths that must destroy idolatry; for the Unity of God, the qualities of the true God, and a state of blessedness and condemnation, are all in the Veda. But the truths which are found in this book are *only scattered* there like grains of gold in a heap of sand." (Max Müller, "Science of Language," vol. 1, p. 177.)

Thus at first the Hindoos admitted one Supreme Being. Nevertheless, in the Vedic hymns, the gods are innumerable; still they are immortal; but as time elapsed this immortality was obtained for many of them by exterior agency, as by the good acts and sacrifices of their worshippers, while at a still later period their religion has become such that even Rationalistic writers say their creed, if not elevated to its original standard at least, must "inevitably end in the total degeneration of the Hindoo race." They worship human beings, beasts, birds, rivers, fish, stones, and even the piece of wood used for removing the husk from rice. In honor of Siva, the adorers' tongues and sides are bored, so that swords, snakes, bamboos, are put through their tongues, and into their sides the pointed handles of iron shovels. On the festival of Juggernaut, devotees throw themselves under the ponderous wheels of the idol's car, to be crushed to death, and the car itself is covered with indecent emblems. Prostitution forms a part of the religious ceremony on this occasion. Widows are burned on the death of their husbands, as a sacrifice to the god Ram. Suicide is a most meritorious act, deserving immediate admission to heaven. Infanticide is practiced as a sacrifice to Gunga. (Religions of the World. India.)

In Egypt there were twenty gods of the first and second rank. Those of the third rank were beyond counting. Every district had its special gods: cats, dogs, owls, crocodiles, storks, and the like; and sometimes, to support the honor of their deities, most bloody wars were waged to decide whether a monkey or a crocodile or a cat was the greatest deity. It was from their slavery in Egypt that the Jews got the idea of adoring the golden calf while Moses was communing with God. Yet, four hundred and thirty years before, when Abraham visited Egypt, the Pharaoh of that time seemed to have the knowledge of the one true God. How does this accord with Colonel Ingersoll's assertion that man progresses by the aid of reason, in religious matters? Lucian, a heathen of the second century, writes: "You may enter into one of their most magnificent temples, adorned with gold and siver, but look around you for a god and you will see a stork, an ape, or a cat." The very history of the Egyptians themselves will tell you how they deteriorated, for it is recorded that men rebelled against the gods and drove them out of heaven! The gods then fled to Egypt and concealed themselves under the forms of these various animals, on account of which those creatures are now worshipped. Juvenal, in Satire XV, thus ridicules the Gods of Egypt in his time:

> Who has not heard, where Egypt's realms are named,
> What monster gods her frantic sons have framed?

> Here Ibis, decked with well-gorged serpents: there,
> The crocodile commands religious fear.
>
> * * * * *
>
> A monkey God, prodigious to be told,
> Strikes the beholder's eye with burnished gold.
> To godship here, blue Triton's *scaly herd;*
> The river progeny is there preferred.
> Through towns, Diana's power neglected lies,
> While to her dogs aspiring temples rise:
> And should you leeks or onions eat, no time
> Would expiate such sacrilegious crime.

Perhaps no nation was more thoroughly of Colonel Ingersoll's religion of "Humanity" than these same Egyptians: none believed more thoroughly in decorating the tombs of the dead, which is the Colonel's *beau ideal* of religious worship. (P. 277.) This is proved by the existence of the pyramids, erected in memory of their princes; and, in proportion to their ability, this respect for the dead was imitated by the lower ranks.

The rites of worship of Isis and Osiris were of so indecent a character as to have been deemed disreputable, and therefore to have been finally repudiated in Rome, though indeed it is hard to imagine that they could have been much worse than those of the Romans themselves.

Such, then, are the religions that Colonel Ingersoll considers so much superior to the Religion of the Bible.

I might continue this sad picture by giving a sketch of the Assyrians, Babylonians, Persians, Chinese, Japanese, etc. I will, however, only add a few rites from some of the most cultivated and civilized nations.

The Carthaginians and Phœnicians offered human

sacrifices to Moloch or Saturn. Children were burned in a furnace of fire, or placed on the hands of a brass statue of the god, from which they fell into the midst of a great fire, where they were consumed.

Diodorus relates that when, in 311 B. C., Agathocles invaded Carthage, the people, reduced to great extremity, attributed their misfortunes to the anger of Saturn, because slaves and foreigners had been offered in sacrifice to him instead of the nobly born. As an atonement, two hundred children and three hundred citizens of the noblest families were offered up by fire.

These practices did not cease even with the destruction of the city, 146 B. C.

This would seem to be the most appropriate place to answer a difficulty which Colonel Ingersoll, following Paine and Voltaire, brings against the Pentateuch.

God "commanded the Hebrews to kill the men and women, the fathers, sons, and brothers, but to preserve the girls alive." (P. 253.)

He then states that the girls were to be given over to the licentiousness of the soldiers and priests, and concludes:

God "gave thousands of maidens, after having killed their fathers, their mothers, and their brothers, to satisfy the brutal lusts of men." (P. 255.)

To prove this he appeals to Numbers, 31st chapter. The 18th verse is the passage meant: "But the girls, and all the women that are virgins, save for yourselves."

There is not one word of their being delivered to the "brutal lusts of soldiers and priests." Knowing the strict law against such crimes, it is the height of impudence for Colonel Ingersoll to make such an assertion. He must rely very much on the stupidity of his readers when making it. Perhaps he will find the American people not so stupid as he imagines. The maidens were destined to lawful marriage with the Jews.

But what are we to say of the command to kill the men and women, and even the male children of the Madianites? Is not this worse than anything in the hideous rites of India, Egypt, and Carthage?

I answer: 1. This was no part of the religious rites of the Jews. It was an act of warfare.

2. The utter extermination of this nation, and of the Canaanites and others was not the usual mode of warfare of the Jews. The extermination of these nations was therefore a transient fact, while the barbarous rites of the heathens of which I have spoken were permanent, and part of their religion.

3. The treatment of the Madianites and Canaanites, etc., was the punishment of the grossest crimes committed by men and women. Three detestable crimes at least, are implied as committed by the women when it is said, "they made you transgress against the Lord by the sin of Phogor," or "to commit trespass against the Lord in the matter of Peor." (Num. xxxi, 16.)

The Israelites were made by God the executors of his law. When Colonel Ingersoll undertook the command of a regiment in the civil war, he did not hesitate to take the sword under authority of the United States Government, and to make speeches to incite others to do the same. The authority of God was Supreme to the Jews, and by that authority they inflicted merited punishment.

The killing of the children was different. They were innocent of the crimes of their parents; but after all God is the Arbiter of life and death. We must all die, and it, in reality, is the same in the end whether death come to us naturally or by accident of fire or drowning or by the sword. In any case it is by God's decree. Even if God were the "constellation dreamer" imagined by Mr. Ingersoll, be it Law or Chance or Nature, death is His decree passed on all mankind. The manner of death is but a secondary consideration. It is true, man cannot have the right of inflicting the death penalty without sufficient cause of guilt, but God has that right; and He cannot be accused of injustice or cruelty when He inflicts it. He has given life gratuitously: gratuitously He may take it away. God might have permitted their destruction by a flood or a conflagration. He could do so in any manner He chose to select, and no one should presume to arraign Him for it.

The same objection is brought by Mr. Paine (Age of Reason, p. 15), and also by Voltaire. Of course this answer is equally good against them all.

What I have said of these children applies still more strongly to the cattle and other animals destroyed either by the plagues of Egypt or by the Noachian deluge. The cattle were made for man's use, and man was punished by their destruction. We cannot question in either case the authority of the Supreme Arbiter of life and death. (Ex. xii, 29; Gen. vii, 23.) Colonel Ingersoll's queries on this point, therefore, are of no weight:

"Why should the cattle be destroyed?" etc. (P. 205; see also p. 143.)

Let us now return to our review of the morals of Pagan nations.

The worship of Venus and Bacchus by the Greeks and Romans was conducted with unbridled licentiousness and drunken orgies and processions. The initiations and mysteries of these Gods were immoral beyond description.

One fact will serve to illustrate the degrading influence exercised by this worship on public morals. After the retreat of Xerxes from Greece, the poet Simonides wrote the inscription which commemorated the fact:

"The prayers of the priestesses, who interceded with Venus saved Greece." These priestesses are known to have been women of ill-fame.

In these countries also, Religion degenerated; for these deities were not adored by the most ancient Romans, and when the worship was introduced it grew worse and worse in every age. Thus Colonel Ingersoll's pretended fact of the progress of religion by the influence of Reason, is but the product of his own imagination.

A word now on the Colonel's assertion that human sacrifices were commanded to the Jews. (P. 267.) In proof of this he appeals to the last chapter of Leviticus. Now, in the last chapter of Leviticus no such statement is made. The 29th verse is the only one by which it might be supposed that such sacrifices were to be offered. The first part of this chapter speaks of the simple vow, called in the Hebrew original *Neder*. (Verse 2.) A clean animal so offered was sacrificed. An unclean animal, a field or a man was redeemed by a price. In verse 28 a special vow is spoken of, called *Cherem*. Under this vow there was no redemption. An unclean animal was sold. A field or a house became the property of the temple.

Human beings, that is children and slaves, the only persons whom a master could devote, were dedicated to serve the temple.* In verse 29 this special vow is not concerned. It is the *penal vow* relating to those who are by public authority condemned to death for their abominable crimes, as in the case of the Madianites and Canaanites. This penal vow is pronounced against the people of Jericho in Jos. vi, 17, 18; against idolatrous Israelites in Ex. xxxii, and Deut. xiii. Another example is in Judges xxi, 5. The Jews understood their own laws, and such is the meaning they give these words. (Jews' Letters to Voltaire, p. 362.)

But Mr. Ingersoll also adduces the order given to Abraham to sacrifice Isaac:

"And a murder would have been committed had not God, just at the right moment, directed him to stay his hand and take a sheep instead." (P. 183.)

Surely the quoting of a passage where God did not allow a human sacrifice, is a strange way of proving that human sacrifices are to be offered!

God tried Abraham's faith and found it complete. Abraham recognized God as the Master of Life, and was ready to obey; but God, who delights not in such sacrifices, stayed his hand. Thus He taught to Abraham, His horror for such sacrifices. (Gen. xxii, 12.)

Voltaire in his Philosophical Dictionary says: "Jephtha devoted his daughter as a whole burnt-offering" in consequence of a vow he made "to sacrifice the first person who should go out of his house to wish him joy of his victory."

In this Voltaire is followed by the whole host of infidels.

Let us look into the text and see whether this be

the case. It is found in the eleventh chapter of the Book of Judges.

During the wars of the Ammonites against Israel, Jephtha was called on by the Israelites to be their prince and judge.

After a victorious career, a decisive battle was to be fought near Aroer, and Jephtha made a vow:

"If thou wilt deliver the children of Ammon into my hands, whatsoever cometh forth from the doors of my house to meet me when I return in peace from the children of Ammon, the same shall I offer as a holocaust to the Lord." (Hebrew text, verses 30, 31.)

The vow which Jephtha makes refers us to the law in Leviticus xxvii, whereby a person vowed to God must under certain circumstances be redeemed, or under other circumstances be dedicated to serve the temple; but a clean animal which could be sacrificed was to be thus offered up. He gained the victory, and on his return Jephtha's only daughter was the first to come to meet him "with timbrels and dances." Whereupon he rent his garments and said: "Alas my daughter . . . . I have opened my mouth to the Lord, and I cannot do otherwise." And she answered, "do unto me whatsoever thou hast promised . . . . Grant me only this that I may go about the mountains for two months, to *bewail my virginity*, with my companions." Here, we do not find, that she laments the loss of life, but she "bewails her virginity." Assuredly this implies that as a virgin she is consecrated to God. This, to the Jewish maidens was a source of grief, because under the expectation of the future Messias, all hope was lost that they should be of the ancestral line from which the Messias should spring. (Duclot, Bible Vindicated iii, 425.)

Her request was granted; "she mourned her virginity in the mountains, and the two months being expired, she returned to her father, and he did to her as he had vowed, and she knew no man." (Verses 38, 39.)

There is no statement that she was sacrificed. The grief is for her virginity.

It is true that some learned commentators have interpreted that the maiden was offered really as a burnt-offering; but these commentators for the most part admit that Jephtha mistook his obligation, arising from such a vow. It was against the law to offer human sacrifice. God says:

"When the Lord thy God shall have destroyed before thy face the nations . . . . . Beware lest thou imitate them . . . . and lest thou seek after their ceremonies saying: As these nations have worshipped their gods, so will I also worship. Thou shalt not do in like manner to the Lord thy God. For they have done to their gods all the abominations which the *Lord abhorreth, offering their sons and daughters, and burning them with fire.* What I command thee, that only do thou to the Lord; neither add anything nor diminish. (Deut. xii, 29 to 32.)

I will bring evil upon this place . . . . . Because they have forsaken me . . . . . and have burned incense in it unto other gods . . . . and have filled this place with the blood of innocents. They have built also the high places of Baal, to burn their sons with for burnt offerings unto Baal, which I commanded not, nor spake it, NEITHER CAME IT INTO MY MIND, ETC." (Jer. xix, 3, etc.)

"And they sacrificed their sons and daughters to devils. And they shed innocent blood; the blood of their sons and daughters which they sacrificed to the idols of Chanaan, and the land was polluted with blood, and was defiled with their works .... And the Lord was exceedingly angry with his people." (Ps. cv. 37, etc. Prot. Bible cvi. See also Lev. xviii, 22; xx, 2.)

Surely, if God desired human sacrifice, He would have allowed Abraham to offer up Isaac. He would have detailed the rights to be practiced on the occasion, as he did for all the sacrifices of the law, and the pious kings, David, Josias, Asa, etc., would not have neglected so powerful an engine to propitiate God in the critical circumstances in which they so frequently found themselves.

No, Mr. Ingersoll, God did not command human sacrifice. This abomination was left to the "civilized pagans" you so much admire.

How sad, indeed, is it that nations whose progress in the arts was so great, should be morally so degraded! Only one obscure people knew the moral law! and they received it from Revelation. Then came on earth our Redeemer, and He sent His messengers of peace to spread throughout the world the knowledge which was so much needed. Christianity is the result.

A few philosophers discovered some germs of truth: but these were so mixed with gross error that they could do little good. And if some had discovered the truth, what effect would it have had on the world? None whatever, unless they had appeared with their authority from God. They lacked unity. The history of philosophy is a history of contradictions. The modern philosophers are in as woful confusion as the ancient. Spinosa, Bailly, Hegel, Darwin, etc., have no surer basis than the Epicureans, Pythagoreans, Platonists, Pyrrhonists, etc. They have no unity. They cannot speak with authority to teach. They have no motive to offer, of rewards and punishments to those who accept or reject their teaching. Indeed, Revelation is sadly needed, if we want even the "Religion of Humanity."

CHAPTER X.
NECESSITY OF REVELATION.—RESULTS OF INFIDELITY.

"The destroyer of weeds, thistles and thorns, is a benefactor whether he soweth grain or not." This is the motto which Colonel Ingersoll has placed on the title page of his book. I think we have already said enough to show that the Colonel is doing his best to destroy the grain and plant thistles; however, we are not finished yet.

In 1792, a noble, Christian country, France, was ruled by Atheists and Deists. The kind-hearted king, and soon after his widowed queen were cruelly beheaded. Christianity was formally deposed, and with sacrilegious rites, the worship of Reason was solemnized in 1793. Thomas Paine was a member of the Legislative body which did all this; though to give him the credit he deserves, we must admit he voted against the execution, but for the deposition of the king. A triumvirate composed of the most depraved and cruel men who ever wielded power were now at the head of the government, and inaugurated the celebrated "Reign of Terror." Terror was King. The country was deluged with the blood of the virtuous, and indeed of many of the vicious votaries of Infidelity. All was done under the name of Liberty and Humanity. Crowds of citizens who had fought for this new order of things, were accused of incivism and without proof were piled in dungeons where the air was pestilential from ordure. Men, women and children were thrown into the Loire, in which, as it was too shallow to afford instant death, they sprawled like toads and frogs in the spring, praying to be thrown into deeper water. 300,000 were thrown into prison, of whom 150,000 were executed. Thomas Paine was himself a sufferer, and was undoubtedly saved from execution by the fall and execution of Robespierre on July 27th, 1794. He attests that among the tyrant's papers there was a record signifying his intention to demand a decree against Mr Paine, as had been done against the other Girondists Death would have been the sure result.

Such was France under Infidel rule. Infidelity removes all responsibility to God, and this responsibility gone, the natural consequence is that men render an account only to their own passions.

The Commune of Paris of 1871 was a repetition of the reign of terror. It was another exemplification of the rule of Atheism. Its results were not so disastrous as those of the first Reign of Terror, because its rule was shorter. France, taught by the events of 1792 and succeeding years, rose in her might and crushed the serpent in its infancy; but it lived long enough to exhibit its spirit.

In the face of these facts, Colonel Ingersoll has the effrontery to assert that Christianity is of persecuting spirit:

"Christianity cannot live in peace with any other

form of faith." . . . Christianity has "wet with blood the sword He (Christ) came to bring." (Pp. 7, 8.)

With these assertions I dealt already in chapter 3.

It may be that a few Atheists or Deists would not be as wicked as their principles, but let a nation be indoctrinated with such principles, and the result must be the same as occurred in France Without Religion, man becomes a wild beast.

Thomas Paine, dishonestly enough, attributes the cruelties of his irreligious confreres to the early teachings of religion, not fully eradicated from their minds. Let us set against this the expressed opinions of some Infidels of note.

Voltaire and Frederic of Prussia I quoted before. De l'Ambert says:

"I attribute irreligion to the desire to have no curb to the passions, to the vanity of not thinking like the multitude, rather than to sophistical illusions. When passions and vanity cease, faith returns."

J. J. Rousseau says:

"Christianity renders men just, moderate, lovers of peace, benefactors of society." (Lettr. de la Montagne, l. 4.)

Similarly, Montaigue, Fontenelle, Byron, Bayle, and Maupertius have expressed themselves.

Besides the doctrines we have already referred to, Reason alone cannot give us positive information on such questions as these:

How is God to be honored and worshipped? What is man's ultimate end? How may sin be expiated?

Colonel Ingersoll says we are bound by no creed (p. 28); but we have only his word for this. We need to be enlightened by Revelation. He maintains that God cannot demand our worship. We have refuted this in chapter 2. He also holds that there is no forgiveness for us if we offend Natural Law. He is for inexorable justice. To decide such matters we need the teaching of Revelation.

CHAPTER XI.

MYSTERIES IN RELIGION.

AT this stage we are confronted with a difficulty against Revelation, which is most resolutely urged by all Rationalists, and it seems proper to remove it before proceeding further. Rationalists maintain that all mysteries in Religion should be rejected; that is to say, all doctrines which we cannot fully understand.

In chapter 1, I gave some reasons why a mystery is not to be rejected merely because it is such. Colonel Ingersoll says:

"We are told we have the privilege of examining it (the Bible) for ourselves; but this privilege is only extended to us on the condition that we believe it whether it appears reasonable or not. . . . . We have no right to weigh it in the scales of reason—to test it by the laws of nature, or the facts of observation and experience." (Pp. 41, 42.)

"It seems to me . . . . that if there can be any communication from God to man, it must be addressed to his reason. It does not seem possible that, in order to understand a message from God, it is absolutely essential to throw our reason away." (P. 60.)

The clergy are obliged "to despise reason." (P. 20.)

They induce "all to desert the standard of reason." (P. 23.)

They teach "the wickedness of philosophy, the immorality of science." (P. 19.)

"The Church has said: 'Believe and obey. If you reason you will become an unbeliever, and unbelievers will be lost."

It is scarcely necessary to say that these statements are false. The Church does not teach that we must despise reason, desert the standard of reason, etc. Col. Ingersoll has a way of saying what is false, and at the same time of suggesting, besides, what he does not dare to assert plainly. This he does, as we have seen, when he suggests that there is no God. He hopes thus to evade responsibility for propagating doctrines which he knows to be dangerous and disastrous in their results. He evidently thinks that he will thus make it more difficult to refute him. On the present occasion he is guilty of following the same course. I must call this course by its proper name. It is both cowardly and dishonest. In the above extracts he asserts that the Church says, "If you reason, you will become an unbeliever." This is tangible, but it is false. The Church permits and encourages the use of reason in its proper sphere, as I have already shown; and it is perfectly reasonable that we should believe the dogmas of Christianity. But besides Col. Ingersoll's assertion, he evidently wishes to convey the impression that *mysteries of religion are necessarily unreasonable.* This he knows to be untenable, and therefore he does not assert it boldly. However in another place he says:

"The clergy must preach foolish dogmas." (P. 25.)

Here he commits himself to a positive statement.

He attempts no proof, we must take his word for it. This is precisely what I do not intend to do. If only the Colonel's difficulties were to be met, it would be enough to deny his unproved assertions; but as I wish further to prove Revelation, I will refute the conclusion which he evidently intends his readers to draw from his assertions. For this purpose I will cite from T. Paine's "Age of Reason" his views on this subject. Paine, with all his faults, unlike Col. Ingersoll, has the courage of his convictions. My answer to Mr. Paine will refute what Mr. Ingersoll intends to convey. Mr. Paine says:

"Mystery cannot be applied to the moral truths of Religion."

"Mystery is the antagonist of Truth, and Religion cannot have any connection with Mystery." Age of Reason.

In Nature, which is man's own sphere, there are Mysteries. This is acknowledged by Mr. Paine.

"Everything we behold is in one sense a mystery to us. Our own existence is a mystery. The whole vegetable world is a mystery. We cannot account how it is that an acorn when put into the ground, is made to develop itself and become an oak. We know not how it is that the seed we sow unfolds and multiplies itself and returns to us such an abundant interest for so small a capital."

"The fact, however, as distinct from the operating cause, is not a mystery, because we see it, and we know also the means we are to use, which is no other than putting seed into the ground. We know, therefore, as much as is necessary for us to know, and that part of the operation which we do not know, and which we could not perform, the Creator takes upon himself and performs for us. We are better off than if we had been let into the secret and left to do it for ourselves." *Ibid.*

Thus Mr. Paine's own acknowledgment disproves his position in regard to Mysteries in Religion; for the same reasoning applies precisely to Religious truth. In Nature which is man's own sphere, we are so enveloped in Mysteries that Mr. Paine says "everything we behold is a mystery to us." Our existence, the vegetable and animal worlds, the influence of our soul on our body, the circulation of our blood, the action of Gravity in the Universe, Chemistry, Natural History, all are mysteries which we cannot penetrate. Electricity, that wonderful agent, many of whose uses we know, and of which we can avail ourselves, is so mysterious a power that we cannot tell its nature. The greatest scientists can only theorize and speculate upon it. Thus in a matter which pertains specially to man, that is to say in the works of nature, we are in a world of mystery. Is it to be supposed that in the sphere which belongs to God we can understand everything? that there must be nothing mysterious or incomprehensible to us? God would not be God: He would not be infinite in His immensity and knowledge if we could understand all that relates to Him. It is, therefore, preposterous for Mr. Paine to assert that there must be no mysteries in Religion. God is infinite. He knows truth which we cannot understand. Our highest wisdom is to acknowledge that the number of truths unknown to us is infinite. If God reveals such it is reasonable for us to believe and unreasonable to reject them. In fact we owe to God the homage of our whole being, of our understanding, as of all our other faculties; and the only way in which we can pay Him that homage, is to believe on His unerring word all that He has revealed, however incomprehensible it may be to us.

Reason and Revelation unite in attesting "how incomprehensible are His judgments and how unsearchable His ways." Rom. xi, 33.

Mysteries in Religion are not against Reason: they are above Reason. It is therefore useless and absurd to attempt to penetrate and understand them by our weak powers of Reason. We may, however, use our Reason to know that God has revealed them; and also to understand what is meant when a mystery is proposed for our belief. Any further than this we cannot go, and it is not reasonable to require that we should understand it fully before believing it. We do not require to understand all about the mysteries of nature before we believe. We accept them on the word of those who have to some extent penetrated them, or who have discovered that the facts exist. The testimony of God is greater than that of men. We are therefore bound to receive His testimony, even though we do not understand the truths He reveals.

It is from this evident that Col. Ingersoll speaks nonsense when he says:

"It does not seem possible that in order to understand a message from God it is absolutely essential to throw our reason away." (P. 60.)

We are not required to throw our reason away; but it is absurd for us to ask to understand all the consequences and relations of a truth that is revealed. We do not require this in things natural, neither must we require it in things which are above nature.

"How can any man accept as a revelation from God that which is unreasonable to him?" *Ibid.*

We are not required to accept that which is unreasonable, that is to say against reason, but we are required to accept that which is above reason, if God reveals it. We know that God is Truth itself, and that He can neither deceive nor be deceived. We are therefore safe in receiving truth on the sole assurance of His word that it is truth.

Mr. Paine says: "Mystery is the antagonist of Truth." Has he not himself proved that mystery is in every truth? Does he not say "Every thing we behold is in one sense a mystery to us?" How then can mystery be the antagonist of truth? Mystery is, on the contrary Truth's constant companion.

Mr. Ingersoll also, while endeavoring to make his readers believe that mystery "must be rejected by every honest man" admits that there must be mystery in the act of Creation, for he says "I do not pretend to tell how all these things really are." (P. 60.) Why then does he constantly ask, when Mysteries are in question, such queries as these?

"What was God doing" in eternity? Where did the water come from? Did Moses know anything about the stars? Can any believer in the Bible give any reasonable account of this process of Creation? etc., etc. (Pp. 57, 64, 81, 95, etc.)

The question is not how revealed truth exists, but: Is this truth revealed? If so, then we should believe it.

CHAPTER XII.

POSSIBILITY OF REVELATION.—IMMEDIATE AND MEDIATE REVELATION.—HISTORICAL CERTITUDE.

THOMAS PAINE makes a distinction of two kinds of Revelation which we may conceive: *Immediate Revelation* is that which God reveals directly to any man: *Mediate Revelation* is that which is received by any man, not directly from God, but through a third person who received it from God.

Let us first consider the possibility of Immediate Revelation.

On the part of God there can be no obstacle to immediate Revelation; for being infinitely wise and powerful, He must know many ways of making known to us truths which relate to Himself, and of manifesting His will.

Men can communicate their thoughts to one another. It follows, then, that God who is infinitely powerful and wise can do so also.

On the part of man there is no obstacle to receiving Revelation; for man is endowed with reason and intelligence. He may therefore receive from God the knowledge which God desires to communicate, just as we can receive the knowledge which other men communicate to us.

Among the things which God may desire to reveal to us, there may be truths which will lead us to a more intimate knowledge of God himself, truths which will increase the manifestation of God's glory, and other truths which it will be for our own welfare to know. There is therefore no obstacle to Revelation in the nature of the truth to be revealed to us.

There is no other source from which an obstacle can arise to the possibility of Revelation except one of the three we have indicated. Such obstacle must necessarily be either in God's nature, or in human nature, or in the nature of the truth revealed; and as none of these presents an obstacle to Revelation, it follows that Immediate Revelation is possible.

The common sense of mankind confirms the possibility of Revelation, for we find from the history of all nations, that Revelations, whether true or false were believed in.

Mr. Paine admits the possibility of Immediate Revelation, but denies the obligation of belief in Mediate Revelation. He says:

"Revelation when applied to Religion means something communicated *immediately* from God to man. No one will deny or dispute the power of the Almighty to make such a communication if he pleases. But admitting for the sake of a case that something has been revealed to a certain person and not revealed to any other, it is Revelation to that person only. When he tells it to a second, a second to a third, a third to a fourth, and so on, it ceases to be a Revelation to all these persons. It is Revelation to the first person only, and hearsay to every other, and consequently they are not obliged to believe it."

He further gives a reason for believing in the possibility of Revelation:

"To the Almighty all things are possible."

The possibility of *Mediate Revelation* Mr. Paine denies. He says:

"It appears that *Thomas* did not believe the Resurrection, and as he would not believe without having ocular and manual demonstration, so *neither will I*, and the reason is equally as good for me, and for every other person as for Thomas."

It is true the reason is as good for every one as it was for Thomas: but if the reason was bad for Thomas, it is also bad for Mr. Paine and for every one else.

Thomas, when he demanded ocular demonstration, had already the testimony of witnesses who were not deceived, and were not deceivers. This was sufficient to justify belief. When miraculous events are related, it is not advisable to be too credulous, but if they are certainly attested by witnesses of whom it is certain that they could not have been deceived, and that they are not deceivers, incredulity becomes a folly. Thomas appears to have been too incredulous: hence he is rebuked:

"Because thou hast seen me, Thomas, thou hast believed. Blessed are they that have not seen and have believed." (St. John xx, 20.)

If something useful to man were revealed, is it not clear that by Mr. Paine's incredulity, himself, not God the Revealer, would, by his refusal of belief be the sufferer and loser. More wisely would we try to ascertain whether or not the Revelation be real. There may be among the truths revealed, some that will be of great benefit to us. There may be duties to be fulfilled compliance with which will bring its own reward.

Mr. Paine seems totally to mistake our relations with God. He seems to consider it an act of condescension and kindness to God to accept Revelation: so he dictates to God the terms of acceptance with as much cool consciousness of superiority as the Emperor Napoleon I. exhibited toward the Austrian Plenipotentiary at Campo-Formio, when the Austrian did not accept the conditions of peace which the Emperor offered. Napoleon threw upon the pavement a precious vase, saying:

"The truce is ended, and war declared. But beware: I will shatter your empire into as many fragments as that potsherd."

Mr. Paine's language: "Unless you give me ocular and manual demonstration, neither will I believe," is equally the outcome of presumptuous pride.

Col. Ingersoll holds the same doctrine as Mr. Paine, and with equal presumption dictates to God the terms on which he will accept his teaching:

"God cannot make a Revelation to another man for me. He must make it to me, and until he convinces my reason that it is true, I cannot receive it." (P. 60.)

The absurdity of requiring God to adduce a series of arguments, and to listen to the Colonel's quibbles and to refute them has been shown in the last chapter. We must receive Revelation on God's unerring word. We are now treating of the possibility of Mediate Revelation. The consequences of the pride which raises itself against God cannot be better illustrated than by the example of Nabuchodonosor (or Nebuchadnezzar.) This King received from God a forewarning of the punishment that awaited him for his impiety, and when the vision which he had seen was interpreted to him by Daniel, he answered:

"Is not this the great Babylon which I have built to be the seat of the Kingdom by the strength of my power and in the glory of my excellence? And while the word was yet in the king's mouth a voice came down from heaven: to thee, O King Nabuchodonosor it is said, thy kingdom shall pass from thee. And they shall cast thee out from among men, and thy dwelling shall be with cattle and wild beasts. Thou shalt eat grass like an ox." (Dan. iv.)

The prophecy was fulfilled.

The king's "body was wet with the dew of heaven, till his hair grew like the feathers of eagles, and his nails like birds' claws."

I know, of course, that the Colonel will make little of this piece of scriptural history; nevertheless it has been confirmed by Babylonian monuments in a remarkable manner. These monuments do not give the whole history, but they record the sudden insanity of the king.

Are we, then, at liberty to reject God's Revelation on the mere plea that it was not made directly to ourselves? A little reflection will show that we are not. The belief that God illuminates directly the minds of all true believers has been the fruitful source of error, absurdity and crime in every age. This belief was the cause of the dreadful tragedy at Pocasset, near Boston in April, 1879, when Charles F. Freeman claimed to have received a Revelation to sacrifice his child, and, to the horror of this whole continent, he acted on his hallucination. Other such atrocities characterized the same belief in Germany and England: and now we have Mr. Paine and Col. Ingersoll among these prophets!

It cannot be denied that God could so enlighten all men; but it is more consistent with His general course to teach Religion as we are taught natural truth. Especially inconsistent is it for one who, like Mr. Paine, says that the book of Nature is the only Revelation, to require that God should proceed in Religion in a way quite contrary to that which he follows in opening to us the book of Nature.

How then do we learn from Nature? Much we may learn by study, much by the teaching of others; and some by these means become more learned than others. Children acquire knowledge by degrees. For the purpose of teaching them, schools are established and competent teachers selected. The knowledge of Religious truth must be acquired in a similar manner.

Let us now see the consequences of Mr. Paine's method as applied to the laws of a country.

Revelation consists of truths and precepts, the truths comprising doctrines and events. Laws consist of precepts, but they also frequently enumerate facts, and they are always essentially connected with the facts of history on which their force depends.

Now, according to Mr. Paine's and Col. Ingersoll's treatment of Revelation, we are at liberty to reject the laws unless ocular and manual demonstration of these facts be brought home to each one of us. It follows that when a new law is passed in the Congress of the United States, for example, the President and the members of Congress should be required to march all over the country to prove to the occupants of each hamlet that the laws of Congress have been validly and properly passed.

As the case stands, these dignitaries give us, individually, very little satisfaction. The President approves the laws after they have been passed in Congress. The originals are placed in the archives of the country and there they stay. Newspapers may or may not publish them. Some lawyers obtain copies and that is all; but they must be obeyed all the same.

Mr. Paine had some experience as a legislator, and I presume he would say that enough had been done for their promulgation. He therefore demands from God the fulfillment of conditions which he would not have dreamed of requiring from the inferior ruler of an earthly State.

Mr. Paine and Colonel Ingersoll seem to imagine that God's arrangements would have been much improved if they had been consulted about them.

Another person was of the same opinion, an Atheist who had been discussing with a Christian companion about the Existence and Providence of God.

The two, in their travels, were obliged to rest for the night under an oak tree, near which spread out a pumpkin vine from which grew a number of very large pumpkins. The Atheist said:

"Now there is satisfactory evidence that Nature or God did not arrange the world as wisely as it might have been ordered. You see that magnificent oak tree, yet what a miserable fruit it produces! an insignificant acorn! but on the grovelling vine that grows along the ground, you find large and beautiful pumpkins. If I had been consulted, I would have had the pumpkin grow on the oak, and the acorn on the pumpkin vine."

The Christian argued that the evidences of wisdom are innumerable in Creation, and that undoubtedly there must be a wise end in view in the arrangement of the growth of the oak and the pumpkin even though we cannot see it at first glance.

The two lay down to rest after their discussion and fell asleep; but during the night the Atheist was suddenly awakened by a painful sensation, caused by the fall of an acorn upon his nose. The Christian was awakened also by the Atheist's cry of pain. On ascertaining the cause, he addressed the Atheist:

"You may be well satisfied that it was an acorn and not a pumpkin that fell upon you, for if you had had your way it would have been a pumpkin that would have fallen upon you, and your head would have been broken."

So Messrs. Paine and Ingersoll would scarcely have made the world and the laws by which it operates, any better fitted for man if they had been consulted about their construction. If God had followed the course they insist upon as necessary to make the acceptance of Revelation obligatory, miracles would need to be multiplied, and Mr. Paine would say as he has said already, that these were "tricks unworthy of God;" and Colonel Ingersoll would say as he says on page 59, that the Revelation must be a "lie;" for "Truth does not need the assistance of miracle." They would be as far from believing as they ever were.

The question of the possibility and obligation of *Mediate Revelation* depends upon this: Can we be certain of events which we have not ourselves witnessed? Undoubtedly we can; and it is only thus that we know of the existence of cities and countries we have never seen: for example, it is only by such certitude that most people know of the existence of London, Paris, Rome, Constantinople, etc., or of such events as the Franco-Prussian, Russo-Turkish and Napoleonic wars.

Euler, the celebrated mathematician, explains that there are three kinds of certitude: Intellectual, Sensible and Historical, which by other writers are called Metaphysical, Physical and Moral. Intellectual certitude is that which regards truth which cannot even be conceived as false. Sensible certitude regards events which depend upon natural laws. Historical certitude is that which depends upon human testimony, and when the witnesses to a fact are not themselves mistaken, nor deceivers, and when they could not deceive even if they would, the fact must be admitted. If there exists such testimony that a Revelation has been given to man by God, the fact of Revelation becomes undeniable. Now, there may be such evidence, and therefore *Mediate Revelation* is possible.

But besides the ordinary motives for believing that certain events have occurred, there are two others special to Revelation: namely, Miracles and Prophecy. Of these we shall speak in the next two chapters.

CHAPTER XIII.

MIRACLES.

"Miracles are impossible. It is absurd to suppose that any power can change the laws of Nature." So say nearly all Rationalists, whether Atheists, Pantheists or Deists. Of course Messrs. Paine and Ingersoll follow in the wake of their *coryphæi*.

Mr. Paine considers miracles as mere "tricks." Col. Ingersoll considers belief in their possibility "an error." He says:

"All worship is necessarily based upon the belief that some being exists who can, if he will, change the natural order of events." (P. 49.)

A little lower down he styles such belief 'an error.'

"A fact never went into partnership with a miracle. Truth does not need the assistance of a miracle." (P. 59.)

If there is any sense in this, it means that truth is so evident to men that as soon as it is proposed it will be accepted without a miracle. Is this the case? Every one knows that the world is filled with delusions and errors. No one is more determined than the Colonel in showing up the errors, real or pretended, which prevail with the whole human race, Christians, Jews, Pagans and Mahometans:

"Every religion has for its foundation a misconception of the cause of phenomena." (P. 48.)

Colonel Ingersoll claims to be a "philosopher." If such nonsense and inconsistency be the result of his philosophy, the sooner he cease to philosophize for the world's benefit, the better.

Again, he says:

"All miracles are unreasonable . . . . The possible is not miraculous." (P. 145.)

"The more reasons you give, the more unreasonable the miracle will appear." (P. 160.)

The miracles of Moses are "feats of jugglery." (P. 194.)

Col. Ingersoll's estimate of miracles is therefore patent to all. Even in the hypothesis that there is a God, Infinite in power, He cannot change the "natural order of events."

Let us see how this "philosophy" will stand the test of Reason.

A miracle may be defined: *a sensible and extraordinary effect exceeding the usual order of Providence and the laws of Nature.*

The possibility of miracles, I thus prove. The Infinite power of God can do whatever involves no contradiction. But a miracle involves no contradiction: therefore God can perform a miracle. I show that a miracle involves no contradiction, thus: A miracle is an event which the usual laws of Nature could not produce; but as God's power exceeds the ordinary powers of Nature, He can produce effects exceeding the effects of ordinary Natural laws. Even it is possible for Him to suspend or change the Natural law, for the same power that made the law can suspend or change it. Therefore there is no contradiction involved in a miracle. It follows, then, that miracles are possible to God.

In fact, the government of the world by God is not the mere government of genera and species, which are abstract ideas, but of individuals, which are alone realities. Hence the cessation of the ordinary course of nature, when decreed by Him is no departure from the universal law of nature, properly speaking. When He created the universe and established the ordinary laws which govern matter, He certainly did not resign His power of exceeding their operation when circumstances justified His intervention in that way. This power is in fact an essential part of the universal law of nature.

Col. Ingersoll does not advance the ghost of a proof that God cannot do thus. He expects his readers to accept his dictum as conclusive. Other Rationalists do attempt to prove the impossibility of miracles.

Thus it has been said, "the laws of Nature are God's own decrees, and they must therefore be unchangeable."

I answer to this that these laws are indeed decrees

of God, but these decrees of God include the provision that God may intervene to stay their operation under certain circumstances.

The laws of Nature owe their existence to God, acting freely. He must, therefore, have the power to intervene to stay the operation of those laws when He deems it advisable. In the establishment of the true worship of God, miracles are necessary to establish the authority of him who claims to be the messenger of God.

Thus, when Moses appeared before Pharaoh, Pharaoh knew nothing of the God of the Israelites; for he said:

"Who is the Lord that I should hear his voice and let Israel go? I know not the Lord, neither will I let Israel go." (Ex. v. 2.)

Only by miracles could Moses have convinced him that there is a Jehovah, and that he was his accredited ambassador.

Man, even, is endowed with a power of interfering with the ordinary working of the laws of nature. This is conspicuous in Botany. Sometimes an insignificant wild plant is so completely transformed by cultivation as to produce magnificent flowers, so that it is hard to believe that the original wild flower could by human industry be so changed. The Camellia Japonica is an example of this. They who object to miracles on the ground of their apparently contravening the laws of nature, make man more powerful than God.

Next we come to the consideration of the force of miracles as a testimony to the divine authority of Revelation.

Miracles are superior to the ordinary operations of

the laws of Nature. Now as these laws of Nature are the effects of God's will, the surpassing of these laws must also be the effect of His will. Therefore only God Himself, or some one acting by His authority can surpass these laws: and as God is the Truth, He cannot surpass these laws for the propagation of error. Therefore, when miracles are wrought, and are appealed to in attestation of a doctrine, such doctrine has the sanction of God, and is divine

Sometimes prodigies have been enacted which have perplexed beholders, and have passed for miracles; but since the whole human race have the invincible propensity to adjudge real miracles to be the work of God, God will not permit even demons so to use their preternatural powers as to lead man into invincible error on this subject. The power of demons must therefore be limited in this regard.

Against all this it has been objected that man does not know all the powers of nature, and that in consequence of is he can never judge a result to be miraculous.

It is true we do not know all the powers of nature, so that we cannot say of all how far their efficacy extends: but we know that her powers cannot attain a certain known effect. Rationalists delight in generalizing on this subject in order to mystify it; but we may take special cases. We do not know all the powers of medicine; still we know that no physician can by a word or sign heal the sick, or raise the dead to life, as in the case of Lazarus, recorded in St. Jno. xi, when the body had been four days buried and was already corrupted. Would even the Deists and Rationalists deny a miracle in such cases? Thus when a philosopher proved to a certain audience that motion is impossible, one present walked to the platform and said: "by walking, I prove that motion is possible." Similarly, when such facts happen as those which I have mentioned, it is proved that miracles are possible. The witnesses are reliable, and the facts, being public, were such that the witnesses could not have deceived, if they had wished to do so.

Examples of pretended miracles have also been adduced as a proof that we should give no credit to the true miracles mentioned in Holy Writ.

Base coin is circulated in the country. Does this prove that there is no sterling gold or silver? We should be cautious not to be too credulous, but we must also be cautious not to be too incredulous.

From all that has been said, we must infer that when a sufficient object is to be attained, we must admit that God may employ a miracle. The attestation of a Revelation is certainly a sufficient object; and when Moses appeared before Pharaoh to declare that he had a commission from heaven, the credentials of an ordinary ambassador would be of no avail. Hence God chose to attest his mission by such wondrous works, that the Israelites were obliged to acknowledge him, and that Pharaoh and the Egyptians should "know that there is none like to the Lord our God." Ex. viii. 10.

Jean Jacques Rousseau was so struck with the absurdity of denying the possibility of miracles, that he penned the following:

"Can God work miracles? Can he derogate from laws which he has established? This question seriously treated would be impious, if it were not absurd. . . . . Who has ever denied that God can work miracles?"

Lyttleton, another Rationalist, speaking of the miracles of Christ, says:

"The Jews and Pagans could not evade the notoriety of the miracles of Christ, but by saying that they were the effects of magic, or the works of demons. So, after the apostles and the Evangelists, the most irrefragable witnesses to the evidence of their truth are Celsus, Julian, and other ancient adversaries of the Christian Religion, who, being unable to contradict or deny the authenticity of Christ's miracles, found themselves reduced to invent causes for them as absurd as they were ridiculous."

In fact the testimony of every historian of the church, of all Jews and Christians, both Catholics and Protestants and of the Sacred Scriptures attest that there have been miracles. Ought not this to be enough to make Colonel Ingersoll hesitate before proclaiming that they are "impossible, puerile and foolish?" pp. 160, 194. At least would it not be reasonable for him to give some proof of so dogmatic a statement?

During the reign of Terror one La-Revieillere Lepeaux instituted the sect of Theophilanthropists, which was intended as a substitute for Christianity. In spite of the high-sounding name and money spent to propagate it, but little progress was made. The founder complained to Barras, one of the most famous Revolutionists, that his followers did not increase, whereas Christ's disciples were faithful even to death. He therefore asked Barras' advice. The blunt warrior answered reflectingly: "Well, I do not wonder at it. I think, however, I can give you good advice on the subject."

"Have yourself killed on a Friday, buried on Saturday, and on Sunday morning try your best to rise again. If you succeed, I assure you, you will not have to complain of want of devoted followers."

The advice of Barras was not followed, and Theophilanthropism is dead; but Christianity lives.

CHAPTER XIV.

PROPHECY.

A Prophecy is the *sure manifestation of a future event which could not be foreseen by natural means.*

To constitute a Prophecy, 1. the prediction should be certain, not merely conjectural. 2. The event should be free, so that it may not be known by natural science. 3. The prediction should be determinate, so that it may not be accommodated to any event that may occur.

The Possibility of Prophecy follows from God's knowledge of all things. Being Infinite in Perfection, He cannot acquire new knowledge. All things past, present and future must therefore be known to Him, and from what we have proved in chapter 12, He is able to manifest His knowledge to man: Therefore Prophecy is possible.

Prophecy is an irrefragable proof of Divine Revelation; for God alone can foresee the contingent future; therefore He alone can foretell it or cause it to be foretold. Consequently Prophecy is an evidence of Divine Mission on the part of him who employs it to attest the truth of his teachings.

Against this it is sometimes objected that Prophecy is the result merely of a vivid imagination, or of extra natural sagacity, and that therefore no certain argument for the divinity of Revelation can be deduced from it.

In answer to this we must remark that such a case is excluded from the sense in which we receive the term prophecy, since what is mere conjecture is not prophecy, nor is that prophecy which is the result of scientific knowledge or natural sagacity.

From what we have said on this subject it is clear that prophecy can only be appealed to as a proof of Divine Revelation, after its fulfillment, for then only can its truth be scientifically proved. But when the prophecy is vested with the conditions we have mentioned, when it regards events which could not be foreseen by conjecture or any other natural means and when it has been fulfilled by the events, the conclusion is irresistible that it has been made by the foresight of God, and that the Revelation which is delivered under sanction of such prophecy is Divine.

The facts that a prophecy was made, and that it has been fulfilled can be proved critically. The same criterion by which the value of human evidence is tested can be applied to the testimony by which these facts are substantiated, and thus their truth may be demonstrated; and though the impious and ignorant may ridicule belief in them, the evidence will remain unshaken.

Among the prophecies which are found in the Pentateuch, and which prove the Divinity of the Religion established by Moses, the following may be here pointed out.

We read in Deuteronomy xxviii, 45, etc.

"And all these curses shall come upon thee, and shall pursue and overtake thee till thou perish: because thou heardest not the voice of the Lord, thy God, and didst not keep his commandments and ceremonies which he commanded thee.

"And they shall be as signs and wonders on thee and on thy seed forever.

"Thou shalt serve thy enemy whom the Lord will send upon thee, in hunger and thirst and nakedness, and in want of all things; and he shall put an iron yoke upon thy neck, till he consume thee.

"The Lord will bring upon thee a nation from afar, and from the uttermost ends of the earth, like an eagle that flieth swiftly: whose tongue thou canst not understand:

"A most insolent nation, that will show no regard to the ancient, nor have pity on the infant,

"And will devour the fruit of thy cattle, and the fruits of thy land: until thou be destroyed, and will leave thee no wheat, nor wine, nor oil, nor herds of oxen, nor flocks of sheep; until he destroy thee,

"And consume thee in all thy cities, and the strong and high walls be brought down, wherein thou trustedst in all thy land.

"Thou shalt be besieged within the gates in all thy land, which the Lord thy God will give thee."

The fulfillment of all this is well known to have occurred in the crimes with which our Blessed Lord reproaches the Scribes and Pharisees, and especially in the crimes committed in persecuting to death the Saviour of the world and His followers.

These crimes are enumerated in the New Testament and even by the Jewish High-priest Josephus.

Thus we read in St. Matt. xxiii, 2, etc., the following description of these Scribes and Pharisees given by Christ Himself:

"The Scribes and Pharisees have sitten on the chair of Moses.

"All, therefore, whatsoever they shall say to you, observe and do, but according to their works, do ye not; for they say, and do not.

"But wo to you, Scribes and Pharisees, hypocrites, because you shut the kingdom of heaven against men; for you go not in yourselves, and those that are going in you to suffer not to enter. (Verse 13.)

"Wo to you . . . hypocrites . . . you devour the houses of widows, making long prayers: therefore you shall receive the greater judgment. (Verse 14.)

"Wo to you, Scribes and Pharisees, hypocrites, who pay tithes of mint and anise and cummin, and have let alone the weightier things of the law, judgment and mercy and faith. These things you ought to have done, and not to leave those others undone. (Verse 23.)

"So you also outwardly appear to men just; but within you are full of hypocrisy and iniquity. (Verse 28.)

"Behold I send to you prophets and wise men and Scribes, and some of them you will put to death and crucify: and some of them you will scourge in your synagogues, and persecute them from city to city. (35.)

"Amen I say to you all, these things shall come upon this generation. (36.)

"O, Jerusalem, Jerusalem, thou that killest the prophets, and stonest them that are sent unto thee! how often would I have gathered together thy children, as the hen gathereth her chickens under her wings, and thou wouldst not? (37.)

"Behold your house shall be left to you desolate. (38.)

"All the chief priests and ancients of the people held a council against Jesus to put him to death. (xxvii, 1.)

"They all say: Let him be crucified. The governor said to them: Why what evil hath he done? But they cried out the more, saying: Let him be crucified." (Verse 23.)

We see by all this, not only the fulfillment of the phophecy of Moses, but also that Christ Himself made prophecies concerning the same matter, which were fulfilled within a very short time. The prophecies of Christ, proving Christianity divine, also prove the divinity of the Mosaic Religion, which is an essential part of Christianity.

But the fearful punishments to be inflicted upon the Jews for these crimes were yet to come. The insolent nation which was to consume the Jewish people in their cities, and to reduce their strong walls are yet to do their work of havoc. This came to pass when the war with the Romans began. A few extracts from Josephus will show how the prophecy of Moses was literally fulfilled.

"Then came Vespasian .... and commanded them to kill the old men, together with the others that were useless, who were in number one thousand and two hundred." (Wars of the Jews, 3 Book, x, 10,)

"And 30,400 .... the King sold as slaves." *Ib.*

"There arose such a divine storm as was instrumental to their destruction .... a great number despaired of escaping, threw their wives, and their children and themselves down the precipices .... but the anger of the Romans appeared not to be so extravagant as was the madness of those who were captured, for while the Romans slew but four thousand, the number who threw themselves down were five thousand." (Book 4, i, 10.)

"God had blinded the minds (of the Jews) for the transgressions they had been guilty of . . . . a famine also was creeping upon them . . . . a great many had died already for want of necessaries." Book 5, viii, 2.

Josephus himself, within hearing of the Jews exhorted them to surrender, because on account of their crimes they were punished by God:

"Nay, the temple itself, this divine place is polluted by the hands of those of our country." ix, 4.

"The famine was too hard for all other passions . . . . children seized the very morsels that their fathers were eating, so did the mothers do to their infants. . . . . They drank the blood of the populace to one another, and divided the dead bodies of the poor creatures between them." x, 3.

"The famine widened its progress and devoured the people by whole houses and families." xii, 3.

We have next the literal fulfillment of the prophecy "thou shalt eat the fruit of thy womb, and the flesh of thy sons and daughters . . . . in the distress and extremity wherewith thy enemy shall oppress thee." Deut., xxviii, 53. See Josephus, Book 6, iii, 3, 4.

Again we learn from St. Matthew, xxiv, 2, that when the disciples came to show Jesus the buildings of the temple,

"He answering said to them: Do you see all these things? Amen I say to you there shall not be left here a stone upon a stone, that shall not be thrown down."

This was fulfilled by the total destruction of the

of the temple, though Titus himself desired to save it. Josephus, Book 6, etc.

The number of captives is stated to have been 97,000, and the number slain 1,100,000. ix, 3.

The walls were then so completely demolished that no trace of a city was left. Book 7, i.

In chapter 19, it will be seen that Moses foretold the period when the Israelites would demand a king, and gave laws which should be observed on such occasion. He foretold also the possession of the promised land.

In Deut. xviii, 15, 18, the coming of Christ is promised, and a command given to hear Him, and in Gen. xlix, 10, the very period of Christ's advent is foretold for it is there promised that the royal line will remain in the house of Juda till Christ's coming.

Numerous other prophecies literally fulfilled might besides be quoted. I will merely indicate a few passages. The sufferings of the Jews are further described in Deut. xxviii, 68; Jerem. xliv, 7; Osee (Hosea) viii, 13; ix, 3; xi, 3 to 7.

The visit of Christ to the second temple is foretold in Mal. iii, 1; Aggeus (Haggai) ii, 4 to 10. Thus it is shown that the coming of the Christ or Messias is an event of the past, since this temple was utterly destroyed.

The prophecy of Daniel, ix, 21 to 27 relates that within 70 *hebdomades*, or weeks (of years) from the going forth of the word to build up Jerusalem again, Christ the Prince shall appear. This is the very period which elapsed between these two great events, as nearly as Chronology has been able to fix these dates. These *hebdomades* are interpreted to mean each, seven years, because such is the meaning of the word in other parts of Holy Scripture; besides which it could not be supposed that the events described should occur within 490 days.

CHAPTER XV.

THE FACT OF REVELATION.

We have proved that *Divine Revelation* is possible and that it is necessary for man in his present condition, to enable him to know and to fulfill his moral duties. We have, further, pointed out that there are certain characters and marks by means of which we can know true Revelation and distinguish it from the spurious article. It is now proper that we should apply these characters and marks for the discovery of the truth.

Is Revelation a delusion? Has God, Infinitely Good and Merciful, being wanting to man in his great need, or has He supplied us with that supernatural help which we so much require? It is a question of fact which must be solved by an appeal to historical monuments, and to testimony.

Christians maintain that such a Revelation has been given. Jews as well as Christians maintain that to the Jewish nation, God revealed Himself, and that Moses, in the first place, recorded this Revelation, and that in the writings of Moses consisting of five books, known as the Pentateuch, we find this record.

The Revelation given through the hands of Moses was supplemented by the later historical and prophetical books, which with the Pentateuch constitute the Old Testament. Thus far Jews and Christians agree.

But Judaism was to be further supplemented by the advent of a Messias, a prophet of whom Moses speaks:

"The Lord thy God will raise up to thee a prophet of thy nation and of thy brethren like unto me, him thou shalt hear .... And the Lord said to me: .... I will raise them up a prophet out of the midst of their brethren like to thee: and I will put my words in his mouth, and he shall speak all that I shall command him. And he that will not hear his words, which he shall speak in my name, I will be the revenger. Deut. xviii, 15, 19. The old law was known only to the Jews, but through this prophet, the Messias, the light of Revelation was to be spread among the nations:

"Behold I have given him for a witness to the people, for a leader and a master to the Gentiles. Behold, thou shalt call a nation, which thou knewest not; and the nations that knew not thee shall run to thee, because of the Lord thy God, and for the holy One of Israel, for he hath glorified thee." Is. lv, 4, 5.

These prophecies were fulfilled in Christ, and the Christian believes that His Apostles and immediate disciples have handed down His teachings in the New Testament.

As it is our intention to answer Colonel Ingersoll's assaults against Moses, and as the five books of Moses constitute the first part of Revealed Religion, we will begin the proof of the fact of Revelation with this part of Holy Scripture. I will show: first, the Authenticity of the Pentateuch; secondly, its Historical Truth; thirdly, the Divinity of the Mosaic Religion.

CHAPTER XVI.

AUTHENTICITY AND INTEGRITY OF THE PENTATEUCH.—SEPTUAGINT TRANSLATION.—ANTIQUITY OF WRITTEN LANGUAGE.

INFIDELS attack very fiercely the authenticity and integrity of the Pentateuch. By authenticity we mean that it belongs to the period of, and that it was written by the author whose work it claims to be. By integrity of a book we mean that it is, substantially, at least, the same work as that composed by the author.

Colonel Ingersoll says, point-blank:

"The Pentateuch was written hundreds of years after the Jews had settled in the Holy Land, and hundreds of years after Moses was dust and ashes." (P. 228.)

He does not deny that the Hebrews may have been enslaved, and that many plagues afflicted the Egyptians, as the locusts and flies, the death of many of their cattle, the visit of a pestilence to their country, etc., but he asserts that all this was superstitiously attributed to God, that the history of the events and their superstitious belief were handed down "from father to son simply by tradition." He adds:

" By the time a written language had been produced thousands of additions had been made, and numberless details invented; so that we have not only an account of the plagues suffered by the Egyptians, but the whole woven into a connected story, containing the threats made by Moses and Aaron, the miracles wrought by them, the promises of Pharaoh, and finally the release of the Hebrews, as a result of the marvellous things performed in their behalf by Jehovah." (Pp. 208, 209.)

Again:

"As a matter of fact, it seems to be well settled that Moses had nothing to do with these books, and that they were not written until he had been dust and ashes for hundreds of years." (P. 46.)

It thus appears that the Colonel asserts:

First, that the Pentateuch was written only "several hundred years after the time of Moses."

Secondly, that it is a compilation from the legends that were handed down by tradition among the Jews.

Thirdly, that the miracles related in it are false and superstitious.

Fourthly, that this unauthenticity is a well settled fact.

These do not represent all the opinions of Infidels regarding the authenticity of the Pentateuch. Colonel Ingersoll concedes the existence of Moses; for he says that he was "dust and ashes for hundreds of years" when the Pentateuch was written. Voltaire, in his Encyclopedia, denies the very existence of Moses. A tract (No. 108) published by D. M. Bennet in his collection, presumptuously asserts that the Pentateuch could not have been written before the reign of Josias, about 625 B. C., and that it was unknown "until a priest named Hilkiah said that he found the book of the law in the house of the Lord." In proof of this he cites 4 Kings xxii, 8, and 2 Paralipomenon xxxiv, 14. (Protestant Bible, 2 Kings, 2 Chronicles.) He adds that it was burned a few years afterwards, and "was never recovered." The same writer (Preston) states that "none of the (present) books were heard of previous to the translation of the Septuagint." 280 B. C.

Another tract from the same collection by A. L. Rawson says that "there has been presented clearly and unmistakably a startling array of facts which argue the conclusion that the Hebrew language was simply a creation of the Rabbis, and was never a living language in use by any people." No. 104.

Again:

"The Hebrew language was an artificial structure framed by scholars in the priesthood for the private use of the Church."

"All these writings were written during the time of the Maccabees and the Herods .... in Greek." *ibid.* i. e. 170 B. C.

A squab-pie cannot be made of more discordant materials, than he has to swallow who would be an Infidel or Agnostic of the nineteenth century. The desire for truth is professedly the motive of Infidel teachings, yet the above doctrines, irreconcilable with the known facts of history and with each other are given as the pabulum on which so-called "Truth-seekers" are fed. How could the Old Testament be translated into Greek in 280 B. C., if it did not exist until 170 B. C? And if it was first written in Greek, what need had Ptolemy Philadelphus to get interpreters to translate it from Hebrew into that language? In fact not only does Josephus, who had ample means of information on a fact comparatively recent, testify that the Septuagint translation was made in Ptolemy's reign, but Philo and Aristobulus attest the same, of whom Aristobulus flourished before the time the Maccabees. Aristæus, also, who was an intimate friend of the King, and who took part in the transaction, gives a detailed account of it. Josephus, Ant. xii, 2. In the face of all this it is certainly a piece of cool effrontery for these Infidels, be they Atheists or Deists, to tell us that there were no such books till the time of the Maccabees, or that there was no Hebrew language, or as Colonel Ingersoll suggests that there was no Hebrew copy from which the translation was made. In fact the Colonel manifests the most blind ignorance of this whole history on which he dogmatizes so positively, for he states that the Septuagint was translated after the "Latin Bibles were found in Africa." I will not add to his blunders the statement that this translation was made two or three years before Christ, because that might be a typographical error. The other is certainly not.

These last assertions of the Colonel are to be found in his lecture, "Mistakes of Moses," published in 1882, by Messrs. McClure & Rhodes, of Chicago. (P. 115.)

Such are the straits to which Agnostics are reduced.

A. L. Rawson's discovery that Hebrew was never a spoken language is a peculiarly happy hit; and he deserves some recognition from his fellow Infidels. If Voltaire deserved a monument in Paris in recognition of his discoveries in theology, Mr. Rawson deserves one in the moon.

Just as the Latin language has its children, Italian, Spanish, Portuguese, French, Wallachian, and Romanesque, and just as these children would testify to the existence of their mother language, if Latin had not been preserved to us by the classic works of the Augustan age, so the children of the Hebrew language would attest to the satisfaction of all linguists the former existence of Hebrew as a spoken language.

The Syriac of Mesopotamia and Kurdistan, the Tigre and Amharic of Abyssinia can be accounted for only by the former existence of Hebrew. The Hebrew has besides its sister tongues, Arabic, Aramæan (Chaldee,) and Himyaritic, besides the Sinaitic inscriptions and the monuments of Assyria. To these must be added the Phœnician, which has handed down its monuments which have been discovered in Malta, Sardinia, Carthage, Algiers, Tripoli, Athens, and Marseilles, proving that the Phœnician as originally spoken was substantially identical with Hebrew. With these facts scholars are familiar.

Let us take a few cases to illustrate how philologists can draw inferences from modern tongues to the character of the tongues from which they are derived. Certainly new languages are not formed by the agreement of learned men that such or such a form of speech should convey such or such an idea. They are formed by the gradual changes of forms already in existence.

Thus the French adverbial termination *ment* added to adjectives to form adverbs, has an origin, yet this termination is not in Latin. *Fort, strong,* is clearly from the Latin *fortis,* but whence comes *fortement* in Latin *fortiter, strongly?* We find in Latin such forms as "*bona mente,*" "in good faith," "*forti mente,*" "with strong will," in "*alia mente*" equivalent to "*altera mente,*" otherwise, or with other intention. It is now easy to see how the French got into the custom of using the words *bonnement, fortement, autrement,* and of applying the termination to other cases, as *figurément, figuratively, librément, freely,* etc. Italians and Spaniards, both use the termination *mente* in the same sense. Who cannot see that these all bespeak their common parent, Latin? Who cannot see that the French *vingt*, the Spanish *veinte*, and the Italian *venti* are all derived from their common parent, the Latin *viginti* twenty? In precisely the same way could philologists infer the existence of the Hebrew parent, from its derivative tongues which exist to-day. See Max Müller, Science of Language.

Besides all this, the Phœnician letters are, with three or four exceptions, identical with those used in Old Hebrew.

To all this we may add, that in the earliest Greek, there are words which are evidently of Hebrew or Phœnician origin. This is the case, especially, when the articles were imported from the East. Thus we have *nether*, Greek *nitron*, *nitre*; *kinnamon*, Greek *kinnamomon*, *cinnamon*; *mor*, Greek *myrrha*, *myrrh*; *shushan*, Greek *souson*, *a lily*; *gamal*, Greek *camelos*, *a camel*; *nevel*, or *nabal*, Greek *nabla*, *a lyre*; *kinnor*, Greek *kinyra*, *a harp*; with many others. See Prof. Hirschfelder's *Biblical Commentary*, p. xxxvi.

Now we come to a discovery of Colonel Ingersoll which is on a par with that of Mr. Rawson, and which would be as deserving of Infidel recognition, only for the fact that the wonderful discovery was made by Voltaire before him. It is that the Hebrews had no written language till long after the time of Moses. See the passage quoted above from pp. 208, 209.

This makes clear also what Colonel Ingersoll states on page 49, which would be otherwise obscure:

"Many systems of religion must have existed many ages before the art of writing was discovered, and must have passed through many changes before the stories, miracles, prophecies, and mistakes became fixed and petrified in written words. After that, change was possible only by giving new meanings to old words, etc., and in this way Christians of to-day are trying to harmonize the Mosaic account of creation with the theories and discoveries of modern science."

In chapter 35 I will speak of the Mosaic account of Creation. At present I have to deal with the assertion that there was no writing in the time of Moses.

No writing in the time of Moses! Ponder well on this assertion. The Colonel says, page 235, that the Egyptians had a code of laws, better than the Mosaic code, *thousands of years* before Moses was born. What? were those laws not written? How then does he know that they were superior to the Mosaic code?

Surely, Colonel, you have a bad memory. You say: "Moses received from the Egyptians the principal part of his narrative" of creation, "making such changes and additions as were necessary to satisfy the peculiar superstitions of his own people." (P. 51.)

And how do you know all this? Oh! "Moses was instructed in all the wisdom of the Egyptians:" (Acts vii, 22,) and then:

"The story had been *imprinted in curious characters* upon the clay records of Babylon, the gigantic monuments of Egypt, and the gloomy temples of India." (P. 58.)

What? The story had been recorded in Babylon, Egypt and India, and Moses had got it there, yet there was no written language yet!

Such is the brilliant reasoning of Col. Ingersoll, who being "an intelligent man," knows that there is no "science" in the Bible, and that "it was produced by ignorance" and "believed and defended by" ignorance also. (P. 242.)

Of course the Colonel's blunders are the product of profound science! The clergy, forsooth, "deliver weak and vapid lectures upon the harmony of Genesis and Geology." There is nothing weak, nothing vapid about Col. Ingersoll's lectures!

Elsewhere, in his lecture on skulls, the Colonel asserts that the Hindoo Vedas were *written* 4,000 years before the Pentateuch; and on page 165 he says: "An account of a general deluge was discovered by George Smith, translated from another account that *was written* two thousand years before Christ." He adds:

This account is "without doubt much older than the one given by Moses." (P. 165.)

All this before written language was invented!

Surely, Colonel, you must have been asleep when you wrote all this. I fear you would have made a sorry work if you had written the Pentateuch, which you say you could have done so much better than Moses.

In Judges i, 11, we read that the ancient name of the town of Dabir (or Debir), was Cariath-Sepher (or Kirjath Sepher), that is to say the "City of Books," and in Joshua xx, 49, the same town is also called "Cariath Senna (or Kirjath-Sannah), the City of Learning. It could scarcely have received such names unless it had some celebrity for its *written* lore.

It is well known that our letters A, B, C, are through the Latin derived from the Greek letters. These are named Alpha, Beta, Gamma, Delta, etc., which in turn are derived from the Phœnician or Hebrew: Aleph, Beth, Gimel, Daleth. Further back we cannot trace them; for in Hebrew these names all have a meaning, and in the old Hebrew, the letters bore a certain resemblance to the objects designated. Aleph is an ox; Beth, a house; Gimel, a camel, etc. Here, then, we have the Alphabet traced to its source. If it was in turn derived from the Egyptian hieroglyphics, as some suppose, the period must be very far back; but this is a mere supposition. The fact remains that in the time of Moses writing was in use in many nations. COL. INGERSOLL IS MISTAKEN.

It will be remarked that this fact is another torpedo to explode A. L. Rawson's theory.

It may be advisable here to point out Mr. Preston's error concerning the first appearance of the Books of the law. He quotes the following passages of Scripture to prove that they were unknown previous to the time of King Josias:

"Helcias, the high priest, said to Laphan the scribe: I have found the book of the law in the house of the Lord, and Helcias gave the book to Laphan, and he read it."

Laphan read the book to the king and the king said:

"The great wrath of the Lord is kindled against us, because our fathers have not hearkened to the words of this book, to do all that is written for us." (4 Kings xxii., 8, 13; Protestant Bible, 2 Kings.)

The second passage which he refers to gives us the explanation of this, viz: that the book found was "by the hand of Moses," that is to say it was the original written by Moses himself.

"Helcias the priest found the book of the law of the Lord, by the hand of Moses." 2 Paralipomenon xxxiv., 14. (Prot. Bible, 2 Chron.) This is further confirmed by what we read in Deuteronomy xxxi., 9, 24.

"And Moses wrote this law and delivered it to the priests the sons of Levi, who carried the ark of the covenant of the Lord."

"Therefore after Moses had written the words of this law in a volume, and finished it: He commanded the Levites, who carried the ark of the covenant of the Lord, saying:

"Take this book and put it in the side of the ark of the covenant of the Lord your God: that it may be there for a testimony against thee."

That this view is correct is further evident from the fact that before this time the law was regularly read, which certainly would not have been the case if it had no existence. Thus:

"Wheresoever there is question concerning the law, the commandment, the ceremonies, the justifications: show it them," 2 Par. xix, 10. (2 Chron.)

"And they taught the people in Juda, having with them the book of the law of the Lord." xvii, 9.

See also 1 Par. (Chronicles) xxiii, 32.

The book of the law was the civil and religious code of the nation. David, Solomon, Asa, all the kings down to Josias made it the basis of their government, and so did Josias himself. It is in the hands of the magistrates as the rule of their judgments. King Amasias, bases on it his judgments in criminal causes (4 Ki. xiv, 6; Prot. Bible 2 Ki.), and even the impious Achab is restrained by it, so as to go through a form of law when committing an injustice. (3 Ki. xxi, 3, 4, 9, 10. Prot. Bible, 1 Ki.) In the reign of Osee, the prophets constantly recalled the ten tribes from idolatry by appealing to the law. (4 Ki. xvii, 13: Prot. Bible, 2 Ki.) In fine we everywhere find the law of Moses to be the rule by which all the conduct of the Jews was regulated, and even under wicked kings, great numbers of Israelites were faithful to it. (2 Par. xxix, xxx, xxxi, 4 Kings xxi; Prot. Bible, 2 Chron: 2 Kings.)

If it be objected that I am here appealing to the Bible as evidence, I reply :

1st. That the objection is drawn from the Bible, and we have therefore a perfect right to have the Bible explain itself.

2ndly. These books of the Bible which I am quoting are the public records of the nation, and are attested as such. They have, therefore, independently of their inspired force, all the force of historical monuments, and more: they have the force of authentic documents treasured in the archives of the nation, besides being made public by their authority in the religion of the State.

It is simply absurd that there should have been only one copy in the reign of Josias.

How then are we to account for the peculiar impression made on Josias by the reading of the law before him?

We have similar examples every day before our eyes. The king was a young man of twenty-three or twenty-four years old, not knowing as yet that Mr. Preston would discover, through the information that Voltaire gave him, that there was no law yet written. He had been trained to respect that law as the work of God, and now the very original, written by Moses is brought before him! Can we wonder that he is filled with reverence and awe, and that the peculiar circumstances brought more vividly to his mind the enormity of the transgressions which had been committed against it? The circumstances prove most decisively that the law was the same which the Jewish people had been accustomed to reverence, but which during the troubled times through which the nation had passed had been partly forgotten, or not sufficiently respected.

At the accession of Josias to the throne, not more than 50 years of persecution of believers had elapsed, and certainly there would be many Priests, Levites, Magistrates and people who would have the memory of the law, and a false law could ,not be imposed on them by Helcias. If this had been the case, the successors of Josias who restored Idolatry would have exposed the trick of this High-Priest. But besides all this, as we shall see in the next chapter, the Samaritans, hostile to the Jews would not have been imposed on in this way.

CHAPTER XVII.

AUTHENTICITY AND INTEGRITY OF THE PENTATEUCH.—TESTIMONY OF THE LATER SACRED WRITERS.

THE testimonies we have enumerated, in the preceding chapter fully demonstrate that the Old Testament was translated into Greek about the year 277 or 280 B. C. It was represented by Demetrius to Ptolemy Philadelphus that these books were of very great value as they contained the history of the Jews from the earliest period. He further informed the king that the Hebrew language which the Jews spoke, and in which the books were written was difficult, and that it would be necessary to incur considerable expense to obtain the translation. The king then, by the advice of Aristæus, who as well as Josephus relates the facts, paid for the emancipation of the captive Jews in his dominions, and thus secured the good-will of the High-Priest Eleazar, and obtained the desired translation.

We need not enter here upon further details. Suffice it to say that the history proves that the Septuagint had a Hebrew original: that the Hebrew language was a reality, a spoken language, and that the Jewish national law was founded on not only the Pentateuch but the whole Old Testament. I say it proves that Hebrew was a spoken language; for though the dialect then spoken was greatly changed by intercourse with the Assyrians, it nevertheless was the child of the old Hebrew tongue. We have then the Jewish nation in the year 280 B. C., with a history and code of laws, and its monuments, its temple, its altars, its ceremonies, all of which proclaim the then antiquity of the law, as loudly as the Egyptian monuments and those of Assyria tell us to-day that these nations have a history too. The law must necessarily have been hundreds of years old then.

But the evidences of the Antiquity of the Sacred writings do not end here.

There exists to-day a little nation that dates from the year 972 B. C. They are the Samaritans of Holy Writ. In the year named, according to the best attainable Chronology, ten tribes revolted from the king of all Israel and formed a new kingdom of Israel, leaving to Roboam the kingdom of Juda. This new kingdom was afterwards named Samaria. 3 Kings (Prot. Bible, 1 Kings), xi; xvi, 24. These Samaritans preserved religiously the Pentateuch, and have preserved it to this day, while they reject the other books of the Old Testament. They became at a later period mixed with the Assyrians. The constant hostility between them and the Jews is a sufficient proof that they did not, by collusion with the latter, adopt the Pentateuch: and indeed they refused even to adopt the more convenient letter which Esdras (Ezra) introduced, and they still retain the old characters, which were used from the earliest period.

There are, it is true, some differences between the Hebrew text and the present Septuagint and Samaritan texts, but they are substantially identical. The Samaritans, we know, corrupted their text in many places to justify the monstrosity of their religion, mixed of Paganism and Judaism: but while these corruptions do not destroy the validity of the true text, the existence of the Samaritan copies, and their *substantial* identity with the Hebrew text, absolutely demonstrates that the true text, whichever it may be, dates from before the separation of the tribes into a distinct kingdom.

Moreover: the existence of the Samaritan Pentateuch proves that already, nine hundred and seventy-two years before Christ, the Pentateuch, the basis of the laws of two nations, must have been ancient: for then also the monuments were extant which attested the antiquity of the nation founded on those laws. Solomon's temple was not the result of a day's belief. The ark of the covenant placed in it, the sacred vessels, the cherubim, the stone tables of the law, etc., were all evidences of the same. Thus we have traced the Pentateuch to nearly seven hundred years earlier than the date allowed by Col. Ingersoll and Mr. Preston, and over eight hundred years earlier than Mr. Rawson allows. But it must have been already hundreds of years old, as the numerous monuments and feasts still kept sufficiently attested: and as the separation of the ten tribes occurred only four hundred and seventy-seven years after the death of Moses, we are already brought to within a short time of the date of Moses himself.

The books of Samuel and Kings and Paralipomenon or Chronicles are the public records of the nation. They differ in this from other national records: that they raise the mind to contemplate how human things are governed by Divine Providence. They were written, as we learn from the last-named books, by Samuel, David, Nathan, Gad, and other prophets, recognized by the authorities of the synagogue as the prophets of God. They made use of other public documents of a similar character, apparently, in their compilations.

The fact of these compilations being authentic is evident from their intrinsic character. The language in which they are written is the intermediate language between the Hebrew of Moses and that which was spoken by the Jews after the Babylonish captivity. They were besides read and venerated as their sacred records by the Jewish people of the time, and they enter upon details of government and conduct of the Jews that none but those who were familiar with the events could write.

In addition to all this, many of the events therein recorded, especially those which refer to foreign nations, are also referred to by profane authors, or monuments; and though it is not to be expected that foreigners would take so deep an interest in the Jewish domestic affairs as the Jews themselves, yet in pagan monuments remarkable confirmations of many principal facts are to be found.

Thus, in 3 Kings iii, 1 (Prot. Bible, 1 Kings), we have an account of Solomon's marriage with the daughter of the King of Egypt; and an extant fragment of Eupolemus relates that friendship existed between the two kings, so much so that there was friendly intercourse between them by letter, and that Solomon, by letter, acknowledged the share the Egyptian workmen had in the construction of the grand temple which he brought to completion. Thus the traces of primitive Revelation found in Egypt would be easily accounted for by the friendly intercourse of the two kings, especially as, according to the account given by Eupolemus, Solomon is in no way backward in announcing to Vaphres, the Egyptian Pharoah, the power of the Most High, "through whom he succeeds to the throne of David." Colonel Ingersoll says (p. 50) that Moses borrowed these traces from the Egyptians. It will be proved in chapter 23 that this is not the case; so we may well suppose that the Egyptians learned these things imperfectly by means of their inter-communication with the Jews. Similarly were communications held with Phœnicia, Syria, and Ophir. To the temple Libanus sent its cedars, and Arabia its perfumes.

We need not here transcribe Solomon's letter to Hiram, King of Tyre; but Hiram's answer, which accedes to Solomon's desires to have a large number of workmen "to cut down cedar trees out of Lebanon," etc., blesses the "Lord God," who has placed Solomon on the throne. It is, therefore, not to be much wondered at if there were in these countries some traces of primitive religious truth, but they were only traces, as they have reached us.

The records of Tyre fully confirm these statements; for in them is found an account of the building of the temple by King Solomon at Jerusalem, one hundred and forty-three years and eight months before the Tyrians built Carthage.

Dius, moreover, relates in his history of Phœnicia that Hiram, King of Tyre, had much timber cut in Libanus for the building of temples, and that between Hiram and Solomon there was much intercourse.

Menander, the Ephesian, relates the same circumstances in great detail.

These facts are in perfect accord with the Scriptural history of Solomon. Menander's chronology also agrees with that of the public records of Tyre, and coincides very nearly with the best modern estimates on these dates.

Berosus, Philostratus, Megasthenes, and the Phœnician records give details concerning the Assyrian invasions of Judea, which agree wonderfully with the Scripture history. All these testimonies may be read in Josephus "against Apion," Book i, 20.

Hermippus, Theophrastus, Herodotus, Cherilus, Aristotle, Agatharicides, all mention various customs of the Jews; from which it is seen that they were strict in the observance of the Mosaic law, and Hecateus wrote an entire book on the same subject. Extracts from these ancient writers may be found in Josephus, Book I, against Apion.

Josephus adds that, besides the above, "Theophilus, Theodatus, Mnases, Aristophanes, Hermogenes, Euhemerus, Conon, and Zapyrion, all of whom, though making many mistakes in their accounts of the Jews, nevertheless attest many things which are true, and which prove their antiquity as a nation; while Demetrius, Phalerius, the elder Philo, and Eupolemus have come very near the truth.

To these writers may be added Cheremon, Polybius of Megalopolis, Strabo, Nicolaus of Damascus, Timagenes, Castor, and Apollodorus.

The place of the temple is now perfectly well-known. It accords with the place whither the Jews were accustomed to repair every Friday to pray, near St. Stephen's gate. Messrs. de Saulcy and Foret describe the immense stone blocks, twenty-nine and one-half feet in length, which are to be seen to-day, and which, with the exception of the blocks at Baalbec, are the largest ever used for building.

Aristæus describes the fountains of the temple in detail, and calls them "a marvel of hydraulics."

Mr. de Saulcy recognizes perfectly in the ruins now visible, the works which Solomon constructed over the valley of Millo. The first indication of the special name of an Egyptian King, is in 3 Kings, xi, 40. (Prot. Bible, 1 Kings.) We are told here that Jeroboam fled to Shishak, King of Egypt, to escape from Solomon's wrath. Champollion has identified this King with Sheschonk, the first King of the 22d dynasty: so that is readily understood that Solomon's father-in-law being dead, Jeroboam should look to the new dynasty for protection against Solomon.

This Shishak invaded Jerusalem in the fifth year of Roboam and carried away the treasures of the temple and of the King. (xiv, 25, 2 Par. xii, 2. Prot. Bible, Chron.)

The existence of Shishak was unknown to profane

historians until Champollion's discoveries, and Infidels of the last century, ridiculed the Bible in this point as inconsistent with history. But at Karnak, Shishak is represented as holding by the hair a crowd of captives whom he is in the act of destroying. Another group is beside this with their hands tied, amongst whom is one with a decidedly Jewish face, bearing a shield with the inscription *Jeoudhamelek, the King of Juda.* See Rosellini and Champollion. The latter adds that this Shishak is undoubtedly the Sesonchis of Manetho. This discovery is a remarkable proof that the Jewish records contained in the Kings and Chronicles are authentic and correct records, written at the period when the events occurred.

The monumental history of Assyria gives similar testimony. Tiglath-Peleser, Shalmaneser, Sargon, Sennacherib and Esarhaddon carried their arms into Palestine, according to the Bible. All these kings are named on the tablets discovered in Assyria, and the events thereon recorded confirm in every respect the Biblical account. Of course the Assyrian accounts are given from the Assyrian point of view, and some slight discrepancies are found on comparing them with the Bible. Thus the total loss of Sennacherib's army when 185,000 men were dead in the morning is not recorded by the Assyrians, whose national pride did not permit them to transmit the memory of their great humiliations, but even this fact is corroborated by Herodotus. The invasion itself is, however, mentioned in detail on the Assyrian tablets.

The oldest monuments extant in Assyria are probably to be attributed to about 1350 B. C. The two centuries which precede the reign of Asshur-idannipal are without monuments. The monuments which have been discovered in connection with Assyrian history since that period, are recognized by Messrs. Layard, Rawlinson and de Saulcy as corroborating the Biblical records to an astonishing extent. The intimacy of the sacred writers with the manners of the various nations of whom they write, is surprisingly manifested in the incidental mention of facts which could not have been thought of by persons who had not witnessed them; and yet facts have been elicited by the discovery of ancient monuments which have fully substantiated the description of the Biblical writers. Thus, for example, the description of King Solomon's litter, (Canticle, iii, 9, 10. Prot. Bible, Song of Solomon,) with pillars of silver, the seat of gold, the covering of purple, is a correct picture of oriental monarchical magnificence of the period. The lions around Solomon's throne, (3 Kings, x; 19, 20,) are the same emblems that covered the walls of Nineveh. The spear and shield and helmet and battering-ram, were all war-like instruments in common use. Moveable towers, such as described by Ezechiel, iv, 2, were also employed in warfare. The Assyrian horses, celebrated from the earliest times are aptly described in Job, xxxix, 19. Habb., i, 8, and the scriptural account of the Kings that reigned in Assyria is perfectly consistent with the story told by the latest monumental discoveries. Mr. Layard has read on the Assyrian tablets the equivalent of Scriptural names of the Syrians: Khitti=Hittites, and the siege of Lachish and succeeding events described in Is. xxxvi, 2, 4 Kings, xviii, 14, etc., Prot. Bible, 2 Kings, are circumstantially described on the Assyrian monuments and many other events mentioned in Holy Writ, on which Mr. Layard's "Nineveh and its Remains" may be consulted.

Numerous other instances might be adduced to show the accuracy of details in the books under consideration, but we need only add that the main facts recorded in Scripture undeniably accord with known history: such as the rise and fall of the Assyrian, Babylonian and Persian Empires, the springing up of Greece as a nation, the rise of the Roman Empire and the diffusion of Phœnician and Greek civilization. All this shows that the Jewish records are a faithful account of the fortunes of the people of Israel.

The wonderful accord between these books as to the facts related, and the prophecies of Isaias, Jeremias, Amos, etc., proves that if one book is rejected as spurious, all must be spurious, which, in the history of literature would be unprecedented.

I have dwelt thus on the character of these books on account of the fact that they cover a great part of the period between Moses and the establishment of the Samaritan Kingdom. There are besides the books of Josue, Judges and Ruth, during the same interval. All these books are based upon the authenticity of the Pentateuch, and as they form a continuous record of Jewish history, confirmative of each other, and all having similar intrinsic evidences of authenticity, they constitute an irrefragable proof of the authenticity of the Pentateuch also.

CHAPTER XVIII.

AUTHENTICITY AND INTEGRITY OF THE PENTATEUCH. — TESTIMONY OF THE LATER SCRIPTURES.—PAGAN TESTIMONY.

Among the many passages of the later Scriptures which testify to the authenticity of the Pentateuch, during the period which elapsed from the death of Moses to the separation of the twelve tribes, the following may be instanced; and it must be remembered that they are from the public records of the nation, both civil and religious: records more sacred, and as carefully preserved as the archives of any nation of to-day.

From Josue we have:

(Jos. i, 1.) "Now, it came to pass, after the death of Moses, the servant of the Lord, that the Lord spoke to Josue, the son of Nun, the minister of Moses, and said to him: 'Moses, my servant, is dead; arise, and pass over this Jordan,' " etc.

(i, 3.) "I will deliver to you every place, ... as I have said to Moses."

(7.) "Observe and do all the law which Moses, my servant, hath commanded thee."

(13.) "Remember the word which Moses, the servant of the Lord, commanded you."

(viii, 30 to 35.) "Then Josue built an altar to the Lord, the God of Israel, in Mount Hebal, as Moses, the servant of the Lord, had commanded. . . . . And he wrote upon stones the Deuteronomy of the law of Moses. . . . . He left out nothing of those things which Moses had commanded."

(11, 15.) "As the Lord had commanded Moses, his servant, so did Moses command Josue," etc.

We find in Judges:

(iii, 4.) "And he left them, that he might try Israel by them, whether they would hear the commandments of the Lord, which he had commanded their fathers by the hand of Moses, or not." etc.

We find in 1, 2 Kings, or Prot. Bible, 1, 2 Samuel:

(1 Kings xii, 6, 8 Prot. Bible, 1 Samuel.) "It is the Lord who made Moses and Aaron, and brought our fathers out of the land of Egypt."

"And the Lord sent Moses and Aaron, and brought your fathers out of Egypt: and made them dwell in this place."

(ii, 6.) "The Lord killeth and maketh alive." This is quoted from Deut. xxxii, 39.

(vi, 6.) "Why did you harden your hearts, as Egypt and Pharaoh hardened their hearts?" Quoted from Ex. iv, 21, etc.

(2 Kings xi, 4, Prot. Bible, 2 Saml.) "She was purified from her uncleanness." This is in accordance with Lev. xv, 18.

(xii, 6.) "He shall restore the ewe fourfold." This is in accordance with Ex. xxii, 1.

From Ruth we find:

(iv, 5.) "Thou must take also Ruth the Moabitess, ... to raise up the name of thy kinsman in his inheritance."

This is to fulfill the law. (Deut. xxv, 7.)

See also verse 10, 11; and in verse 12, reference is made to Gen. xxxviii, 29.

In 1, 2 Paralipomenon or Chronicles.

(1 Chron. vi, 49.) "But Aaron and his sons offered burnt-offerings, etc., according to all that Moses the servant of God had commanded."

(xv, 15.) "And the sons of Levi took the ark of God, as Moses had commanded."

It will be here seen, and throughout Kings and Chronicles, that the ark of God was a standing monument of the law given by Moses. The same is to be remarked of the two monuments mentioned in the next quotation:

(xxi, 29.) "But the tabernacle of the Lord, which Moses made in the desert, and the altar of holocausts was at that time (B. C. 1017) in the high place of Gabaon."

(2 Chron. i, 3.) "He went .... to the high place of Gabaon where was the tabernacle of the Lord which Moses the servant of God made in the wilderness."

In v, 10, another important memorial is mentioned as being kept in the ark: "the two tables which Moses put there at Horeb."

I need not quote more. It is perfectly well known that not only these books, from which I have cited a few out of many passages, but also all the books of the Old Testament, constantly refer to the Mosaic writings as the law which every Hebrew was bound to obey. The 3d and 4th books of Kings, the Psalms, Ecclesiasticus, the books of Proverbs, Esdras and Nehemias, the prophecies of Isaias, Jeremias, Ezechiel, Daniel, and the minor prophets, besides Tobit, Judith, Baruch, Wisdom, and the books of the Maccabees, all quote the law and writings of Moses, as the basis of religion and patriotism. Can we, in the face of this constant tradition and the historical archives of a nation, deny the authenticity of the Pentateuch?

Surely even Col. Ingersoll who accepts as authentic

the Koran, the Vedas, the sacred and political fragments of Egypt and China must acknowledge that there is for all these no such evidence as for the Pentateuch. Cæsar's commentaries, Cicero's literary and philosophical writings, the annals of Tacitus, Xenophon, and Herodotus, the poetry of Homer and Virgil, might possibly be put in doubt, as works of these authors, but not the Pentateuch, which is proved by authorities so constant, so positive and so numerous; and be it remembered, that if the books of Moses are not authentic, the whole of a nation's records, civil and religious, must be rejected also, together with their public monuments and traditions.

The testimony of Christ and His Apostles we need not insert, as it is universally acknowledged that they recognized the entire Old Testament; and not only is this authenticity acknowledged by Jews and Christians of all denominations, but it is admitted by Mahometans and Pagans. Celsus, Porphyry and Julian never called it in question while writing against Christians, though they would certainly have done so if they had anything to allege against it. On the other hand, the most ancient writers of every nation recognized this fact more or less fully.

Of the Egyptians, Manetho, their oldest historian, states from the sacred writings of Egypt, much that is found in the Pentateuch, though he adds much that is erroneous. However, as far as his account is accurate, it is a strong confirmation of the authority of the Pentateuch, and even his mistakes imply the truth of the leading facts.

He relates that the captive Hebrews left Egypt during the reign of Tethmosis, and that they occupied Judea, and built Jerusalem. Their leader, he says, was born in Heliopolis the same as On (Gen. xli, 45,) the city of the Sun. His name was Osarsiph, which he changed to Moses. He forbade the worship of the Egyptian Gods, and established many customs which were opposite to those of the Egyptians and even killed the animals which the Egyptians held sacred.

Diodorus of Sicily says that "The Jew Moses pretended to have received from the God Jahal (corrupted from Jehovah) the laws which he gave to his nation." Nicholaus of Damascus speaks of "Moses the legislator of the Jews." Strabo praises "the sanctity of the worship which Moses established, when at the head of a vast multitude, he left Egypt to fix himself in Judea, as he detested the profane customs of the Egyptians."

Polemon, Hellanicus and Philochorus and Castor, all spoke of Moses as a man highly to be esteemed, and as having a divine character. The Koran of Mahomet also frequently speaks of Moses as a prophet of God.

Who doubts of the existence of a Confucius, a Zoroaster, a Lycurgus, a Solon, a Numa, a Mahomet? Yet the existence of Moses and his authorship of the Pentateuch are proved by testimonies much more worthy of credit, much more numerous and universal than those which attest the life and actions of these celebrities.

The books of the Old Testament, and especially the Pentateuch contain the laws, the doctrines, the morality of the Jewish people, their genealogies and their title-deeds. The kings and priests were obliged to make themselves familiar with them. They were read frequently to the people. Many copies of them were preserved with the greatest care among them, and history attests that such was their respect for the sacred volume, that every letter was regarded as so sacred, that no alteration was tolerated in the most minute particulars. Every circumstance combines to prove that they must be authentic.

CHAPTER XIX.

AUTHENTICITY AND INTEGRITY OF THE PENTATEUCH.—OBJECTIONS OF MESSRS. PAINE AND INGERSOLL REFUTED.

Let us now see on what grounds do infidels maintain that the Pentateuch is spurious.

A few—very few—passages are found which, they say, must evidently have been written by a later hand, and the last chapter of Deuteronomy records the death of Moses.

If it were the case that slight variations from the original were made by a later hand, the substantial accuracy and authenticity of the work would not be in the least impaired. Other books, especially those of ancient date have suffered changes, which do not prevent us from acknowledging that they are, as a whole, authentic.

It is not pretended that the last chapter of Deuteronomy may not have been written by Joshua or some other prophet, as a supplement to Moses' work: though I must say I would see no difficulty in admitting that Moses himself should have written it in the spirit of Prophecy, as he lived in an atmosphere of Prophecy and Miracles.

In either case the authenticity of the work itself, in substance, cannot be impugned.

It is not, however, claimed, either by the book itself, or by the Christian Church that Moses wrote this chapter. In fact, the sixth verse of the chapter seems to imply that at all events the fifth and following verses were added after Moses' death:

"No man hath known of his sepulchre until this present day."

Josephus is, however, of the opinion that Moses himself wrote the account of his death " through fear that the people should venture to say that because of his extraordinary virtue he went to God." Antiq. Book iv, 48.

This is the opinion of Josephus, individually, and Philo embraces the same view; but this is not necessarily the opinion we must entertain. It is usually believed among Christians that this part of Deuteronomy is the supplement by another. Thus Col. Ingersoll's witticism is harmless, though it was intended to be conclusive against the authenticity of the Pentateuch. He says (pp. 265 to 268,) in an *elegant* sentence of nearly six pages:

"Let us admit .... that God .... did not secretly bury a man, and then allow the corpse to write an account of the funeral."

Under either hypothesis there is no question whatever of a "corpse writing an account of his own funeral."

Among the other objections which are brought against the authenticity of the Pentateuch, on the plea that certain passages must have been written at a later period, we find the following in Col. Ingersoll's book:

"In the 30th chapter of Exodus (verse 13,) we are told that .... each one must give a half shekel after the shekel of the Sanctuary. At that time no such money existed, and consequently the account could not, by any possibility have been written until after there was a shekel of the Sanctuary, and there was no such thing until long after the death of Moses." (P. 229.)

On what authority does Col. Ingersoll declare that there was no shekel of the Sanctuary? In Exodus God begins to regulate everything relating to the Sanctuary, and He here ordains the shekel of the Sanctuary and declares that it shall be twenty gerahs or obols. Undoubtedly the weight of the shekel was then determined by a standard to be kept for the purpose in the sanctuary. This is evident also from Lev. v, 15; xxvii, 3, 15; Num. iii, 47.

Col. Ingersoll evidently blunders here by following Voltaire blindly. If the shekel was not a coin in our modern form, might it not have been a weight? The verb shakal from which it is derived means to weigh, and it was the custom to carry weights in a bag for the purposes of traffic. (See Deut. xxv, 13; Mic. vi, 11; Prov. xvi, 11.) In the sanctuary, the standard weights were kept.

"No shekel of the sanctuary in the time of Moses," Col. Ingersoll tells us. What could have induced Moses, then, to have spoken of such a weight? His testimony is sufficient to prove that it did exist. In fact there is every reason to believe that there was no difference between the shekel of the sanctuary and the ordinary shekel, except that the shekel of the sanctuary was the standard; and we find the shekel used over 400 years before the time of Moses, in Genesis xxiii, 15, 16, xxiv. 22. Such are the puny objections by means of which Col. Ingersoll would wish to destroy the credit of the Bible.

These two absurd objections, together with the equally absurd objection, which I have refuted in chapter 16, that in the time of Moses writing was unknown, are the only arguments, absolutely, which Col. Ingersoll can find against the authenticity of the Pentateuch.

Mr. Thomas Paine, however, finds some difficulties of similar character, which it may be well to refute here. The pages are from the New York edition of "Age of Reason," 1878.

Mr. Paine says:

"I mean not to go out of the Bible for evidence of anything, but to make the Bible itself prove historically and chronologically that Moses is not the author of the books ascribed to him." (P. 68.)

"I will not go out of the Bible for proof against the supposed authenticity of the Bible. False testimony is always good against itself." (P. 75.)

The following is the first evidence of unauthenticity:

"In the 14th chapter of Genesis," v. 14, we read that "Abraham pursued (the captors of Lot) unto Dan. . . . . . There was no such place as Dan till many years after the death of Moses; and consequently Moses could not be the writer of the book of Genesis." (P. 69.)

"The place that is called Dan in the Bible was originally a town of the Gentiles, called Laish; and when the tribe of Dan seized upon this town, they changed its name to Dan in commemoration of Dan, who was the father of that tribe." (P. 69.)

He then refers to Judges xviii, 27, 29. "They (the Danites) came unto Laish . . . . and burned the city with fire, and they built a city . . . . and they called the name of the city Dan, after the name of Dan, their father, howbeit the name of the city was Laish at the first." (P. 70.)

Certainly, if the Dan to which Abraham pursued Lot's captors was the same place which was named Dan by the Danites, it would prove one of two things: viz., either Moses, by inspiration, knew that the Danites would occupy the site of Laish, and call it Dan, or else subsequent copyists introduced the word Dan as an explanation of the word Laish, in order that the reading might be better understood. But, surely in either case, the whole work is not on this account to be rejected as spurious. There are in Josephus, Tacitus, Virgil, Homer, passages which some suppose to be interpolated accidentally or intentionally, but no one dreams of rejecting their whole work on this account. Why then should the entire work of Moses be rejected, merely because an explanatory change of a word were made in this case, possibly even, by authority? But considering that Moses is throughout conscious that the Israelites will possess the territory of the Chanaanites, it is not at all unlikely that he could foresee that the spot would be called Dan.

However, there is another answer to this. Mr. Paine assumes that the Dan spoken of in Genesis is the same place as the Dan mentioned in Judges. This supposition is entirely gratuitous, and therefore his whole argument falls to the ground.

In fact St. Jerome, a perfect scholar in Hebrew, who wrote fifteen hundred years ago, tells us that the

Dan of Genesis xiv., and the Dan of Judges xviii., are two different places, in all probability.

The river Jordan is certainly JOR-DAN, and it means the river *Dan:* and though the Hebrew syllable *Jor* differs from the spelling of *Jor* a river, as applied to the Nile, it has the same meaning. Jordan is therefore the river *Dan*, and it had this name before the time of Moses. It is even called by this name in the very history of Lot, wherein the pursuit of the four kings by Abraham to Dan is recorded. (Gen. xiii., 11, 12.) Why then, should not the Dan mentioned in Gen. xiv., 14, be some locality in the neighborhood of the Jordan, or the Jor-Dan itself. This is perhaps the most probable view to be taken of the narrative: for we may far more readily understand that the four kings were pursued to Jordan or Jor-Dan, than to the Dan in the extreme north of the land of Canaan, which was altogether in a different direction from the country of the four kings.

This opinion is further favored by the fact that there was a town Dannah (Jos. xv., 49,) the feminine form of Dan, as Moses wrote both words: *Dn; Dnh.* The town Dannah and the river Jordan may possibly, both have been named after Dan before Jacob and Dan left Canaan to make their dwelling in Egypt.

Is this the kind of objection that is to upset all the positive proofs we have given of the authenticity of the Pentateuch?

Mr. Paine's next objection is against Gen. xxxvi., 31:

"And these are the kings that reigned in Edom before there reigned a king over the children of Israel."

On this Mr. Paine says:

These words "could only have been written after the first king began to reign over them; and consequently the book of Genesis, so far from having been written by Moses, could not have been written till the time of Saul at least." (P. 71.)

He then points out that the writer of Chronicles i, 43, uses the same words through several verses.

He infers that Genesis is not so old as Chronicles. (P. 72.)

He does not attempt to explain how the Chronicles have managed to quote the Pentateuch so frequently as we have shown (Chap. 18,) if the Pentateuch were written after it. However, in Deut., xvii., 14, Moses expressly says to the Israelites:

"When thou art come into the land which the Lord thy God will give thee . . . . and shalt say. I will set a king over me, as all nations have that are round about. . . . Thou mayest not make a man of another another nation king."

Is it a very inconsistent thing to suppose that he who could foretell that they would wish for, and would have a king, should also be able to say, such and such kings reigned in Edom before Israel had a king?

In Deut. xxviii, 36, he repeats his prediction of the same event.

Let us look at the matter from another point of view. Moses did not write in English, but in Hebrew. The word *Melek*, which we translate king, does not necessarily mean the ruler of 50,000,000 of people. The *Melek* was a ruler of a nation, even a small one, and Moses is himself called by this name in Deut. xxxiii, 5. "He shall be king with the Most Right, the princes of the people being assembled with the tribes of Israel." Now, since Moses is called a king, cannot it be that the expression "these are the kings that reigned in Edom before there reigned a king over the children of Israel," means "these are the kings of Edom before my rule began in Israel?"

Whichever view we take of this matter the authenticity remains intact.

Mr. Paine's next objection is not against the authenticity of the Pentateuch, but against the character of Moses, who is accused of atrocity in his dealings with enemies. It is drawn from Num. xxxi, 13. We answered this in chapter 9.

The next objection against the authenticity is founded on Ex. xvi, 34.

"The children of Israel did eat manna until they came to a land inhabited; they did eat manna until they came unto the borders of the land of Canaan."

Mr. Paine says:

"Moses could not write this account, because the account extends itself beyond the life and time of Moses. Moses .... died in the wilderness, and never came upon the borders of the land of Canaan." (P. 74.)

REFUTATION. Moses reached Mount Pisgah "over against Jericho." (Deut. xxxiv, 1.) This mountain was therefore on the borders of Canaan. Pisgah was in Moab, "a land inhabited." Moses was therefore with the Israelites when they reached "a land inhabited" on "the borders of the land of Canaan." The account, therefore, does not extend beyond the life and time of Moses, and there was no difficulty about his writing Exodus up to the date of the arrival of the Israelites at that spot. It is indicative of a bad cause to have recourse to such petty special pleading.

Mr. Paine himself acknowledges virtually that this last objection, as well as the next, is worthless, for he first says that the next objection is more remarkable than this one (p. 75,) and immediately afterwards he adds that his historical difficulty in the next is "not so direct and positive as in the former cases." (P. 75.) He adds, however:

"It is nevertheless very presumable and corroborating evidence, and is better than the *best* evidence on the contrary side."

Mr. Paine seems to forget that he has undertaken to *prove* the non-authenticity of the Pentateuch. We have given positive evidence of its authenticity and will in the next chapter give more. His indirect and un-positive proofs are therefore of no weight. However, let us see what he has to say that requires this apologetic introduction. He quotes Deut. iii, 11:

"For only Og king of Bashan remained of the race of giants; behold his bedstead was a bedstead of iron; is it not in Rabbath of the children of Ammon? Nine cubits was the length thereof, and four cubits the breadth of it after the cubit of a man."

He adds:

"A cubit is 1 foot 9.8881 inches; the length, therefore, of the bed was 16 feet 4 inches, and the breadth 7 feet 4 inches."

"The writer, by way of proving the existence of this giant, refers to his bed, as an *ancient* relic, and says, is it not in Rabbath (or Rabbah) of the children of Ammon? meaning that it is, for such is frequently the Bible method of affirming a thing. But it could not be Moses that said this, because he could know nothing about Rabbah, nor of what was in it. Rabbah was not a city belonging to this giant king, nor was it one of the cities that Moses took. The knowledge, therefore, that this bed was at Rabbah, and of the particulars of its dimensions must be referred to the time when Rabbah was taken, ... 400 years after the death of Moses." (P. 75.)

To confirm this, he quotes 2 Sam. xii, 26.

The difficulty implied, but not positively stated, in regard to the existence of giants will be treated in its proper place, chapter 28. The difficulty about the impossibility of Moses' obtaining knowledge of Rabbah is but a miserable subterfuge, as all must see who have the least notion of the means by which the general of an invading army can obtain the knowledge of the enemy's country. During the Austro-Prussian and Franco-Prussian wars, the knowledge displayed by Baron Von Moltke of every detail of the enemies' countries is acknowledged to have been wonderful. If he were to write a book descriptive of these wars, and were incidentally to mention some such fact regarding the city of Lyons as that which Mr. Paine selects from Deuteronomy, if one would say, "Von Moltke could know nothing of Lyons, since it was not captured by him," the discernment of the skeptic would be justly ridiculed. We would merely answer that the General's knowledge of details was remarkable. Why, then, should the ignorance of Moses be so positively assumed? Certainly the minuteness of details related by him regarding many transactions shows him to be a man of great observation. The admirable suitableness of his laws to secure the health of the Jews, manifests no little skill in Hygiene, the excellence of his moral code, exhibits general wisdom, especially if, as Infidels maintain, his writings are merely human: why then might he not have known even by human means something about Og's domestic arrangements? Is not information sometimes obtained from spies? Sometimes do not deserters or prisoners relate such incidents? And even if all other means of information failed, we know that Moses was instructed by Revelation, or special information given him by Almighty God. But after all, there could not have been very much hostility between the Israelites and the Ammonites, which would prevent the former from obtaining such information. The Israelites were expressly forbidden to make war upon the Ammonites (Deut. ii, 19, 37); and though the latter showed the Israelites no favors, war was not waged against them. Intercourse, therefore, could not have been difficult between the two nations, especially as Rabbath was less than twelve miles from Aroer, less than nine miles from Jezer, two cities of the tribe of Gad, and only about three miles from the confines of the Gadites. Mr. Paine, therefore, utterly fails in his proofs against the authenticity of the Pentateuch.

Mr. Paine adds, however, that the bed of Og is referred to as an *ancient* relic. It is not very clear what length of time is requisite to justify a writer in stating that an article may still be seen. Much depends, I presume, on the estimation in which articles of the kind are usually held. A bedstead is not usually cared for with much veneration. If, therefore, Og's bed had been preserved with unusual care, for a year, or perhaps more, I see no absurdity in calling attention to the fact that it was still kept as a memorial of the last giant of the locality. Surely Mr. Paine rests his case, as he himself acknowledges on arguments that are not very positive or direct.

I have answered all the arguments on this subject which have been advanced by Mr. Paine and Col. Ingersoll. The next chapter will be devoted to the further evidence that the Pentateuch is the work of Moses.

CHAPTER XX.

AUTHENTICITY AND INTEGRITY OF THE PENTATEUCH.—PROOF FROM JEWISH FESTIVALS.

We already proved in chapters 21 and 22 that the Jews have their history as a nation, dating back from the time of Moses. That history is so interwoven with events that happened in the time of Moses, that it is an indubitable proof that the record is his work.

If all our books were burned, the annual celebration of the fourth of July by the people of the United States would tell of a remarkable occurrence in the life of the nation. It would tell that in the year 1776 the great Union of States ceased to be so many colonies and became a nation. Future generations would know by this means alone, of the great event which occurred on the day of the Declaration of Independence.

What Christian is there who does not call to mind, every Christmas-day that a Saviour was born on that day for our Redemption? Who does not remember on Good-Friday that the same Saviour was crucified between two thieves? And on Easter-Sunday, who forgets to recall the remembrance that the same Saviour rose from the dead glorious and triumphant? And when year after year we change the date of our letters from 1883 to 1884, and from this again to

1885, is there any one who is not reminded that these dates are intended to inform us that so many years have elapsed, with perhaps a slight error in the number, since that same Saviour appeared on earth?

The feasts of a nation record its history as if it were written in ink. But these festivals are known also, by historical records, to have reference to the events they commemorate. This union of historical testimony, and annual observance affords the strongest possible chain of evidence to the truth of the events thus attested.

The Jews also keep at this day similar festivals.

On the fifteenth day of the month Nisan or Abib, the Jews celebrate to this day the Passover or Pasch, called by them Pesach. This feast corresponds with our Easter, with the difference that Easter Sunday is the Sunday following the Pesach. This festival was celebrated when Judea was a nation, as attested by Josephus, Philo and all other historians who have written on Jewish customs. In the Old Testament which is the historic record of the nation, there is constant reference to its observance throughout the ages that have elapsed since the Exodus from Egypt. It is well known that the festival is to commemorate the deliverance of the Jews from their Egyptian bondage, their miraculous passage through the Red Sea, and the death of the Egyptian first-born. It is in the Pentateuch that the festival is commanded, and the reason given for its observance. Could such a festival and with such memories have been established if the Pentateuch were a spurious work, first known 170 or 280 years before Christ? You might as easily persuade the American people that the Declaration of Independence never occurred.

In fact it was in remembrance of these transactions that the month Nisan or Abib was made the beginning of the year, as we read in Exodus xii: the year beginning before that with the month Tishri, corresponding with our September and October. This is evident from Ex. xxiii, 16, xxxiv, 22. Hence the manner in which the Jews begin the year is a testimony to the authenticity of the Pentateuch. The civil year begins in Tishri, and the religious year in Nisan. See Josephus Ant. B. 1, c. 3.. The change of the beginning of the year was made precisely in memory of the Passover. (Ex. xii, 1.)

It is a remarkable fact that down to the close of the fifth century of the Christian era, and probably to a later period, the Egyptians observed the vernal equinox with mourning for a great calamity, on account of which they spread red clay on their houses and the trees. It would appear to be an imitation of the means by which the Hebrews averted the death of the first-born in their houses. This is attested by St. Epiphanius.

The feast of Pentecost on which the Revelation of the law on Mount Sinai is celebrated, the fast of expiation on the 10th of Tishri, and commanded in Lev. xxiii, the feast of tents or tabernacles commanded in the same chapter, and other feasts are all additional evidences of the authenticity of the Pentateuch. To these may be added the weekly observance of the Sabbath, which is commanded Ex. xvi, 23 to 29; xx, 8, 11, and elsewhere.

Thus also, to this day, in obedience to the commandment of Moses circumcision is observed, and the eating of unleavened bread is also practiced; but perhaps above all the observance of the Sabbatical year was a testimony to the authority of the Pentateuch which cannot be gainsaid. Every seventh year it was commanded that the land should rest, and that crops should not be sown. It was promised that in the sixth year there should be a triple crop to enable them to observe the law: and all history attests that as long as the Jews were a nation this law was observed. Thus the authenticity of the Pentateuch was attested by a standing miracle.

That the Sabbatical year was observed is evident from many testimonies. I may select the following from Josephus B. 11, c. 8. It is here related that on the occasion of the visit of Alexander the Great to Jerusalem, B. C. 334, the Jews obtained the privilege of not paying tribute in the seventh, i. e. in the Sabbatical year. The Samaritans, hearing that the Jews had obtained such favors, also made a petition for the same privilege, because, they said, they also were Jews, and did not sow during that year. It does not, however, appear that the Samaritans gained the favor.

In this same chapter is related another circumstance which may be added to the proofs of the authenticity of the other books of the Old Testament; for it is related that Jaddus, the high-priest, in consequence of a vision from God, went forth in his priestly robes, to meet Alexander as the latter approached the city, and that Alexander saluted Jaddus with great respect. When the king's attendants observed this they were much surprised, but Alexander, answering Parmenio, replied: "I did not adore him, but that God who hath honored him with this high priesthood; for I saw this very person in a dream . . . . at Dios in Macedonia, who . . . . exhorted me to make no delay, but boldly to pass over the sea thither, for that he would conduct my army and would give me dominion over the Persians," etc.

"In the temple the high-priest showed to Alexander the book of Daniel, wherein Daniel declared that one of the Greeks should destroy the empire of the Persians, and he supposed that himself was the person intended."

It is here worthy of remark that the peculiar privilege of the sabbatical year no longer preserved the Jews from famine, after the time of Christ, as we learn from Josephus, B. xv, 9; xx, 2.

CHAPTER XXI.
AUTHENTICITY AND INTEGRITY OF THE PENTATEUCH.—INTRINSIC EVIDENCE OF ITS LANGUAGE.

BESIDES the extrinsic proofs of authenticity which we have already given, the Pentateuch affords many intrinsic evidences of the same point.

To ascertain by intrinsic evidence whether a given work is authentic or not, we examine whether it is such a work as agrees with the circumstances under which the author writes. In examining the Pentateuch, we may fairly ask:

Is its language such as might have been written by Moses?

Does the writer show such acquaintance with the life and history of the Israelites and Egyptians and other nations with whom he came into contact as justify us to attribute the work to Moses?

Is he as familiar with the geography of the country

as we would have reason to expect from the leader of the Israelites at that time?

If the Pentateuch was not written by Moses, or at least by some one living very close to the time of Moses, we would naturally expect that in all these respects it would vary much from what might be expected from Moses. In fact none but a cotemporary could so write as to conform with what Moses would be likely to write under the three aspects which I have mentioned; and that cotemporary should be perfectly intimate, as Moses was, with Jewish and Egyptian history, and with the secrets of Moses himself, and should be acquainted with the geography of the countries described, as none could be except one who had travelled with the Israelites on their departure from Egypt. Now no cotemporary could possibly have palmed his work on the Israelites as the work of Moses, unless he were authorized by Moses himself to do so, in which case the work would have to be regarded as Moses' work, since it would be promulgated by his authority.

If, then, we can show that these three questions are to be answered affirmatively, it will follow that the Pentateuch is authentic.

First, then, let us see whether the language is such as we might expect Moses to write.

For the correct understanding of this question, it is necessary to say something of the entire Old Testament. There are seven books received by Catholics, but rejected by Protestants and the Jews of to-day, namely, Tobias, Judith, Wisdom, Ecclesiasticus, Baruch, and two books of Maccabees. There are, besides, some chapters of Esther and Daniel in the same position. These chapters and books were not found with the Hebrews of Palestine at the time the New Testament canon was formed, though the Jews of Alexandria received them. They were therefore translated from the Greek. Even Protestants acknowledge that they are historical monuments, though they refuse to them the authority of Inspired Scripture; and some of them are quoted by Josephus as sacred books. However, it is not to our purpose here to enter upon any disquisition on the authority of these books; for it is readily seen that as we have not their Hebrew originals, they do not bear so directly upon the subject we are at present considering, the language in which Moses wrote.

The other books of the Old Testament were written in Hebrew, except a few chapters of Esdras and Daniel, and a verse of the prophecy of Jeremias. These are written in Chaldee, called Biblical Chaldee because of the many Hebraisms found in it.

Chaldee is a language, cognate with Hebrew, being very similar to it: still it is not Hebrew. The Hebrews when in the Babylonian or Chaldean captivity from 605 B. C., to 536 B. C., lost their language, and spoke a mixed dialect of the two tongues. Hence we find different gradations of language in the Old Testament according to the amount of intercourse with the Assyrians, Persians, Hindoos and especially the Chaldeans or Babylonians: and even in the Chaldee there are dialectic varieties, according to the period to which it belongs.

This is what happens in all languages to this day. Horace tells that it has always been, and always will be the case "that new words will be coined with the stamp of the present day" (Ars Poetica):

> "Ut silvæ, foliis pronos mutantis in annos,
> Prima cadunt ; ita verborum vetus interit aetas,
> Et juvenum ritu florent modo nata vigentque."

"As the earliest leaves of the forest fall, while its foliage changes with progressing years, so do old words perish, and by the usage of rising generations, new ones take their place and flourish."

Thus by phonetic decay, the English word *Lord* has been derived from the Anglo-Saxon *hlaf-ord*, i. e., *bread origin*, for *hlaf* is *bread*, and *ord* is *origin :* and lady is from *hlaf-dige*, from *hlaf*, *bread* or *loaf* and *dige* from *dugan*, to *serve*. Thus *Lord* and *Lady* signify originally the *bread-winner* and the *bread-server*. (Max Müller, Science of Language.)

Some languages change rapidly, others very slowly. Thus, Du Ponceau says that the Huron and Iroquois languages did not change at all in two hundred years; while in Central America, some missionaries formed with great care a dictionary of a language, but when they returned to the same tribe in 10 years, the language was so changed that the dictionary was antiquated and useless." (Max Müller, *ib.*)

Hebrew, being fixed by the respect paid to the sacred books, did not change very much from the date of the giving of the law on Mount Sinai 1491 B. C., to the Babylonish captivity, 605 B. C. Nevertheless, the changes have been sufficient to enable us to trace the period to which each book belongs. Thus we are furnished with a powerful and irrefragable evidence of the authenticity of both the Pentateuch and the following books of the Bible.

A genuine book bears about it the impress of the time when it was written, so characteristic that an impostor cannot imitate it; and, with the necessarily limited means at command, which an impostor in the time of Esdras (Ezra) must have had, and indeed at any other period, it must have been absolutely impossible to imitate the characteristics of the period of any of the books of former days, and much more was it impossible to imitate those of the most ancient times. We must bear in mind that literature was confined to a much narrower sphere when printing was unknown, and when books were therefore necessarily scarce. Besides, the forger would have to know perfectly the history of the nations of which he treated, when it was impossible for him to obtain accurate information. He would need to know the geography of countries which he had not visited, and the manners and customs of people concerning whom he could have no sure information; for they were dust centuries before he lived. Besides he would have to provide for a contingency which has actually occurred. His writings would have to stand the test of comparison, on all these points, with monuments of ancient days which have lain buried in the bosom of the earth for centuries, nay even for thousands of years. This contingency, it is impossible he should have foreseen, and if he had foreseen it, it is a contingency for which no imposter would ever dream of providing.

I intend, principally, to show here that the Pentateuch possesses these characteristics; but while doing so, many proofs will occur to show that the other books of the Old Testament possess them also.

The Chaldaic parts of the Old Testament refer to matters which relate to Babylon. This may be seen by referring to them. The portions are Jer. x, 11. Dan. ii, 4 to the end of vii. Esdras iv, 8 to vi, 18, and vii, 12 to 26.

How natural was it for Jeremias to furnish those Jews who were just carried into captivity, with an answer to the Babylonians in their own tongue, when the latter would endeavor to persuade them to forsake the true God?

"Thus then shall you say to them: the Gods that have not made heaven and earth, let them perish from the earth, and from among those places that are under heaven." (x, 11.)

The Chaldee of Daniel is very different from the Chaldee of the reign of Antiochus Epiphanes, as is pointed out in the able Biblical Commentary of Professor Hirschfelder of Toronto University.

Usually the opponents of the Bible place the appearance of their pseudo-Daniel in the reign of Antiochus, about one hundred and sixty years B. C. Now at this time the Hebrews had lost their original language. The Hebrew portion would only be understood by the learned, and even the Chaldee, being of a style then not in use, would have to be translated for the more modern Hebrews. If the prophecy of Daniel were of the late period, it would undoubtedly have been written in the language then current, which is the language employed in the Targums which were written soon after the time indicated. Indeed there would have been no reason for writing in two languages, if it had been of the modern period.

The time of the closing of the Jewish canon is placed by Josephus in the reign of Artaxerxes, king of Persia, i. e., about 435 B. C., and he counts the prophecy of Daniel with the other books, and we have already seen that he states that it was shown to Alexander the Great in 334 B. C. and he adds, when speaking of the canon: "during so many ages as have already passed, no one has been so bold as to add anything to them, or to take anything from them, or to make any change in them; but it becomes natural to all Jews, immediately from their very birth to esteem those books to contain divine doctrines, and to persist in them, and, if occasion be, willingly to die for them." (Against Apion i, 8.)

It is asserted in the Talmud that the great synagogue of one hundred and twenty members, chosen for their eminence in learning, was established by Ezra to enforce the religious observances. Is it possible that Daniel, and other prophecies could have been introduced into the canon, if they were spurious, without being noticed by the members of this assembly, or of the Sanhedrim which succeeded it?

The book of Ecclesiasticus was written about two hundred years before Christ. The writer refers to the three divisions of the Canon of the Jews, "the law, the prophets, and other books of our fathers;" (Prologue), and in chapter xxxix, 1 to 15, the portrait is so closely drawn to the life that there can be little doubt that in his description of the wise man, he has Daniel in view.

All these intrinsic and extrinsic proofs combine in pointing out that both Daniel and Jeremias were written at the time claimed for them, that is to say during or near the time of the captivity of Babylon; for the reasons we have given for the authenticity of Daniel, nearly all apply likewise to the prophecy of Jeremias.

The books of the Old Testament which intervene between the time of Moses, and that of Daniel and Jeremias show all the gradations of language which might be reasonably expected between the ancient and more modern forms; and when we reach the Pentateuch the evidences of the greatest antiquity become very positive.

Thus, with the extension of commercial intercourse with foreign countries, it is natural to expect that foreign words would be introduced into a language. The time of Solomon was especially such a period, and hence we find just in the books which are attributed to him, and to his cotemporaries, the beginning of the frequent use of such words. Thus, into English, the word damask was introduced with the rich silk of that name, originally made at Damascus. *Mandolin* and *boomerang* are words borrowed from the countries where the things expressed were used.

Thus also in the reign of Solomon and afterwards, evidences of the more extensive intercourse of the Hebrews with foreign nations, are to be found in the Bible.

In 3 Kings x, 22 (Prot. Bible 1 Ki.), we have mention of "ivory, apes and peacocks," brought from Tharshish: "*shen-habim ve-kopim ve-thukiyim*," where the words *habim, kopim, thukiyim* are Sanscrit or Hindoo words, with the Hebrew plural ending.

In Sanscrit, *ibhas* is an elephant, *kapi* is an *ape*, and *togei* a peacock in the Malabar tongue.

The same words occur in 2 Par (Chronicles) ix, 21.

Ahalim, aloes, from the Hindoo *Aghil* (probably), is also used in Prov vii, 17; Ps. xliv, 9 (Prot. Bible, Ps. xlv); Cant. iv, 14 (Prot. Bible, Song of Solomon); 2 Par. (Chron.) ii, 7.

Argavan and *argaman, purple*, occur in Dan. v, 7, 16, 29; 2 Par. (Chron.) ii, 6; Ex. xxvii, 16; Prov. xxxi, 22; Jer. x, 9. This word is found in Sanscrit: *ragaman, ragavan*. Wilson's Sanscrit Dictionary.

In the Pentateuch, Joshua, Judges and Ruth such words are very rarely found, though *aloes* are mentioned in Num. xxiv, 6, and in iv, 13 we find *argaman, purple*, and in many places in Exodus, where it is ordered for ritual purposes.

In 2 Par. ii, 7, *Algum* wood is spoken of as *algumim*. In 3 Kings x, 11, 12; 2 Par. ix, 10, 11, (Prot. Bible 1 Kings, 2 Chron.) *almugim* is used.

Persian words are also found; thus, *achashtranim, mules*, from Persic *estar* or Sanscrit *acwatara*, Esther viii, 10. The usual Hebrew name for a mule is *phered* used 19 times, the first occasion being 2 Kings, xiii, 29. (Prot. Bible, 2 Samuel.) This is an additional proof of the authenticity of the preceding books, as well as of those in which the word occurs, for it was the law not to bring together animals of different species, for the production of mules, though the use of the mule itself is not forbidden. Hence not until there was considerable intercourse with foreign nations, could mules be common.

Darkmon and *adarkon* are used for the Persian coin *daric* in 1 Esdras ii, 69; viii, 27; 2 Esdras vii, 71; 1 Par. xxix, 7. (Prot. Bible, Ezra, Nehemiah, 1 Chron.)

Satraps, achashdarphim, are spoken of in 1 *Esdras* (*Ezra*) viii, 35; *Dan.* iii, 2, 3. 28; vi, 1, 2, 4, 7; *Esther* iii, 12·· viii, 9; ix, 3

Pecha a governor, from the Persian *pashaw*, a noble, *puchten* to care for, or Sanscrit *paksha* a companion is also found in 3 Kings x, 15; xx, 24; 4 Kings xviii, 24; 1 Par. ix, 14; (Prot. Bible 1 Kings, 2 Kings, 1 Chron.) 1 Esdras viii, 36; v. 3, 14; vi, 6, 7, 13; 2 Esdras, ii, 7, 9; v 14, 15, 18; xii, 26; (Prot. Bible, Ezra, Nehem.) Is. xxxvi, 9; Jer. li, 2, 3, 28; Ezech. xxiii,

6, 23; Esther viii, 9; ix, 3; Aggeus (Haggai) i. 1, 14; ii, 2, 21; Mal. i, 8; Dan. iii, 2, 3, 28; vi, 7.

Bag, food, and *pathbag,* the *king's food* are used, the former in Ezech. xxv, 7, the latter in Daniel i, 5, 8, 13, 15, 16; xi, 26.

Pethigil, a fine cloak is used in Isaias iii, 24.

Pithgam a *decree* is used in Esther i, 20; Eccli. viii, 2; 1 Esdras (Ezra) iv, 17; v, 7, 11; vi, 11; Dan. iii, 16; iv, 14. (Prot. Bible iv, 17.)

All of these are Persian words. The Targums use *pithgam* for a *word,* and in other respects differ even from the latest books of the Bible. *Parthmim, nobles* is also a Persian word. Dan. i, 3, etc.

From all that we have said it follows that the books of the Bible are all older than the Targums, and indeed as regards Esdras and Nehemias, as their writings are of comparatively modern date, and were written just before the appointment of the Great synagogue of 120 members, it is clear that they cannot be spurious. The other books of the Old Testament are evidently older still, and Daniel, Esther and Jeremias must date from near the beginning of the Babylonian Captivity.

The books of Samuel and Kings, Chronicles or Paralipomenon, must necessarily be intermediate between the time of the Judges and the Captivity; and, as we have seen that they record with wonderful accuracy the events which they describe, they must belong respectively to the periods to which they refer. Thus we arrive at an incontrovertible proof of their authenticity.

The other prophetic books for similar reasons, evinced by their language and by their descriptions of passing events, sufficiently demonstrate that they also belong to the periods to which they are ascribed, and that they were written either by the authors to whom they are attributed, or by their authority.

The books of Josue and Judges, by means of the proofs we have given, are also evidently seen to be older than the books of Samuel and Kings. They belong evidently to a period when there was little or no intercourse with foreigners, and just such a period the books themselves show the Hebrews to have been in at that time.

This argument might be extended almost indefinitely and the greatest nicety in date could be thus ascertained. Besides the gradual introduction of Chaldaisms into Hebrew might be shown, and thus the intrinsic evidences of authenticity would be very greatly accumulated. I have, however given proofs enough to establish the dates of the principal historical books of the Old Testament, and of some of the prophecies, I will therefore proceed in the next chapter to show the intrinsic proofs that the Pentateuch is above all the others in antiquity.

CHAPTER XXII.

AUTHENTICITY AND INTEGRITY OF THE PENTATEUCH.—INTRINSIC EVIDENCE OF ITS LANGUAGE CONTINUED.

I have next to show that the language of Moses betokens an earlier stage than that of the other books of the Old Testament. The method of proof is similar to that adopted in the last chapter.

The name *Medinah,* a province, occurs in the Old

Testament 36 times: yet its first occurrence is in 3 Kings xx, 14. (Prot. Bible 1 Kings.) It is a Persic word and was introduced about king Solomon's time, or soon after, into the language.

Nebel a musical instrument is used 25 times in the Old Testament. Its earliest use is in King David's reign, Psalms xxxii, 2. (Prot. Bible Psalm xxxiii.) It is the name, in Hebrew, of the "instrument of 10 strings."

The *tabernacle* which Moses erected was a very fine structure, and was built with the voluntary offerings which the Israelites supplied from the spoils of the Egyptians, which they brought with them on their departure from bondage. Ex. xxxv; xxxvi, 3, etc. The Hebrew words by which this tabernacle was named were *Ohel* and *Mishkan*.

But in Kings i, 9 (1 Samuel,) we find a new word applied to this tabernacle for the first time, *Hikal*, the *temple;* and this name is afterwards constantly applied to it as well as the names by which it was hitherto known, the older names being from this time forward but seldom used.

I might multiply instances where new words began to be used as soon as the Israelites came forth out of the troublesome times they passed through under the Judges, but I will merely mention a few more, all of which will substantiate my thesis that a marked change in the language took place at the date when the Israelites became settled as a prosperous nation. Thus we have seen several stages through which the language passed. I may give the following examples further:

Matsad, the *summit* of a mountain, occurring thirty-three times in the Old Testament, is first used in

Judges vi, 2. *Nagid*, a *leader*, used forty times, occurs first in 1 Kings ix, 16 (Prot. Bible, 1 Samuel.) *Nathab*, a *path* occurring twenty-five times, is first used in Judges v, 6.

Finally, the Jewish year began in March or April, as explained above in chapter 20. The names of the Months are *Nisan, Zif, Sivan, Tammuz, Ab, Elul, Tishri* or *Ethanim, Bul, Kisleu, Tebeth, Shebat,* and *Adar*, with a supplementary month, *Veadar*, every three years, to make the year of these *lunar* months accord with the *solar* year.

The first mention of these months occurs in 3 Kings vi. (Prot. Bible, 1 Kings.) The only exception is but an apparent one. The month *Nisan* is called *Abib* at an earlier period: but *Abib* means "*the new corn*," and is a purely Hebrew word, while the other names are borrowed from the Chaldeans. Hence the first month was naturally called *Abib*, the month of new corn, before names were really given to the other months. Until the Chaldean names were adopted, the months were known as First, Second, etc. This, then, is another important change of language during or about Solomon's reign.

Now what forger, writing the books of Moses, Joshua, Judges, and Ruth, in the reign of Josias, or at the time of Ptolemy Philadelphus, would have succeeded in giving to them these characteristics of antiquity?

But I must further show that the Pentateuch is older than the other books here enumerated.

Many of the more recent words I have already quoted are used first in Judges. This of itself stamps the books of Moses and Joshua as of much higher antiquity than Judges. We need further only show the very great antiquity of the Pentateuch above all the rest. Of course the fact that both Judges and Joshua rest upon the Pentateuch as on their foundation is sufficient evidence, but we wish here to see what testimony the language of the books themselves will give on this subject.

In the later Hebrew, *hua* signifies *he;* *hia*, *she*, as pronounced by those who do not use the Masoretic points. These two words are, of course, exceedingly frequent in the Old Testament, especially as there are but two genders in the language, but in the Pentateuch *hua* is *nearly always* used for the feminine, as well as the masculine, as the form *hia*, according to the Masora occurs only eleven times in the whole Pentateuch, while *hua*, outside of the Pentateuch, is used for the feminine only in three places at most: 3 Kings xvii, 15; (Prot. Bible, 1 Ki.) Job xxxi, 11; Isa. xxx, 33. Here, then, is an evident change towards definiteness in the language. (See Lexicon of Gesenius.)

Naar, a *boy*, stands in a like position to *hua*. The feminine is *Naarah*, a *girl*. In the Pentateuch, *Naar* is used indiscriminately for a *boy* or *girl*. It means, therefore, a young person or a child. In the later Hebrew the distinction of meaning is observed between the two words.

The process of employing what were formerly generic terms for species, and inventing new words for other species is constantly going on in languages. We have examples of its occurrence in English in our own days. Thus we had daguerreotypes, and now we have ambrotypes, photographs, etc. We had formerly velocipedes, now we have velocipedes, bicycles, tricycles, etc. So *naar* must have been the original word, which afterwards became developed into the two words to signify *boy* and *girl* respectively.

The Pentateuch uses the word *tsachak, to laugh*, 13 times. In all the rest of the Old Testament it is only used twice, viz: in Judges xvi., 25; and Ezech. xxiii., 32. In both places the antiquated form seems to be used for boisterous laughing. Thus in Judges xvi., the Philistines call Samson to sport for them, and he sported for them boisterously. He had in this an object in view, namely to prevent their suspicion of his design to destroy at one bold stroke many enemies of his nation. The word in Ezechiel appears to have similar force. The more recent verb is *sachak*.

There is also a contraction *she* or *sha* for the relative pronoun *asher, who, which*. This contraction belongs to the more recent Hebrew, and is first found in Judges.

Thus we have established fully a gradation in the Hebrew language from the time of Moses to the Restoration of Israel. We have shown that there is a well-marked dialectic difference at each of these epochs: 1, the Mosaic, 2, the Judicial, 3, the period of Samuel, 4, the period of Solomon, 5, the Babylonian captivity, 6, the Restoration from captivity. There would be an average of 161 years to effect each of these changes, which I contend is a very reasonable allowance, epecially as it has the history of the times to confirm it. I am therefore quite justified in saying that the language of Moses, and of the other Scriptural writers proves the authenticity of their writings.

Besides what we have already stated, we must not overlook the fact that the Israelites came out of

Egypt, where they had lived for 215 years, out of which they spent at least 80 years in bondage. Now though the territory they chiefly occupied was separate from that occupied by the Egyptians, very many Hebrews lived in the Egyptian territory: and though they were further separated by the difference of religion, we would expect some words to have crept into the Hebrew tongue from the Egyptian, and such is really the case..

The word *Achu*, which occurs in Genesis xli, 2, 18, and *suph* in Exodus ii, 3, 5, are both Egyptian words. *Achu* is anything green, which grows in marshy places. St. Jerome says that he expressly inquired from learned Egyptians the meaning of this word, and was so informed. Hence in translating the Bible into modern Egyptian, or Coptic, the translator uses *achi*. Kindred words in Egyptian are *ake, oke, bulrush, reed.* Lexicon of Gesenius.

Suph is translated in the English bibles respectively, *sedges, flags.* Though transposed as to its letters from the Egyptian *phous*, philologists agree that there is no way of accounting for it otherwise than as of Egyptian origin.

Lashon, a *tongue; Yam*, the *sea; Saris*, a *eunuch*, or *officer; Ephah*, a *measure of grain; Shesh, fine linen;* are all acknowledged to be of Egyptian origin. These words are found respectively in Genesis x, 5; Gen. xiv, 3; Gen. xxxvii, 36; Ex. xvi, 36; Ex. xxvi, 1.

Ior, a *river*, is of constant occurrence. It is the Egyptian *iaro*, and is used almost exclusively of the Nile. Ex. i, 22, etc. Thus even after the Israelites were out of Egypt, *ior* refers to the Nile. See Ex. xvii, 5; and afterwards this use continued as part of the Hebrew language. Is. xix, 7. No one but one who had lived in Egypt could have dreamed of calling the Nile *the river*, and only to a nation coming out of Egypt could this language be intelligible.

In asserting that the Pentateuch is a spurious writing of late origin, Colonel Ingersoll is evidently very much mistaken.

CHAPTER XXIII.

AUTHENTICITY AND INTEGRITY OF THE PENTATEUCH.—TESTIMONY OF HISTORY.—EVENTS IN JOSEPH'S LIFE.

I already proved in chapter 17 that the historical parts of the later books of the Old Testament agree wonderfully with the history of the nations referred to, as recorded in profane authors, and with the monuments of those nations. This of itself is a strong argument in favor of their truth in testifying to the existence and authenticity of the Mosaic record: more especially as these books constitute the archives of the nation, which are always held as most precious, and are preserved with the greatest care. The universal consent of Christians and Jews, Mahometans and Pagans, that Moses is the author of the Pentateuch is a further testimony to the same fact, and the books of the Bible forming a continuous chain of testimony, prove the tradition of their genuineness to be as constant as it is universal.

These texts from the Old and New Testaments will show the spirit in which Jews and Christians unite in this testimony.

"Only take courage and be careful to observe all things that are written in the book of the law of

Moses: and turn not aside from them, neither to the right hand nor to the left." Jos. xxiii, 6.

"There was no king before him like unto him (Josias) that returned to the Lord with all his heart and with all his soul and with all his strength, according to all the law of Moses." (4 Ki. xxiii, 25; Prot. Bible 2 Kings.)

"And beginning at Moses and all the prophets, he (Jesus) expounded to them in all the Scriptures the things that were concerning him." (St. Luke xxiv, 27.)

"And he said to them: These are the words which I spoke to you while I was yet with you, that all things must needs be fulfilled which are written in the laws of Moses, and in the Prophets, and in the Psalms, concerning me." (Verse 44.)

Thus also, as a historian, Josephus attests:

"But now as to our forefathers (the Jews,) that they took no less care (than the Egyptians and Babylonians) about writing such records, ... and that they committed that matter to their high priests and prophets, and that these records have been written all along down to our own times with the utmost accuracy; nay, if it be not too bold for me to say it, our history will be so written hereafter. . . . ."

"For our forefathers did not only appoint the best of those priests, and those that attended upon the divine worship, for that design, from the beginning, but made provision that the stock of the priests should continue unmixed and pure." (Against Apion, book 1st.)

I have already mentioned that Celsus, Porphyry and Julian did not dispute, but took for granted the authenticity of the Pentateuch. Josephus also quotes against Apion the testimony of Manetho, th   extant, who was the oldest historian of Egypt, and who had all access to the Egyptian records.

"Manetho says that the Jews departed out of Egypt (under Moses, as he says elsewhere,) in the reign of Tethmosis, 393 years before Danaus fled to Argos. Lysimachus says it was under king Bocchoris, that is 1700 years ago. Molo and some others determined it as every one pleased." (B. 2.)

The fact is therefore historically attested by old Egyptian records that at a most remote age, very near the period, to say the least, recorded in the Pentateuch, Moses led the Israelites out of Egypt. What record is more likely to give the true particulars than the attested records of the Israelites themselves? There might be some uncertainty regarding the exact date of the occurrence, but there can be none concerning the fact itself; and this outside testimony is one of the collateral evidences of the genuine character of the Pentateuch.

With the history of Joseph we may very properly begin our examination of the accuracy of the historical narrative of the Pentateuch, for with the facilities which Moses possessed for obtaining knowledge, reared and educated in the palace of Pharaoh, it was no hard task for him to trace back the history of Egypt for 215 years. The Egyptians were a civilized people, in a secular sense, and were able to keep a record of events, as the monuments even now extant prove. True, Col. Ingersoll tells us there was no writing then, and therefore Moses could not write, but the monuments of Egypt tell a different story. There can be no doubt that in the archives of the nation records were kept, and that the priests of

Heliopolis were also well able to give to Moses much information, besides what he would learn from the traditions of his own kindred and countrymen.

The grandfather of Moses was one of the seventy who came into Egypt while Joseph occupied the position of Pharaoh's chief officer. Certainly there could be no difficulty about his hearing from his father those few particulars which he relates of that period, in which his grandfather took a prominent and active part. Besides, the evidence that the Israelites had their records to which he had access, is clear from the fact that their genealogies were faithfully kept, and those genealogies are handed down to this day in Genesis xlvi, and Num. i, iii.

Moses had therefore all the facility for writing his history that any zealous historian possesses, who needs only to write a short account of a comparatively recent event, an event in which his own grandfather was a participator.

There are other events in Joseph's history which touch on the manners and customs and history of the Egyptians. Let us see how they accord with the testimony of such history of the time as is within our reach at the present day.

The earliest Egyptian historian is Manetho, who wrote about 350 years B. C. His history is not extant, but there are quotations from it in Josephus, and epitomes by Eusebius and other early Christian writers, which are undoubtedly correct enough to give a good general idea of Manetho's views of early Egyptian events.

Manetho may have been, and in all probability was, an accurate historian of events which came reasonably within the scope of a historian; but when he related events, not founded on historical documents of credit, but on legends which were related as history solely on the authority of the Egyptian priests, he ceases to be a historian.

Thus when he merely names a series of kings whose reigns when summed up amount to 3,555 years from Menes to 350 B. C., he evidently roams in the region of fable.

Thus, also, when he relates that for thirteen thousand nine hundred years Egypt was governed by a dynasty of Gods, Vulcan or Ptah, Helios, the Sun or Ra, etc., he will scarcely be deemed worthy of credit. After these came Menes and the demi-gods. With Menes began a series of kings, three hundred in number, divided into thirty-one dynasties and reigning three thousand five hundred and fifty-five years, when the lengths of their reigns are added up, to the year 350 B. C.

Now, among the memorials of some of these dynasties, some records have actually survived to the present day which cannot be reconciled with Manetho's lists. (See Chambers' Encyclopædia Art. Egypt.) The only way to reconcile them is to suppose that many of Manetho's dynasties are simultataneous, in different parts of Egypt, instead of successive. When once we begin to apply this principle of simultaneous dynasties, the three thousand five hundred and fifty-five years will be very much reduced. Most of his kings have undoubtedly existed, for their monuments have survived to the present day, but in all probability many were mere myths. Probably Manetho copied the lists correctly from the Egyptian sacred books, etc., but in their national pride, to show a fabulous antiquity, **many of** the records were imaginary. Manetho is not wilfully a falsifier, but his sources of information were frequently unreliable.

The illustrious Champollion was the discoverer of the method of reading the Egyptian hieroglyphics, and his method has been fully demonstrated. He declares:

"I have demonstrated that there is no Egyptian monument really anterior to the year 2200 before our era. This is certainly a very high antiquity, but it affords nothing against the sacred traditions, and I dare to say even that it confirms them on all points. It is, in fact, by the adoption and succession of the kings named on the Egyptian monuments that the history of Egypt accords admirably with the Sacred books. For example, Abraham arrived in Egypt about the year 1900 (B. C.), that is, under the shepherd kings. The kings of the Egyptian race would not have permitted a stranger to enter into their country. It is equally under a shepherd king that Joseph becomes the highest official in Egypt, and establishes there his brothers. This could not have occurred under the kings of Egyptian race. The head of the dynasty of Diospolitans, called the eighteenth, is the "new king that knew not Joseph" (Exodus i, 8,) who, being of Egyptian race, would not acknowledge Joseph the official of the usurping kings, and therefore reduced the Hebrews to slavery. The captivity lasted during the eighteenth dynasty, and it was under Rameses V, called Amenophis, at the commencement of the fifteenth century (B. C.,) that Moses delivered the Hebrews. This occurred during the youth of Sesostris, who succeeded immediately his father, and made his conquests in Asia, while Moses and Israel wandered in the desert for forty years. This is the reason why the sacred books cannot be expected to speak of this great conqueror. All the other kings of Egypt named in the Bible are found on the Egyptian monuments in the same order of succession, and at the precise epochs where the sacred books place them. I will add, even, that the Bible gives, more accurately than the Greek historians, their true names. I would be curious to know what answer to these facts will be made by those who have maliciously asserted that Egyptian studies tend to change our belief in the historical documents furnished by the books of Moses. On the contrary, my discoveries come invincibly to their support." Quoted by Cardinal Wiseman in "Lecture Eight, on Science and Revealed Religion."

Rosselini, also well known as an Egyptian scholar, states in his "Monuments of Egypt," that such parts of the early history of Egypt as go beyond the limits prescribed in Genesis, are unworthy of credit; and all Egyptian archeologists agree that there is much obscurity about the Egyptian monumental history even at the period when Moses and the Israelites were in Egypt. Hence there are great difference of opinion as to who was the king reigning at the time of their departure. The facts, however, above mentioned regarding Abraham and Joseph's history are authenticated, and we may thence infer a surprising knowledge of Egyptian history on the part of the writer of the Pentateuch.

Besides all this, we find that Joseph was, in the first place, sold to some Ismaelite merchants of Madian, "on their way from Galaad, with their camels carrying spices, balm and myrrh to Egypt." (Gen, xxxvi., 25.)

This indicates a large commerce in the articles mentioned, and it strikes us, at first, as extraordinary that such articles would be in great demand. Here again the Scriptural account is confirmed by the modern discoveries that it was the practice of the Egyptians to embalm their dead, and that even the poorer classes did this by a less expensive process than was employed by those who were able to afford the more effectual and costly methods.

The museums of Europe are teeming with mummies of the date of the Pharaohs, and the amount of spices used for embalming purposes, must have been enormous.

Madian, situated on the eastern branch of the Red Sea, was the high road from Canaan and Arabia, the two great emporiums of balm and myrrh, and it was celebrated for its camels. "Their camels also were innumerable as the sand that lieth on the sea shore." (Jud. vii, 12.) This part of Joseph's history is therefore quite in accord with the facts of known profane history, and exhibits the perfect acquaintance of the writer of the Pentateuch with the state of all those countries of which he spoke.

Besides all this the fact is attested by Egyptian monuments, that the people of Canaan were frequently held as slaves in Egypt. On the tomb of Imai, a prince of Suphis, three hundred years before the time of Joseph, Canaanite men and women are depicted as posturers, tumblers and jugglers exhibiting before the Egyptian princes, and one hundred and fifty years later hundreds of Canaanite slaves are represented as gladiators fighting before Chetei, a prince of the twelfth dynasty. Jacob and his family dwelt in Canaan. Thus, again, is the accord between sacred and reliable profane history complete.

CHAPTER XXIV.

AUTHENTICITY AND INTEGRITY OF THE PENTATEUCH.—THE TESTIMONY OF HISTORY CONTINUED.

WE have seen, in the preceding chapter, four circumstances of the history of Joseph confirmed by profane history. Other instances of this agreement are still to be found. The Madianites sell Joseph to Potiphar, an officer: in later times a eunuch (*Saris,*) of Pharaoh. (Gen. xxxix, 1.) We already pointed out that the Hebrew *Saris* is an Egyptian word. It is spelled in unpointed Hebrew, as Moses wrote, Sris. Almost letter for letter, this word is found on the tombs of the Egyptian magnates, *Srs* or *srsh*. Israel in Egypt.

The name *Potiphar,* in Coptic *Ptaphre,* means *belonging to the Sun.* This Potiphar may or may not have been the same who is named in Genesis, xli, 45, Poti-pherah. At all events the signification of the word is the same. Potipherah being priest of On or Heliopolis, that is the City of the Sun, is appropriately styled "He who belongs to the Sun, or the Sun's own." Lexicon of Gesenius.

Next, it will be remarked that there are several words in Hebrew to express magicians: *Chartom,* Gen. xli, 8, *Asaph,* Daniel, i, 20, *Chakim,* Dan. ii, 21. Of these the word *chartom* is found in Egyptian under the form *carecton.* Now though it is possible that *chartom* has a Hebrew root, it was natural for one just coming out of Egypt to use that name for the Egyptian magicians which most resembled the Egyptian name by which they were called. Hence we find that whenever Moses speaks of the magicians of Egypt he uses this word, *chartom.* This implies his complete knowledge of Egyptian customs. See Gen. xli, 8, 24; Ex. xi, 22; viii, 7, 18; ix, 11.

In the relation of Joseph's interpretation of Pharaoh's dreams, Gen. xli, the magicians and wise men who failed in interpreting it are spoken of under the names *chartomim* and *chakamim.*

In the same chapter it is related that when Joseph was brought from prison "he shaved himself and changed his raiment, and came in unto Pharaoh." Mr. Tripard in his "Moses" remarks on this that "owing to the reputation of the young Hebrew, for his ability in interpretation . . . . he would, most probably, be presented in the Sacerdotal costume, that is to say in the costume of official Seers."

Herodotus states (Book ii, 36), "in other countries the priests wear their hair; in Egypt they shave. They wear garments of irreproachable whiteness, and every three days they shave their hair entirely, through respect to the Sanctity of the Gods whose ministers they are."

Another expression in the first verse of Gen. xli, is worthy of notice. After Potiphar's name, it is added that he was an Egyptian. This would, at first sight, seem to be an unnecessary piece of information regarding a high official of the Court of Egypt; yet three times in the same chapter he is described by this name. Now in the present case, as we are aware that the shepherd kings, Canaanites, were reigning, and that Canaanites, as well as Egyptians held high offices, it became important for the descendants of Joseph to know that the progenitor of their tribe was not a bond-slave in the house of one of the doomed race of Canaan, but of a prince of Egypt. The epithet, Egyptian, therefore, shows the knowledge of Egyptian history possessed by the author of the Pentateuch.

On the Egyptian monuments a great famine is attested to have taken place, of which we have a more detailed account in Genesis xli, xlii. This occurred in the reign of Osirtesen I. It is remarkable that an Egyptian papyrus of this period is among the modern discoveries of the country in which some of the king's dreams, and other events of his life are recorded. This unusual circumstance of the record of dreams undoubtedly proves that the dreams of this king were regarded as of more than usual importance. Why this should be the case, it would be difficult to surmise if it were not told us in Genesis xli, how his two dreams which Joseph interpreted, were the occasion of saving the country from the dire consequences which the famine would otherwise have entailed upon it.

This famine extended to Canaan, and obliged ten of Jacob's sons to go into Egypt to buy corn, leaving at home Benjamin, Joseph's full brother.

I need not dwell upon the affecting scene which occurred when Joseph beheld his ten brethren coming on such an errand. When these sold him into slavery, they were filled with savagery, frowning upon a helpless stripling, whom they were prevented from slaying by the Providential appearance of the Ismaelite merchants; and even then they changed their plan into another still more cruel and heartless. Now they appear before their brother, wrinkled and grey with age, bowing themselves to the earth before his royal state; but though they are recognized by Joseph, they do not recognize him. Joseph spoke roughly to them and said "Ye are spies; to see the nakedness of the land ye are come."

Joseph was not aware that his brother Reuben had remonstrated against the cruel designs of the rest. Hence it is not to be wondered at that he addressed them roughly, remembering their wickedness towards him. At all events, occupying the position he did as chief adviser of the king, he would be an object of suspicion if he too readily yielded a kind reception to strangers, especially in the then existing political relations of the Egyptians with the Canaanites. Though the shepherd kings were originally from Canaan, with the most of the Canaanites the Egyptians were frequently at war, and on these occasions the Canaanites of Egypt united with the Egyptians. Hence, lest a formidable force should be introduced, it was necessary to be very cautious in the reception of Canaanites coming in, even under the pretext of buying corn. The conduct of Joseph arose, therefore, from the circumstances of the period; and in his narration, Moses manifests a perfect knowledge of the history of the country.

The Egyptian monuments everywhere attest that a great change took place in the position of the Pharaohs from about the date to which we must attribute Joseph's elevation. Only from that period does the power of the kings become real. Hitherto the nobles had been almost independent, but from that time Pharaoh is at the head of every movement. Up to that time the powers of the nobles were so great that the king was like the kings of Europe in the Middle Ages, the vassal of his haughty nobles. Hence there were continual changes of dynasty, anarchy, and wars. All this was changed by the measures of Joseph. During the years of plenty the king bought up the superfluous corn, and sold it again during the years of famine for the cattle and lands of the inhabitants. Then the lands were given back to the people to till, on condition that one-fifth of the proceeds should belong to the king. (Gen. xlvii.)

The land of the priests, however, was not bought up, "for the priests had a portion assigned to them of Pharaoh." (Verse 22.)

In the preceding periods the great works of Egypt were executed by the nobles, and the Pharaohs left few memorials of their existence, save the pyramids in which they were buried; but in succeeding ages the nobles have no monuments of any consequence. This fully accords with the Scriptural account.

Diodorus Siculus confirms this testimony of Scripture and monumental history. He visited Egypt about 20 years before the birth of Christ, and he declares that the king's right at about that time was one-third of the produce, but that it had been commuted by the king receiving one-third of the land. (History i, 73.)

The history of Joseph is so universally known that it would be useless to introduce it here. Suffice it to say, that when his brethren returned to Egypt a second time, with Benjamin, Joseph made himself known, and directed them to return home, and to bring their father back with them, promising, "I will give you the good of the land of Egypt." xlv, 18. "And they came into Egypt, Jacob and all his seed with him," to the number of "70 souls."

The directions which Joseph gave his father and brethren on their arrival in Egypt has often appeared strange to readers of the Bible. He says:

"My brethren, and my father's house, that were in the land of Canaan, are come to me, and the men are shepherds."

"And when he shall call you and shall say, "What is your occupation?"

"You shall answer: We thy servants are shepherds. . . . . And this you shall say, that you may dwell in the land of Goshen, because the Egyptians have all shepherds in abomination." Gen. xlvi, 31, 34.

How could Joseph expect his father and brothers to be received the more favorably by Pharaoh on account of their occupation as shepherds, whereas shepherds were an abomination to the Egyptians?

The answer to this is found in the fact which a stranger to Egypt would not have known. Pharaoh was one of the shepherd kings, a foreign race from Canaan. Thus he would the more readily admit strangers to power in his dominion, and especially Canaanites, though the Egyptians were very jealous against strangers. Thus also the circumstance of these strangers being shepherds, though it would render them odious to the Egyptians, would make them more dear to the king whose family were of the same occupation.

An impostor writing hundreds of years after Moses could never have dreamed of inserting such a circumstance into his history; or if he had done so, he would have given an explanation which would have reconciled the apparent contradiction. The history is told with the simplicity of truth, by one who was conscious that he was telling the truth and that the truth would vindicate itself; and, now, after the lapse of more than 33 centuries, the testimony of witnesses who have been 36 centuries in their tombs has been recovered, and this testimony authenticates the Mosaic record.

CHAPTER XXV.

AUTHENTICITY AND INTEGRITY OF THE PENTATEUCH. — THE BONDAGE IN EGYPT.

AFTER the death of Jacob and his sons, the Israelites "grew exceedingly strong and filled the land." (Ex. i, 7.)

"In the meantime there arose a new king over Egypt that knew not Joseph."

"And he said to his people, Behold the people of the children of Israel are numerous, and stronger than we."

"Come, let us wisely oppress them, lest they multiply, and if any war shall rise against us, join with our enemies, and having overcome us, depart out of the land."

"Therefore he set over them masters of the works to afflict them with burdens, and they built for Pharaoh cities of tabernacles, Pithom and Rameses."

"And the Egyptians hated the children of Israel, and afflicted them, and mocked them." (Exod. i.)

Concerning the exact date of these events there is some uncertainty. It is generally acknowledged that the Exodus of the children of Israel occurred about 1491 B. C. Assuming this as correct, or very nearly so, we would have the date of the decree for the destruction of the male Hebrew children, 1571 B. C., and the king who knew not Joseph would be reigning at that date. This brings us necessarily into the 18th or 19th dynasty of Egyptian history.

There is a great deal of difference of opinion between learned Egyptiologists as to the exact dates when the monarchs of the 18th and 19th dynasties reigned. I do not pretend to settle these differences, but there are some facts which are acknowledged as demonstrated by the testimony of the monuments. We have already shown how aptly the history of Joseph fits the reigns of some of the shepherd kings, during whose reigns Joseph must have flourished. We shall now see how the monumental testimony fits the history of Moses.

"A king arose that knew not Joseph." We have seen how this fact is confirmed by the expulsion of the Shepherd dynasty. A king succeeds to the throne who would naturally be hostile to the Canaanites, who would be supposed to be favorable to the Canaanite dynasty. The Israelites are therefore ill-treated and reduced to slavery. Even an attempt is made to exterminate the nation in a short time by a decree for the destruction of the male children.

The cruelty with which slaves were treated is often depicted on the monuments of Egypt. The huge stones which are found in the walls of the temples and their quadrangular precincts, and those which are found in the colonnades were brought to their places by sheer human force, working on inclined planes, and any dilatoriness or mistake was visited on the unhappy delinquent with most cruel scourgings. This accords exactly with the description given in Ex. i: "Come, let us wisely oppress them," and "he set over them masters of the works to afflict them with burdens."

When the Israelites were thus reduced to slavery, an immense number of men were at once added to the usual number employed on the public works. Indeed, when the Egyptian priests related their history to Diodorus they explained that the great works of Sesostris had been entirely erected by forced labor of his captives. This was to be expected, for such was always the custom, when possible. The memory of Cheops was detested in Egypt because he had employed upon the great pyramid which bears his name, the forced labor of his own subjects. Sesostris would also have been held in detestation if he had done the same. The fact that he was always venerated confirms what Diodorus states.

With the immense number of workmen added to the usual workmen, it is to be expected that the monuments of some one limited period, or of some one king would far exceed the works of many of the most famous building periods together, and if the Bible account be true, we may reasonably look for this to be the case; and if this be the case, we shall have at once a strong confirmation of the Bible history. We shall have a proof that the writer of the Pentateuch was familiar with Egypt and its past history.

Diodorus and Herodotus both visited Egypt, and many of the things they repeat are fabulous. They repeat the stories told them by the Egyptian priests, and many things they say will not stand the crucial test of comparison with the monumental records. Any impostor of later days than Moses would have fallen into similar errors, more especially as the details given are such as would expose to an easy detection as soon as they would be tested by the facts.

What then is the testimony of the monuments in regard to the accession of so many workmen? The entire number must have been about 300,000 or 400,000 at least.

There is a short period in the monumental history of Egypt which in the grandeur and number of its public works excels the ages of all the Pharaohs that came before and after it. This period is the beginning of the nineteenth dynasty. Seti II. reigned probably about thirty years. "He erected the great temple of Osiris, at Abydos, and built the famous hall of columns in the palace of Karnak." His warlike exploits are represented by an immense series of magnificent sculptures. Ramesses II. succeeded him and reigned at least 66 or 67 years. Ramesses was the greatest builder among the Pharaohs. Obelisks, temples and magnificent edifices of all kinds are among his works.

In the Delta, in Nubia and Egypt proper, nearly every mound and every ruin is marked with his name. Truly, then, this must be the period when the "king arose who knew not Joseph." The persecution of the Israelites must have begun with one of the kings of this period, perhaps with Ramesses himself.

Since Champollion's day, learned Egyptiologists have come to the conclusion that the accounts given of Sesostris by Herodotus and Diodorus are grossly inaccurate. In this case the views of Mr. Champollion may need to be modified. It becomes unnecessary to account for the silence of Moses concerning Sesostris. It is now generally believed that Ramesses II. was the Sesostris of the Greeks (American Cyclopædia, Art. Egypt,) and the silence of Moses is sufficiently accounted for by the fact that he belongs to the period previous to where the detailed history in Exodus begins. Ramesses was Ra-merois-sothpre, contracted by the priests into Sesothpre and Hellenized to Sesostris.

The monumental records of the reign of Ramesses Sesostris are so decisive, that a flood of light is thrown by them on the Scriptural account, and they prove beyond shadow of doubt that the Pentateuch which records these facts, without aiming at effect, and without having in view the future discovery and almost miraculous deciphering of the hieroglyphics, must be the authentic record of what took place in the reigns of Ramesses-Sesostris and his successors.

The land of Goshen was undoubtedly the Eastern part of the territory of the Delta, "the good of the land of Egypt," which Pharaoh gave to the children of Israel. (Gen. xlv, 18; xlvii, 6.) The Egyptians occupied the West, near where Ramesses was situated. The use of straw in brick-making has been attested by monuments whereon the process is portrayed, and gangs of Jewish slaves have been discovered pictured at Thebes in the act of brick-making, confirmatory of the account given in Ex. v, 10, etc.

"And the overseers of the works and the taskmasters went out and said to the people: "Thus saith Pharaoh: I allow you no straw: go, and gather it where you can find it: neither shall anything of your work be diminished," etc.

The destruction of the first-born, and the overwhelming of the Egyptians in the Red Sea, are not represented or recorded on the monuments, for the Egyptians of that day possessed a national pride somewhat like that of modern nations. They were ready enough to proclaim their victories, but they wished their disasters and defeats to be forgotten.

The name of Moses was given because he was saved from the water.

Pharaoh's daughter "called his name Moses (in Hebrew *Mosheh;*) and she said, because I drew him out of the water." (Ex. ii, 10.)

In Egyptian *mo* is *water, uses, to deliver,* according to Josephus, and the name is derived from these words, signifying "saved from the water."

When it is borne in mind that the Pentateuch is by far the most ancient record that we have of any nation, it will be readily understood that it is not easy to find corroborative history for all its details. At least six hundred years elapsed before Homer wrote the Iliad. Manetho was eleven hundred years after Moses. Berosus wrote about 268 B. C. The only written records which compare in antiquity to the Pentateuch are the Vedas of India, the brick records of Nineveh, which belonged to the library of Sardanapalus, and the Egyptian monuments. Some of the latter are undoubtedly older than the Pentateuch, but they are disconnected and but a small amount of information so ancient is to be obtained from them. The age of the Vedas is purely hypothetical, though their antiquity is very great, and the Assyrian brick books are in the same position. They state that they were written in the reign of Sardanapalus, that is, about 606 B. C.; but they claim to be transcripts from more ancient copies, which of course would bring their originals back to a very early date. However, few of these, except the Assyrian and Egyptian monuments, and these but incidentally, treat at all of the same subjects as the Pentateuch, so that we cannot look to them for much confirmatory evidence, except as they testify to a common tradition.

We have, therefore, under the circumstances, all the historical evidence we could expect for the genuineness of the Pentateuch. More, however, will be given in the next chapter.

CHAPTER XXVI.

AUTHENTICITY AND INTEGRITY OF THE PENTATEUCH.—THE TEN PLAGUES OF EGYPT.

OUR next proof of the familiarity of the author of the Pentateuch with Egypt will be derived from the history of the plagues which afflicted Egypt, as related in Exodus vii to xii.

Moses had fled to Madian at the age of forty years, because Pharaoh sought to kill him on account of his having slain an Egyptian who was oppressing one of the Hebrew slaves. From Madian, at the age of eighty years, he was recalled by God, who wished to make him the instrument of the delivery of the Israelites from bondage. To prove the divinity of his mission, he was empowered by Almighty God to work miracles. By these miracles the Hebrews were convinced of the truth of his mission, and Moses was enabled to go to Pharaoh as the ambassador of God and the representative of the Israelites.

In the presence of Pharaoh, to prove his divine mission Moses commanded Aaron to cast his rod upon the ground, and it was turned into a serpent. The Egyptian magicians did likewise and their rods were turned into serpents also, but Aaron's rod devoured their rods.

Pharaoh refused to give the Hebrews the permission they demanded to go to the desert to offer sacrifice to God. He oppressed them more than before.

As a further sign, by will of God, the first plague came upon Egypt:

1st. The waters of the river were turned into blood. The magicians imitated this miracle also, and Pharaoh did not yield.

2. The second plague was then brought on: frogs came from the waters and covered the land. The magicians imitated this also and brought a few frogs likewise. Pharaoh promised to accede to Moses' request, if the frogs would be removed, but on the removal of the frogs, he broke his promise.

3. The third plague was of *kinnim* in Hebrew. By this word the modern Hebrews, followed by the Protestant version, understand lice. The Septuagint, the Vulgate and Philo, followed by the Catholic English translator understand sciniphs, gnats. These the magicians could not produce, and they acknowledged that the finger of God was there.

4. The fourth plague was of flies swarming into all the houses. Pharaoh again promised to grant the demands of the Israelites, but broke his faith when the plague was removed.

5. The fifth was a murrain on the beasts in the field so that they died. Still Pharaoh was unmoved.

6. The sixth was of boils on men and beasts. Still Pharaoh remained obdurate.

7. The seventh plague was a storm of thunder and lightning and hail, such "as never before was seen in the whole land of Egypt since that nation was

founded." (ix, 23, 24.) The Egyptians were warned to remain themselves and to put their cattle under cover, for all found abroad when the hail would fall should die. Many paid no heed to the warning and were killed, and so with their cattle. The flax and the barley were hurt but the wheat and corn were lateward and were not injured. Pharaoh made similar promises to those he had formerly made, and broke them in like manner.

8. The eighth was of locusts which eat up everything that was green. Pharoah promised as before but again violated his promise.

9. The ninth plague was of darkness: "horrible darkness in all the land of Egypt for three days." (Ex. x, 22.) Pharaoh still refused the required permission.

10. Lastly God ordered Moses to threaten the Egyptians with the death of the first-born in each house. The threat was afterwards put into execution, and the Egyptians resisted no longer, but hurried the Israelites to go forth.

None of these plagues afflicted the Hebrews.

We notice, first, that on the return of Moses, no effort is made to punish him an account of the act for which the former Pharaoh had sought to put him to death. The Egyptian monuments inform us that after the death of Ramesses, Mernephtha I. succeeded to the throne, leaving his son Seti II. concealed in Ethiopia on account of the troubles of the Kingdom. Seti II. was then 5 years of age. Two usurping kings reigned before Seti came to the throne. American Cyc. Art. Egypt.

In one of these reigns the return of Moses must have taken place, and in any case the Egyptian law relieved him from proscription on the death of the monarch who had proscribed him.

The easy access of Moses and Aaron to Pharaoh can only be accounted for by the fact that Moses was the adopted son of a Pharaoh's daughter, and that Aaron was elevated to noble degree on account of the high position of Moses. We see in all this the perfect consistency of the sacred with profane history.

The Egyptian magicians by their jugglery are able to imitate Moses by throwing their rods upon the ground, on which they are also changed into serpents. God undoubtedly permitted the magicians to imitate this miracle in order to make manifest his superior power: and probably even all the power of the devil was exerted in their aid.

The act of Moses and Aaron was a true miracle, but the devil cannot work real miracles. It was therefore a delusion, and we know that the jugglers of Egypt have surprising powers of deception in their serpent charming to this day. Lane's Modern Egyptians. Moses refers to these powers of jugglery, adding "by their enchantments"

> "They dally with the crested worm,
> They stroke his azure neck, or they receive
> The lambent homage of his arrowy tongue."

In this again the knowledge of Egyptian manners displayed by the author of the Pentateuch is complete.

The same is to be said of the change of water into blood, and of the production of frogs. The magi produced these marvels by their jugglery, most probably by such prestigiation as jugglers usually employ, or possibly by diabolical intervention. Of course they only produced a small quantity of blood and a few frogs: In this respect they did not equal Moses who changed the water of the whole river into blood, and produced frogs to swarm over the land and to corrupt it with their dead bodies. By chemical means, the appearance of blood is readily imitated; and the Egyptians were acquainted with Chemistry at a very early period.

The change of water into blood punished the Egyptians in the sorest of spots; for on the river they depended entirely for the irrigation of the country, and for drinking purposes. Rain does not fall at all except very seldom about Alexandria and Rosetta. This is another evidence of Moses' intimate knowledge of the country.

Frogs are very numerous in the Nile, and were adored by the Egyptians. Hence they were punished in their own superstition. Here also the knowledge of the country possessed by the writer of the Pentateuch is displayed

The sciniphs and flies are common in warm, and the sciniphs especially in marshy countries. Hence both were numerous in Egypt. We remark throughout that God by His power intensifies evils that are in existence already, instead of creating entirely new plagues. Thus also the knowledge of the writer of the Pentateuch with the condition of Egypt is the more manifest.

The murrain on the cattle is simply a *very grievous plague:* in Hebrew, *deber kabel mod.* This pestilence is well known in Egypt, as it occurs when the annual overflow of the Nile exceeds twenty-seven feet. (Chambers' Encyclopædia, Nile.)

The next plague was of boils and blains. This blain was a burning ulcer. In Deut. xxviii, 27, the "ulcer of Egypt" is spoken of as peculiar to the country: in Hebrew *shichin*. This ulcer of Egypt is a kind of black leprosy or elephantiasis. (Lexicon of Gesenius.) Again, the knowledge of Egypt is manifested in both passages of the Pentateuch.

Up to the present the magicians failed in imitating the miracles of Moses, excepting his first three. Now they are stricken with the blains, and the victory over their enchantments is complete.

Of the hail the inspired writer says, "There was none like it in all the land of Egypt since it became a nation." Hereby he insinuates that such storms have been elsewhere.

On the 5th of August, 1514, in Cremona, hailstones fell as large as hens' eggs. Olaus the Great, B. i, 22, states that in Scandinavia, hail fell the size of a man's head. Even in warm countries, dreadful hailstorms sometimes occur. Commodore Porter describes a dreadful hailstorm which he experienced on the Bosphorus in 1831.

The words "since it became a nation," seem to imply that the vanity of the Egyptians in boasting of the immense antiquity of their nation was already intolerable, and therefore Moses insinuates here their comparatively modern origin. In ix, 18, he uses almost the same words in speaking to Pharaoh. It is equivalent to saying, "instead of your boasted antiquity of over thirteen thousand years before Menes, the date of the kingdom is still to be computed. It took its rise from Mizraim, within six hundred and twenty-seven years."

The eighth plague was of locusts. The mere mention of the name of locusts invading the country was calculated to strike terror in a country like Egypt, where their ravages are so well known. Pliny says: "This plague is believed to be a manifestation of the anger of the Gods . . . . even their touch destroying much, and their bite consuming everything." (xi, 29.)

The plague of darkness followed, "horrible darkness in all the land of Egypt for three days," and "so thick that it may be felt." (Ex. ix.) When dense clouds fill the air, saturated with heavy mist, it may surely be said that the clouds are palpable. They are really sensible to the touch. This is precisely what to be felt means. Under such circumstances, therefore, it could be said, the darkness could be felt. But some who have been in Egypt for years tell us of another source of this darkness. The author of "Israel in Egypt" says:

"No one who has been in Egypt to experience it, will doubt for a moment the agency whereby Jehovah wrought. The plague of darkness was a sandstorm. It is impossible for words to describe this fearful visitation more accurately than the passage before us."

"During the whole season of the prevalence of this wind (*hamseen* in the middle of April,) the atmosphere is excessively dry, and *loaded* with the fine particles of the sand of the Sahara, to the great discomfort of the inhabitants of Egypt. But occasionally the west wind suddenly freshens to a perfect hurricane, and sweeping before it the light sands of the desert, precipitates them in columns and drifts upon the Valley of the Nile. The sufferings of man and beast during these dreadful storms, in ordinary years, baffle description. They who are overtaken by them, wrap their faces in their mantles, and lie prostrate on the ground. It is their only chance of life. The light of noon-day is but a red angry twilight. At intervals, though brief ones, the sun is obscured, and the darkness is total while the heavy drifts pass the sun's disc. *We testify that we have seen on this point.* It is impossible by any expedient to keep the sand out of the houses. So saturated is the air with the sand, that it seems to lose its transparency, so that artificial light is of little service. The sand also gets into the eyes, producing ophthalmia; so that men 'see not one another.'"

"We speak from personal endurance, when we say, that for intense and universal misery the plague of darkness would far surpass all that went before it." (Pp. 367, 369.)

Surely this is a "darkness that may be felt." Yet the author says he only describes "the sand-storm of an ordinary year." What language, then, are we to use to describe the special plague sent by the Almighty to punish Egypt? And who could describe the scene except one whose information was most accurate, or who had himself been an eye-witness to it? Moses, then, exhibits familiar acquaintance with the condition of Egypt.

Here we may stop to see what Col. Ingersoll has to say about this plague.

"There could have been no better time for the Hebrews to have left the country," than when Egypt was covered with such darkness. (P. 208.)

True, they might have left at that time, but people do not always do what might be done. Why should the Hebrews be an exception to the general rule?

The fact is, it was God's will that still another penalty should be inflicted on Egypt for the crimes of Prince and people, and until this was done it was not His will that the Hebrews should go.

The Colonel says also:

Moses "speaks of a darkness that could be felt. They used to have on exhibition at Rome, a bottle of the darkness that overspread Egypt." (P. 62.)

"Well: is not the darkness of the *hamseen* a darkness that could be felt?"

Oh! "darkness is simply the absence of light," so that you cannot have "pieces and chunks of darkness on one side, and rays and beams of light on other." Col. Ingersoll, (P. 61.)

"But where did you learn all this?"

We may imagine the Colonel answering:

"Why every naturalist knows that darkness is the mere absence of light."

"Yes, that is undoubtedly correct, in the *conventional language* of modern chemistry; but how long is it since this conventional language was invented?"

"Oh! the Jews in the time of Moses were 'barbarous people:' (P. 1.) Of course they did not talk the language of chemistry. In fact the language of chemistry was really no language at all until this enlightened 19th century."

"Well; would you have Moses talk to them in a language which was not to be invented till three thousand three hundred years after his time?"

"At least an inspired writer should speak in scientifically correct language."

"But if '*darkness*' meant quite a different thing in the language Moses spoke from what it means in the modern *conventional* language; if for instance the word '*darkness*' meant the *atmosphere itself in the condition which would make it impossible for us to see*, would it not be *scientifically correct* to say that such darkness as we have described could be felt?"

I think that even Colonel Ingersoll would be obliged to answer "yes" to this question.

Well such was exactly the case in which Moses stood. The language he spoke, and every other language in the world understood this when they spoke of darkness, and under such circumstances his language was perfectly correct.

The Colonel's assertion that a bottle of Egyptian darkness was exhibited in Rome is a fraud. Perhaps some mountebank of the Ingersoll creed may have made such an exhibition, but if he means, what his words would imply, that there was ever such an exhibition, sanctioned by the Catholic Church, his statement is false. The Colonel is evidently befogged in the Egyptian darkness.

I have already given the reason why the death of the first-born is not mentioned on the Egyptian monuments. The Egyptians were too proud to record their national disasters. But in chapter 20 I mentioned an annual commemoration which existed in Egypt, and was celebrated in sorrow. The only explanation which can be given for this is that it was the effect of a distorted tradition of the facts related in Exodus.

Thus the entire history of the plagues of Egypt agrees wonderfully with the history and condition of Egypt, and manifests on the part of the writer of the Pentateuch a thorough knowledge of the history of that country.

It is true, the circumstances I have pointed out regarding the first nine plagues are true of Egypt at any time and could be ascertained by a writer later than Moses; but many other coincidences already pointed out, and more which will appear after, could not be so ascertained. Taken altogether they establish my point fully.

CHAPTER XXVII.

THE TEN PLAGUES OF EGYPT.— REFUTATION OF OBJECTIONS.

As Colonel Ingersoll takes occasion, in the twenty-second chapter of his book, to draw certain objections against the truth of the Pentateuch, from the history of the ten plagues of Egypt, this will be the most appropriate place to answer them.

He begins by stating the cruel treatment undergone by the Jews, particularizing the destruction of *all* the male children.

The Colonel is not accurate here. He should state a case properly. I hope he does not thus bungle his cases when he pleads before the bench. Surely he did not do so in the "Star Route" cases.

All the male children were not destroyed. Orders were given that they should be destroyed, but the orders were not obeyed. (Ex. i, 17.)

If the male children had been *all* destroyed, there would have been no nation to leave Egypt forty years after.

Is this statement made in order to make out another inconsistency in the Bible? This would seem to be the case, for so able a lawyer would scarcely make so gross a blunder unintentionally.

The Colonel continues:

"If the account given is true, the Egyptians were the most cruel, heartless, and infamous people of which history gives any record."

Probably he wishes us to infer from this that the history could not have been true. Is such a mode of reasoning to upset all the positive proofs we have given and those which will be seen in the succeeding chapters? The Egyptians were accustomed to throw children into the Nile as a sacrifice. They could, as a rule, have but little scruple about destroying the children of their slaves, who were always treated with heartless cruelty. But that there were tender-hearted persons among them is evident from the fact that the midwives spared the children in spite of the King's decree; and this they did, not because of Infidelity, but because *they feared God.*

The Colonel next ridicules the miracles which God empowered Moses to work.

We proved in chapter 13 the possibility of miracles, and that they attest the divine mission of him who employs them for this purpose. These proofs need not be repeated. Nearly the whole of Colonel Ingersoll's chapter 22d is an attempt to throw ridicule on the belief in the possibility of miracles. He adduces no argument to refute our proof of chapter 13; so that it is unnecessary to refute his chapter on "the Plagues," further than to say: "Once we admit the possibility of miracles, we must infer that there is no absurdity in believing that they have occurred, and that they occurred, through 'the instrumentality of Moses, when he presented himself before Pharaoh as the ambassador of the Almighty."

The Colonel puts his case thus:

"Suppose we wished to make a treaty with a barbarous nation, and the President should employ a sleight-of-hand performer as envoy extraordinary, and instruct him that when he came into the presence of the savage monarch, he should cast down an umbrella or a walking stick, which would change into a lizard or a turtle: what would we think? Would we not regard such a performance as beneath the dignity even of a President? And what would be our feelings if the savage king sent for his sorcerers and had them perform the same feat? If such things would appear puerile and foolish in the President of a great Republic, what shall be said when they were resorted to by the Creator of all worlds?" (P. 194.)

Miracles being possible to God, it was quite fitting that He should confer on Moses the power of performing them; for we can imagine no other way by which the power of God, and the authority of His ambassadors can be so well attested. Col. Ingersoll calls this sleight-of-hand. He blasphemously calls God, when working miracles, "a prestigiator, magician or sorcerer." These terms imply deceit. Now with God there is no deceit. The miracles of Moses were therefore real. There was no deceit about them. The occasion was one which undoubtedly called for the exhibition of God's power over created things; for a Revelation was to be made to man through Moses, Revelation which we have already proved to be necessary for human welfare. Miracles were the means whereby that Revelation was to be attested, and therefore Moses was empowered to work them.

It was necessary that the Jewish people should be impressed with the conviction that Moses had received his authority from God. It is the conviction of the human race that the claimant to authority to promulgate a new Revelation should prove his claim by works surpassing the powers of Nature, that is by miracles.

We have seen in chapter 12 that both Mr. Paine and Col. Ingersoll demand from God a multiplication of miracles in case of Revelation, since they require direct Revelation to each individual.

God has not seen fit to make His Revelation after the fashion these gentlemen require of Him, nor has He seen fit to work exactly the miracles they demand. He is surely as wise as they are, and we may feel satisfied with the way He has chosen to make known to us His will.

All men of good sound sense will acknowledge that God manifests both wisdom and mercy in attesting Revelation, rather by the means that the conviction and sense of mankind have pronounced appropriate, that is by miracles, than by the means demanded so dictatorially by Mr. Ingersoll, especially as we have the Colonel's own word for it that even if God were to accept his terms, and acknowledge the Colonel's right to command Him, he would only be treated as a juggler and sorcerer. (Mistakes of Moses, p. 194.)

But the Colonel calls the miracles which God wrought through Moses small and contemptible. (P. 194.) Let us examine whether this be the case.

The Egyptians adored serpents. How appropriately then did God show the nothingness of this Egyptian deity by proving his control over serpents as over all creation? God made the God of the

Egyptians the means of overthrowing their superstition; for the serpents brought out by Moses devoured the serpents produced by the Egyptian magicians.

The turning of the Nile into blood was likewise a reproof for their superstition in paying divine honors to that river. In fact this and all the following plagues were highly calculated to impress both on Hebrews and Egyptians the conviction that He alone rules all creation, who could make all creatures obey his commands.

"You shall know that I am the Lord your God." (Ex. vi, 7.)

"The Egyptians shall know that I am the Lord." (vii, 5.)

The Colonel tells us the sorcerers did the same feat as Moses. See quotation above, p. 194.

The sorcerers did not the *same* as Moses. Moses performed real miracles; the sorcerers practiced deceptions. "The magicians of Egypt did so (or in like manner) *with their enchantments.*" (vii, 22; viii, 7.)

The Hebrew *ken,* so, or *in like manner,* expresses resemblance, not identity. Besides in each case God showed his superiority over the devils or false Gods on whom the Egyptians relied. Their serpents were devoured. Their juggling trick of substituting a basin of blood for a basin of water was not to be compared with the conversion of the Nile into blood, and the production of a few frogs by similar means does not equal the causing of the whole country to swarm with them. The Egyptian feats could be done by jugglery, those of Moses could not.

If the magicians wished to show the power of their gods, it would have been more to the purpose to restore the Nile to purity, and to drive away the frogs. This they could not do, and they could not even imitate the other wonders of Moses. They were forced to acknowledge that Moses wrought by the power of God, thus confessing that they did not. "This is the finger of God." viii, 18.

It is true, the President of the United States or the Ruler of any great Kingdom would act beneath his dignity if he required his ambassadors to exhibit juggling tricks as his credentials to any king, savage or civilized; but the miracles of Moses were no juggling tricks. The President would rely on the external grandeur of his State, his armies and his navies to command due respect; but Moses appeared before Pharaoh and even before his own countrymen without all these. They had a right to demand from him proofs of his mission of a character such as no earthly Ruler could produce. They had a right to demand, not juggling tricks, but a manifestation of such power as no earthly Ruler possesses; and this they did demand from him, for we read, Ex. iv, that he is empowered to change the rod into a serpent before the Hebrews.

"That they may believe that the Lord God of their fathers . . . . hath appeared to thee." Verse 5.

In case of their unbelief, he is empowered to work a second miracle, and God adds:

"If they will not believe thee . . . . nor hear the *voice of the former sign*, they will believe the word of the latter sign, but if they will not even believe these two signs, nor hear thy voice: take of the river water and pour it out upon the dry land, and and whatsoever thou drawest out of the river shall be turned into blood." 7, 8.

That Pharaoh also demanded signs is evident from vii, 9.

"When Pharaoh shall say to you, Shew signs: thus thou shalt say to Aaron: Take thy rod and cast it down before Pharaoh, and it shall be turned into a serpent."

I already quoted in chapter 13 the testimony of Jean Jacques Rousseau on miracles. Let us now hear Voltaire speak:

"Miracles were necessary to the nascent Church; they are not so for the Church once established. God being among men should act as God. Miracles are for him ordinary actions. The master of nature must always be above nature."

There remains now very little requiring an answer in Col. Ingersoll's essay on the plagues.

We treated of the plague of darkness in chapter 26. Let us now see what the Colonel says in detail of the other plagues:

We are told:

"We are not informed where they (the magicians) got the water to turn into blood since all the water in Egypt had already been so changed." (P. 195.)

Where did the Colonel find that all the waters of Egypt had already been so changed? The Bible does not say so: it speaks only of the waters of the Nile system: so the Egyptians dug wells to procure water which was pure.

"I will smite with the rod .... upon the waters which are in the river; and they shall be turned into blood." Ex. vii, 17.

True, it is said (verse 19) that there shall be blood in the wooden and stone vessels, but this shows merely that the blood remained so when they filled their vessels from the river. Streams, ponds and pools also are said to have been turned into blood, but these formed part of the river system. It is no where said that the water which had previously been in the houses, or that that found in the wells was turned into blood also:

He asks:

Is it necessary to believe all this was done "that a king might be induced to allow the children of Israel the privilege of going a three days' journey into the wilderness to make sacrifices to their God?"

Yes, Colonel. Religious liberty, the liberty to serve the true God is a precious treasure. You would find *millions* in the United States alone, who would sacrifice everything they possess, *even their lives*, rather than be deprived of it. It would appear you do not appreciate it so highly.

Again you say:

"The only claim that Moses and Aaron made for their God was that he was the greatest and most powerful of all the Gods." (P. 196.)

This is not true. In the first chapter and first verse of the Bible we are told:

"In the beginning God (*Elohim*) created heaven and earth." Gen. i, 1.

The God of Israel is the only Creator; therefore he is the only God.

"The Lord he is God, and there is no other besides him." Deut. iv, 35.

In many other passages we find the same doctrine.

We have next:

"All the cattle of Egypt died; that is to say all the horses, all the asses, all the camels, all the oxen and all the sheep." (P. 199.)

After this " boils broke forth with blains upon man and upon beast throughout the land." (P. 199.)

You add that:

"These boils with blains broke out upon cattle that were already dead. It must not be forgotten that all the cattle and all beasts had died with the murrain before the boils had broken out." (Pp. 199, 200.)

If you had read the text carefully you would have seen that the murrain fell upon the *cattle in the fields.*

"Behold my hand shall be upon thy fields; and a very grievous murrain upon thy horses and asses and camels and oxen and sheep." (Ex. ix, 3.)

In verse 6 it is said:

"And all the beasts of the Egyptians died."

This refers to the beasts already mentioned, that "were in the field." There were, therefore, some left on which the boils would have effect. Besides "all the beasts" and similar expressions are often used to signify a very great part, or nearly all.

I suppose that in explaining the coincidence of the Pentateuch with history, geography and language you would say the writer of the Pentateuch was a cunning impostor, and skilful in all these branches of knowledge to put on such an appearance of antiquity: but truly, now, you are making him a stupid blunderer. He could not have been both. Which was he? In truth he was neither. He is the faithful cotemporary historian.

The Colonel's next attack is on God for having slain the first born of Egypt, and the cattle. He says:

"What had these children done? Why should babes in the cradle be destroyed on account of the crime of Pharaoh? Why should the cattle be destroyed because man had enslaved his brother? .... Where can words be found bitter enough to describe a God who would kill wives and babes because husbands and fathers had failed to keep his law?" (P. 205.)

I need only refer the reader to chapter 9 for the answer to this. We may add here: God is the Supreme Arbiter of life and death. He may and does doom all to die. There is no escape. We are liable to die by accident or the malice of others; and if we escape these, still we must die by natural decay. God must not be accused for this. After all, physical evil is no real evil; and for mankind all will be rectified in the future life. The just who suffer here will gain their compensating reward, and the wicked who prosper will meet their merited punishment.

"But this everyone is sure of that worshippeth thee, that his life if it be under trial, shall be crowned: and if it be under tribulation it shall be delivered; and if it be under correction, it shall be allowed to come to thy mercy. For thou art not delighted in our being lost: because after a storm thou makest a calm; and after tears and weeping thou pourest in joyfulness." (Tobias iii, 21, 22.)

The Colonel continues thus:

"Of course God must have known that turning the waters into blood, covering the country with frogs, etc. .... would not accomplish his object, and that all these plagues would have no effect whatever upon the Egyptian King." (P. 207.)

Certainly God knew that the first plagues would not produce a permanent effect on Pharaoh:

"For I know their thoughts and what they are about to do this day." (Deut. xxxi, 21.)

However, He has left man free-will; and Pharaoh

in the exercise of his free-will was hardened. Therefore God did not lessen his punishment, and the punishment of his nation, which also took part in the oppression of Israel. (See also, on this subject, chapters 1 and 38.)

Next, the Colonel says:

"Is it not altogether more reasonable to say that the Jewish people, being in slavery, accounted for the misfortunes and calamities, suffered by the Egyptians, by saying that they were the judgments of God?" (Pp. 207, 208.)

No; for God has revealed that He inflicted them, and He confirmed His Revelation by miracles. It is more reasonable to believe God than to frame fanciful theories, and believe them in preference.

CHAPTER XXVIII.

AUTHENTICITY AND INTEGRITY OF THE PENTATEUCH.—TESTIMONY OF HISTORY, CONCLUDED.

There are still some points of Egyptian history and manners which from the references in the Pentateuch demonstrate the writer's familiarity with the country.

The next evidences of this to which I shall call attention is the answer of Moses to Pharaoh in the following passage:

"Pharaoh called Moses and Aaron and said to them: Go and sacrifice to your God in this land. And Moses said: It cannot be so, for we shall sacrifice the *abominations* of the Egyptians. . . . . Now if we kill those things which the Egyptians worship in their presence they will stone us." (Ex. viii, 26.)

It is evident that the writer of this knew that the Egyptians worshipped sheep and oxen, lambs, cows, etc., which were the chief sacrifices offered by the Jews. He knew that the Jewish sacrifices were sacrilegious in the estimation of the Egyptians, for which reason he calls them the "abominations of the Egyptians." He knew that the Egyptians would be angry at the Jews, and would stone them if they saw them offering these animals. The Egyptian history is in perfect accord with all this. The monuments and all historic records prove the people to have been devoted to their religion. Their religious wars were frequent, and whoever the writer of the Pentateuch may be, he proves that both Moses and himself (if he were another person) knew their character.

Another evidence to this is the worship to which the Jews were addicted when they left the true God. The worship of Baal was in later days their besetting sin. When they were settled in Judea, surrounded as they were by nations that adored Baals and Astaroth (*Baalim* and *Astaroth*) and Moloch, they never dreamed of setting up a calf for worship for over five hundred years. This was the peculiar worship of the Egyptians; and so we find (Ex. xxxii, 4,) that during the absence of Moses for a short time on Mount Sinai, when they forgot the true God, the god they made for themselves was a calf. They had just escaped out of Egypt: they had been constant witnesses of calf and ox worship; undoubtedly many had even participated in it, and nearly all knew the manner in which its worship was carried on. It was the most natural form of idolatry for them to fall into just at that time, and the writer of the Pentateuch must have been familiar with all the events as they occurred.

I have said, for over five hundred years calf-worship was not thought of. I might say for fifteen hundred years, for the only exception was when Jeroboam set up two calves, one in Dan, the other in Bethel, for adoration; but he also learned by his visit to Egypt this mode of worship. This exception is a confirmation of my statement. (See 3 Kings xii, 26, 29; xi, 40. Prot. Bible, 1 Kings.)

My next illustration on this subject will be taken from Num. xi, 5. The Israelites murmured when they were tired of manna. They longed for "the fish and meat, the cucumbers, melons, leeks, onions and garlic of Egypt."

Fish and meat are the staple food of all countries where they can be had. It is therefore no matter of surprise that these should be in their mind first of all. The plants named seem to be rather an odd selection from among garden vegetables, that they should be particularly named as being so much longed for.

Now, it is a fact attested by travellers that these very vegetables are to this day highly prized in Egypt. Cucumbers, melons, and onions are among the leading productions of the country, and they grow in great perfection there, being far superior to the same articles as grown in America or Europe. One traveller says that our onions, in comparison with those of Egypt are as bad turnips to good apples. Onions, in fact, are there exceedingly palatable and agreeable. (Dr. Eadie, Bib. Cyc. Cucumbers, Onions, etc.)

Again: The country between Hebron and Jerusalem was inhabited by a tribe called Anakim, being the descendants of Anak. When the twelve spies of Israel were sent in to view the land of Canaan they returned and reported it to be "flowing with milk and honey," and that its fruits, specimens of which they brought, were of great excellence: yet the land through which they had to pass was inhabited by "men of great stature."

"And there we saw the giants, the sons of Anak of the giants, and we were in our own sight as grasshoppers, and so we were in their sight." (Num. xiii, 33.)

We may add to this the short history of Og, given in Deut. iii, 1, 11. Og is declared to be the only one remaining "of the race of the giants." His bedstead was sixteen feet five inches in length and seven feet three and one-half inches in breadth, more accurately than Mr. Paine states, as we have seen in chapter 19.

Mr. Paine means to suggest that the existence of such giants is a mere myth. We are not to suppose that the sons of Anak described by the Israelite spies were quite as large as they stated. The Bible does not say they were. It merely records the report of the spies. Now these relating, under the influence of their terror, what they saw, very naturally exaggerated the size of the giants. Still there is no doubt that the Anakim must have been of huge size, and Og must have been of immense stature also, though necessarily not so large as was his bedstead.

The writer of the Pentateuch could have had no object in inventing this story about the giants; and if an impostor wished to pass it as the work of Moses he would have omitted these details, which at first sight would throw discredit on his story. Did giants ever exist of the immense proportions described? The traditions of every country kept the memory of such men. Are these traditions entirely baseless, or are they founded on facts which have been considerably magnified and distorted by the vagueness of the traditions? There is certainly strong evidence that the latter is the case. ' Persons and families of great size have from time to time appeared in many countries; Barnum exhibits such men to-day, and the ruins of Baalbek attest that in very ancient days there must have been a *race* of enormous men: that indeed "there were giants in those days" when the edifices of Baalbek were built.

Baalbek is thirty-six miles northwest of Damascus. The greater temple stood upon an artificial platform between twenty and thirty feet high, and extended one thousand feet from east to west. The peristyle is elevated on a platform fifty feet above the surrounding country, and on the western side there are three immense stones whose united length is one hundred and ninety feet, the largest being sixty-four feet long, their average height thirteen feet, their thickness still greater. Am. C˟c. Baalbek.

These stones if no heavier than limestone would each exceed nine hundred tons in weight. Modern science has constructed no engines which could bring from the quarry a quarter of a mile distant, and raise them to their present position. A late traveller, Chester Glass, Esq., a leading Barrister, late of London, now of Winnepeg, Canada, states in his book of travels, that when standing in the presence of these gigantic blocks, he was strongly impressed with the truth of the Scriptural record, "there were giants in those days." Thus does modern science vindicate the Bible.

The record proves by this statement that the writer

was familiar with the history of the days of which he wrote.

To conclude our proof from history, we must not omit the inscriptions found engraved on Mount Sinai, and along the adjacent valley. In the year 530 A. D. Cosmas, an Egyptian Christian had occasion to travel from Alexandria to Thibet, through the Sinaitic deserts. With his varied knowledge he was able to assist in deciphering certain characters which he beheld in great numbers on the Sinaitic rocks. He says:

"On the rocks of Sinai, at the different stations of the Hebrews we encounter rocks covered with inscriptions in Hebrew characters. I passed through these places and testify to the fact. Some Jews who accompanied us read the inscriptions and translated them for us. They were to the effect: 'departure of such, or such a tribe, in such a year and such a month' . . . . and so numerous are the inscriptions that all the rocks are covered with them." The valley and mountain have been named *Wady-Mokatteb, Djebel Mokatteb, Written Valley, Written Mountain.* An Anglican clergyman, Rev. Chas. Forster, B. D., in a work published in London, Eng., 1851 says:

"These inscriptions of the same style, the same character and the same language, are to be counted by thousands, and in the valley of Wady-Mokatteb alone there are several thousand. In length they extend for several leagues. They are at inaccessible heights, ... and many are of such proportions as to have required immense labor and a long time. These inscriptions are almost entirely confined to the route from Suez to Sinai, which must have been the route followed by the Israelites on leaving Egypt."

One of these inscriptions attests the passage of the Israelites through the Red Sea.

"Turned into dry land the sea, the Hebrews flee through the sea." Sinai Photographed.

Another is composed of 41 lines, the letters being one inch in relief, and a foot long. This has a title the letters of which are three inches in relief, and six feet long. The exact translation has not been made for certain, but the title speaks of the horses and riders of Pharaoh being cast down. The 41 lines are believed to be a transcript of the canticle of Moses in Ex. xvi. Undoubtedly when these inscriptions shall be interpreted with the certainty of the monuments of Egypt, they will throw great light upon the history of Israel. Even what is already known of them serves to confirm what is related of it in the Pentateuch. Darras' Unabridged History of Church, vol. i, p. 701.

The testimony of history to the authenticity of the Pentateuch is cumulative. The larger the number of coincidences, the more convincing is the evidence that the writer must have been intimately acquainted with the facts he relates. If he had not been so he would have blundered hopelessly in his narration, as did Herodotus and Diodorus, and he would frequently have said things irreconcilable with facts now known by other means. The fact that he has not thus gone astray is conclusive evidence that the Pentateuch was written in the time of Moses, and by Moses, or by his authority. Col. Ingersoll and Mr. Paine are mistaken.

CHAPTER XXIX.

AUTHENTICITY AND INTEGRITY OF THE PENTATEUCH.—THE TESTIMONY OF GEOGRAPHY.

WE have next to see what testimony the science of Geography affords to the authenticity of the Pentateuch.

1. Let us turn to Exodus vii, 19; viii, 6.

". . . . Stretch out thine hand upon the waters of Egypt, upon their streams, upon their *rivers*, and upon their ponds, and upon all their pools of water, that they may become blood." Ex. vii, 19.

". . . . Stretch forth thine hand with thy rod over the streams, over the *rivers*, and over the ponds, and cause frogs to come up upon the land of Egypt." Ex. viii, 5.

In these two passages for *rivers*, Moses wrote *iorim*, the plural of *ior*, *river*, which, as we explained in chapter 22, is used for the *Nile*. Aaron, then, is commanded to stretch his hand over the *Niles*. The Nile is the only river in the world that for 1,500 miles has no affluent whatever, notwithstanding which it is able to get through the burning sands of Nubia. In the strictest sense, therefore, there is but one *Nile* in Egypt, until the Delta is reached, where it separates into several streams and flows into the sea. How easily would one unacquainted with the facts of the case, blunder in speaking of such a river! Yet the writer, speaking of an occurrence which happened precisely at the place where these branches are, speaks of the *Niles*, that is at the only part of the river where such a term could be used.

2. The Israelites, reduced to slavery "built for Pharaoh cities of tabernacles, Pithom and Ramesses." (Ex. i, 11.)

It is certainly not by mere guess-work that the writer of the Pentateuch attributes the building of the city Ramesses just to the period when a king of that name was reigning, or even if it were not exactly the case that a Ramesses were reigning, Seti I. whose reign was between those of Ramesses I. and Ramesses II., being the Son of one Ramesses, and the father of another might easily be supposed to have so named a city. However, it is almost certain that these cities were built in the reign of Ramesses-Sesostris.

3. The cities of Pithom and Ramesses are named on the Egyptian monuments only after the period we have indicated. This is another proof of the geographical accuracy of the Pentateuch.

4. It has long been a matter of dispute whether Tyre or Sidon is the more ancient city. Both are undoubtedly of very great antiquity. The Tyrians themselves claimed on the strength of their traditions to be the oldest settlement in Phœnicia, dating from about 2750 B. C.

Now if, as Col. Ingersoll and his fellow Infidels pretend, the Pentateuch were a late spurious work, the writer would certainly not wish to meddle with so dangerous a topic as the decision against Tyre at a time when the glory of this city was in its heyday. Yet this he does virtually. From the time of Jeremias, Tyre and Sidon are nearly always coupled together, except when Tyre, on account of its greater importance, is spoken of alone, as in 2 Ki. v, 11. (2 Samuel.) See Jerem. xxvii, 3, xlvii, 4, etc. But before the time of Samuel we find in Scripture only one mention of Tyre, viz: in Josh. xix, 29. Tyre is then called "the strong city." Sidon is spoken of five times in Joshua, and three times in the Pentateuch, without counting the passages where Sidon the father of the Sidonians, is meant. (See Gen. x, 19, etc.) Now this is in perfect accord with Homer, who also mentions only the Sidonians. Probably Tyre, though then important by its strength, was as yet much inferior to Sidon. The prophet Isaias, indeed, calls Tyre "the daughter of Sidon." This thorough self-consistency of the Bible, in opposition to Tyrian boasts, together with the silent testimony of Homer, certainly seem to show conclusively that the geography of the Pentateuch is right here also.

5. In Genesis x, 11, 12, we are told of the beginning of the kingdom of Assyria. One of the cities of this kingdom, Resen, is said to be "between Nineveh and Calah: the same is a great city."

Nineveh, the great capital of Assyria, had perished so completely, that even the classic authors of antiquity now extant, speak of it as an extinct city. Herodotus describes the Tigris as the river on which Nineveh had been, but he knew nothing of the city itself. Xenophon actually encamped on its site, which he calls "a vast deserted enclosure." Strabo was only aware that it was in the heart of Assyria. Alexander the Great overcame the Persians near it, but his historians were not aware of its existence. Lucian says that no one knew of its whereabouts in his day. Yet to-day its site has been fixed by the discoveries of its magnificent palaces and temples, and the very libraries of its ancient kings are ransacked and read. Is not this a thorough vindication of the geography of the whole Old Testament?

6. Again, the city of Calah is spoken of as a city distinct from Nineveh. The monumental records show that Calah, the ruins of which are also now known, was the capital for a long time.

7. Of Resen, history tells absolutely nothing: yet Moses describes it as a great city between Calah and Nineveh. To this description the ruins of Nimrud correspond. The geography of Moses is therefore vindicated, and it precedes all extant profane history.

8. Egypt is in Hebrew called by two names: *Mitsraim* and *Cham.* Mitsraim is plural of *Matsor,* Lower Egypt. The Egyptians called the country Metouro and Kam, the latter name being spelled on the Rosetta stone Km, exactly corresponding to the Hebrew Chm. In Coptic it is still called Chemi, and in Sahidic Keme. This correspondence is a further proof of the accuracy of the Pentateuch.

9. If we were to enumerate the names of places which have been retained from the days of Moses to the Christian era, or even to this day, with but little or no change the list would be swelled to vast proportions, but as many of these names are of places near Palestine, which therefore would be familiar even to a late writer, I will give only a few in illustration, which required a more extensive knowledge. Thus, Ur, Tadmor, Sabtah, Ekron, Lud, Lubim, Pheleseth, etc., are called in modern times:

Ur, Palmyra, (being the Greek of *Tadmor*=a *palm tree,*) Sabai, (so called by Strabo in Greek,) Akir, Lydia, the Lybians, Philistæa, (so called by Strabo), etc. Thus is proved the thorough knowledge of the writer of the Pentateuch, with facts he relates.

10. The tenth chapter of Genesis contains the origin of Nations. The names of Noah's sons and

grandsons need not be repeated here. Suffice it to say, that these descendants of the Patriarch dispersed themselves through the various parts of the world then within reach, and the countries to which they went have retained even to this day the very names of many of Noah's children, or grand-children, as recorded in this chapter: and the tradition of a tripartite division of the world between the descendants of the three sons of Noah, is found interwoven in the history of all Eastern nations. The annals of Phœnicia, Egypt, Greece, Rome, China, pertain to the individual nation, but in this record of Moses the whole world finds its earliest history. We cannot identify the descendants of every one named, but the leading divisions are seen at a glance. They may be found in Darras' Unabridged Church History, i, 336 to 345; or abridged in Eadie's Biblical Cyclopædia, Nations, Origin of.

Thus the Egyptians acknowledge the origin of their nation which is given in the Bible, when they name themselves from Mizraim. The Ethiopians are called Cush. The Medes, Thracians, Ionians, and the natives of Elis acknowledge by their names their descent from Madai, Thiras, Javan, Elishah. The Assyrians, Aramæans, Lydians and Elamites by their very names proclaim their parentage in Assur, Aram, Lud and Elam.

There are estimated to be about 4,000 names of persons and places in the Bible: yet of all these, it has never been shown that there is a single person named who is fabulous, or a locality misplaced, whereas on the contrary, for the most part, both persons and places have been perfectly identified both by history and geography.

There can be no more decisive evidence of any fact than the evidence that the writer of the Pentateuch had access to authentic records of the past, as well as familiarity with the events that were passing at the periods of which it treats, and that none but Moses, or some one writing by his authority, could be in a position to write it. All this I have shown,

First. By its existence from age to age as we go back, first to the time of its translation into Greek, then to the period of the Samaritan revolt, and then to the time of Moses himself. Chaps. 16 and 17.

Secondly. By the authenticated records of the nation which form an uninterrupted testimony to the days of Moses himself. Chap. 17.

Thirdly. By the testimony of Jews and Christians, Pagans and Mahometans. Chaps. 17 and 18.

Fourthly. By the petty character of the attacks of Messrs. Ingersoll, Paine and others, upon its authority. Chap. 19.

Fifthly. By the monuments and feasts of the Jews, which constitute a lasting testimony to the genuineness of the books on which they are founded. Chap. 20.

Sixthly. By the antiquity of the language in which the books are written. Chaps. 21, 22.

Seventhly. By its agreement with the history of the times. Chaps. 23, 24, 25, 26, 28.

Eighthly. By the perfect knowledge displayed in them of the geography of the places described. Chap. 29.

Any one of these proofs would in itself be satisfactory: but combined their evidence is irresistible and overwhelming.

CHAPTER XXX.

TRUTH OF THE PENTATEUCH.—PROOFS OF THE SINCERITY OF MOSES.

The Pentateuch has been proved to be the work of Moses. The next question we have to consider is: Did he write the truth, or was he an impostor, trying, for some purpose, to pass upon the Israelites a tissue of lies? We maintain that the Pentateuch is historically true.

The testimony of a witness must be received as true if he be not himself deceived and he be not a deceiver.

Now, in examining the truth of the Mosaic history we may begin with Exodus, the portion of the narrative in which he was himself the central character. Of course he was an infant when the events occurred which are related in the first ten verses of the second chapter. These events are not complicated nor numerous. They are just such events as a family would constantly talk of, and could not forget, and he would readily be informed concerning them, both by his own family and that of Pharaoh, as well as those of the Israelites in general. The events of the first chapter are in part contemporaneous with him, and part concern the period just before his birth. These were matters of notoriety with both Egyptians and Hebrews. They were merely the prominent facts which regarded the bondage of Israel. Moses could not but be familiar with them, even by ordinary human means. He was, therefore, not deceived in respect to them. The succeeding events of the Pentateuch were events public, obvious to his senses and to those of his whole nation. If his own senses had deceived him, an impossible supposition, he would have been undeceived by the universal testimony of those who surrounded him. Only a confirmed madman could have been deceived concerning such facts. This Moses was not. His writings, his learning, his admirable doctrine, his laws, his skilful leadership of his nation under immense difficulties, prove him to be a man of very great prudence and wisdom. This even infidels admit. If, therefore, the Pentateuch be false, Moses must have been an impostor.

It cannot be supposed that the Hebrews conspired with Moses to pass a fraudulent history upon posterity. A nation never desires to concoct a fraud which is to them perfectly useless, and which indeed would hold them up to future generations in an odious light. Many might indeed be willing to allow themselves to be represented as having received special favors from God, but even then there would be many who would not endure the palpable falsehood: but when the question is unnecessarily to perpetuate a fraud which represents them as a perverse and ungrateful people, the deceit would be at once unanimously repudiated.

Now there are many facts in the Pentateuch which are disgraceful to the nation: such is their inconstancy while Moses was on Mount Sinai communing with God. They could not persevere for forty days in God's service, but they fell into most gross idolatry, setting up a golden calf of their own make and offering up their homage to it with absurd ceremonies; and even Aaron, the brother of Moses, was induced to assist in their delinquency. (Ex. xxxii.)

Thus, also, their many shortcomings brought upon them so strong a reproach from God as this:

"The Lord had said unto Moses: Say unto the children of Israel, Ye are a stiff-necked people: I will come up into the midst of thee in a moment and consume thee." (xxxiii, 5.)

So also in Exod. xxxiv, 9, Moses thus prays to God:

"O Lord, let my Lord, I pray thee, go among us for it is a stiff-necked people."

We find, besides, a mutiny among the people headed by two hundred and fifty princes of the assembly, recorded in Num. xvi; and at a later period a very general delinquency, when a vast number fell into idolatry and other gross crimes, on account of which they were punished by terrible marks of God's indignation. We need not specify other occasions of their fall, justifying the name by which they were called, a stiff-necked people.

One additional fact may be named which, though mentioned in Genesis, would be of itself a reason why the Hebrews would not have conspired with Moses in concocting and preserving a false record.

Respect for one's ancestry is a common feeling among men. Especially is this the case when the ancestors are not very distant from us. Now the twelve sons of Jacob were the ancestors of every Israelite; and as ancestors they were not remote. As ancestors they were held in great veneration. They brought the bones of Joseph with them from Egypt in veneration of his memory and in obedience to his last will. Now it is quite inconceivable that any nation imbued with such sentiments should permit the history of Joseph and his brothers to be handed down to posterity as it is recorded in Genesis xxxvii, unless they were perfectly conscious of its truth: for these ancestors of all the tribes, except Joseph, Benjamin, and Reuben, are represented as plotting together for the perpetration of one of the most heartless acts ever committed by men. Would the other tribes have consented to have their ancestors thus blackened, while those of the three tribes, and especially Joseph and Reuben, were elevated above them all? Yes, even above the tribe of Judah, which was promised to be the royal tribe, and that of Levi, which was already the ruling and priestly tribe, when the Pentateuch was written.

After this read the last of words of Jacob, full of sorrowful and prophetic reproaches, some to be fulfilled in regard to many of the tribes, and this time even the tribes of Reuben and Benjamin do not escape the scathing. See Genesis xlix.

The Pentateuch, therefore, is not the result of a conspiracy between Moses and his people. Was it the deceit, then, of Moses himself? According to the rules of fair criticism a historical writer, especially an eye-witness is to be supposed sincere, unless there are positive reasons for calling his sincerity to doubt. In the case of Moses no such reasons can be given. On the contrary he possesses all the characteristics of sincerity which the most fastidious critic can require.

The first thing that strikes us when we read the Pentateuch is the sublimity and holiness of the doctrines therein taught.

In the first words of Genesis we have the authoritative declaration of the world's origin: "In the beginning God created heaven and earth." Matter then is not eternal. It is God's creation. The world is not made by chance or by the action of blind forces, nor is matter a part of God, as the pantheists say, but matter is creature subject to its Creator, and depending entirely upon Him.

The idea of God the Creator is, as we have already shown, in perfect accord with human reason, and more, it is the only view of God which reason approves and demonstrates. However, it would seem that unaided reason is incapable of rising to this sublime idea. Pagan philosophy never attained it. Its systems always rest on the first existence of a chaotic mass, which the divine power organized. But whence came matter? How came it into the hands of him who organized it and gave it form? These problems Plato could not solve. As we have seen in chapter 7, Col. Ingersoll cannot solve it either.

Moses, on the other hand, lets us at once into the secrets of the Eternal, and teaches this most sublime truth. Yet the Colonel has the hardihood to say that "Moses received from the Egyptians the principal parts of his narrative, (of Creation,) making such changes and additions as were necessary to satisfy the peculiar superstitions of his own people." (P. 51.)

He further explains this by saying that "if some man should assert that he had received from God the theories of evolution, etc." and we should find that "he had lived in the family of Charles Darwin, we certainly would account for his having these theories in a natural way." (P. 51.)

The differences between the two cases are that,

1. The Egyptian Cosmogony is evidently not the original of the Mosaic. The only so-called Egyptian work which could even in a remote degree be compared with the Mosaic record are the Hermetic books

which are acknowledged by learned men to be in great part at least spurious. Wherever Hermes Trismegistus resembles the Mosaic record he falls into absurdities. See Champollion's "Ancient Egypt." Darras' unabridged Church History vol. i, (P. 125.)

Instead of Moses copying, Hermes copied Moses, and failing to copy truly, his mistakes are absurd.

2. Mizraim the father of the Egyptians was one of those who dispersed themselves after the building of the tower of Babel, 587 years before the birth of Moses. The fathers of the human race at that period certainly knew the traditions handed to them by Noah (still alive) and his sons. Is it wonderful, then, that the pagan nations retained some notion, derived from the common ancestors of mankind, of Creation, God, Providence, the Immortality of the soul, etc.? It is thus that we find traces of religion among those people.

But we have seen how men, in spite of human reason, degenerated in their belief, and corrupted it so that the original creed of mankind can scarcely be recognized. That this degeneration took place we proved in chapter 9. This is fully confirmed by the testimony of Sacred Scripture.

"A father being afflicted .... made to himself the image of his son .... and him who then had died as a man, he began now to worship as a god, and appointed him rites and sacrifices. .... Then in process of time .... this error was kept as a law, and statues were worshipped by the commandments of tyrants." (Wis. xiv, 16.)

"And the multitude of men carried away by the beauty of the work took him now for a god that but a little before was honored as a man." (Verse 20.)

"When they knew God they have not glorified him . . . . and they changed the glory of the incorruptible God into the likeness of the image of a corruptible man, and of birds and of four footed beasts and of creeping things." (Rom. i, 23.)

It is the climax of impertinence and dishonesty to say that the religion of the Bible was borrowed from the absurdities and impieties of Egypt.

CHAPTER XXXI.

TRUTH OF THE PENTATEUCH.—CONTINUED.

1. The doctrines, then, of one only God, the Creator of all things, of God's Providence, Holiness, Justice, Mercy, Eternity, Truth, the doctrines and precepts of human responsibility to God, the punishment of the wicked, the reward of virtue, the immortality of the soul, the obligation of worshipping God, the ten commandments are so sublime, so consistent, so elevating, that they must leave their impress on one who had meditated on them like Moses. An earnest belief in them is one of the characteristics of Truth, possessed by Moses.

These doctrines and precepts Moses inculcated on the Jews as necessary for belief and practice. His zeal in promulgating them is seen in innumerable passages of the Pentateuch. How then could he so grossly manifest his own contempt for them by endeavoring to palm on the people such a tissue of falsehoods as the Pentateuch must be if its miracles be untrue? Take out the miracles and the Pentateuch will be a record without a meaning.

2. The wisdom of the Mosaic Laws is acknowledged by infidels. They are well adapted to their object, to attach the Jews to their own country and religion, and to keep them distinct from the idolatrous nations that surrounded them. Their laws of health are so conducive to this end that in countries which have been visited by plagues, the Jews, following the Mosaic Law strictly, have escaped harm on many occasions.

"A contagious distemper raged in Palestine and the neighborhood; the wise precautions of our legistor prevented its communication and our fathers thus .... kept off this scourge." (Jews' Letters to Voltaire, p. 345.)

"In this (Hebrew) legislation there were none of those hereditary professions .... those blemishing distinctions of castes established among the Egyptians and Brahmins; none of those contempts of one order for the other, which caused seditions for a long time in Rome. Everything recalled to the minds of the Hebrews that original equality and those fraternal feelings with which their common descent from one stock ought to inspire them."

"Where can laws be found which require 'the tender care of the Jewish law-giver for the orphan, the widow, the poor and all the distressed?'"

"Almost all ancient governments abandoned .... slaves .... to the lust and brutality of their masters."

"Our laws did not give to masters these tyrannical powers. They watched over the lives and modesty of slaves. Our fathers, for this reason, were almost the only ancient people among whom were never rebellions of slaves which brought so many other states to the brink of ruin." (Jews' Letters, pp. 334, 338.)

Can we suppose that a legislator so prudent, so zealous for justice and mercy among his people, is himself an impudent and characterless liar?

3. Moses seeks in all his acts the good of the nation. His family are not placed in lofty positions. His sons live in obscurity. This does not look like the conduct of one who would lie impudently for self-aggrandizement.

4. An impostor desirous of passing upon the public a false history would not make statements publicly known to be false. The appearances of God to him would be all private, as was the case with Mahomet and Joe Smith, the Mormon Prophet; or at most a very few persons conspiring with him would be the witnesses. So also if there were any miracles professed to have been wrought, they would in like manner be private, or if some strange feats were done in public, they would be mere juggling tricks, and such tricks would need to be but sparingly used, unless indeed the impostor were a man of extraordinary boldness. Even then he would scarcely be able to keep up for long so daring an imposture. Let us look at the deeds of Moses in this light. It is not denied by infidels that the ordinary or non-miraculous events described may be true. Thus we have seen that Mr. Ingersoll does not deny a few of the prominent occurrences, such as the leadership of Moses, the escape from bondage under that leadership, the visitation of a pestilence on Egypt, etc., (pp. 207, 208;) but all that is in any degree miraculous he would reject.

We need, therefore, only specify the miraculous facts. The truth of the non-miraculous facts is shown by exactly similar reasoning.

Moses proclaims miraculous facts the falsehood of which would be known to his people as soon as they were proclaimed, unless they were absolutely true; and he would have been at once confronted by witnesses innumerable who would have refuted them. It was only on the strength of his miracles that he obtained authority among his people. If these had been false they would have been palpable falsehoods, and they would not have obtained his authority for him. Such facts as the turning of the waters of the Nile into blood, the frogs overrunning the whole country, the sciniphs and flies annoying the whole country in so extraordinary a manner, the murrain, the boils and blains on men and beasts, and finally the death of the first-born, were so public, so obvious to all that an impostor would not have dared to relate them as a proof of his divine mission, to the very people who had been witnesses that they had not occurred.

5. Col. Ingersoll maintains, (p. 207) that it is more reasonable to say that the Jews " accounted for the misfortunes and calamities suffered by the Egyptians, by saying that they were the judgments of God."

This is, on the contrary, quite unreasonable. Such calamities do not occur at the command of man, in the ordinary course of nature; but in the account which Moses wrote for the Jews they are described as occurring at his command. This is an essential point of the history, and as his command was public, every one knew whether or not the command was given. It is also recorded of eight out of the ten plagues that they were positively foretold. It is not said whether or not any such warning was given of the other two, the plague of boils with blains, and the plague of darkness: but these two, as well as the others came only at the command of Moses. So certain is it that these plagues were *miracles*, and not ordinary events, that the Israelites are directed to take certain precautions to avert from themselves the death which was imminent upon the first-born; and before the plague of the hail came, the Egyptians were warned to keep their cattle under cover, and the plague injured only those who heeded not the warning.

The same is to be said of the passage of the Israelites through the Red Sea. When Moses holding in his hand his rod stretched it over the Red Sea, the waters divided so that the Israelites passed through, and when the Egyptians following were in the bed of the sea, with the waters on each side as a wall, Moses again stretched his rod over the sea, the Egyptians were overwhelmed by the return of the waters to their place. (Ex. xiv.)

This also was a public fact which the whole nation could have contradicted if it were not true.

The same can be said of the supply of manna which falling from heaven (the sky) six days of each week, kept the nation supplied with food during their forty years' wanderings in the deserts of Arabia: (Ex. xvi:) of the water which gushed from the rock in Horeb: (Ex. xvii:) of the sudden death which befell Nadab and Abihu who were consumed by "fire from the Lord" because they "offered strange fire before the Lord:" (Lev. x, 1, 2:) of the fire that was quenched by the prayer of Moses: (Num. xi, 2:) of the opening of the earth to swallow up Korah, Dathan, and Abiron and their followers, because of their mutiny against Moses and Aaron, (Num. xvi,) besides many other facts equally above nature.

Of all these works, Moses testifies "the Lord hath sent me to do all these works; for I have not done them of my own mind." (Num. xvi, 28.)

6. The miracles of Moses were therefore the work of God. They were the testimony of God that Moses had divine mission. It is evident that in relating such facts, Moses could not have deceived the Hebrews, even if he had wished to do so, and the single fact that they received his teachings and writings as divine is a demonstration that no one could gainsay his miracles. Moses therefore has no hesitation in saying to the nation what an impostor would not presume to say:

"Your eyes have seen all the great works of the Lord which he hath done." (Deut. xi, 7.)

Again: "You have seen all the things that the Lord did before you in the land of Egypt to Pharaoh, and to all his servants, and to his whole land."

"The great temptations which thy eyes have seen, those mighty signs and wonders." (Deut. xix, 2, 3.)

7. These miracles are not attested by Moses alone. Joshua speaks of the passage through the Red Sea as a matter well known even to foreign nations. Thus Rahab of Jericho tells the Hebrew spies:

"We have heard that the Lord dried up the water of the Red Sea at your going in, when you came out of Egypt." (Jos. ii, 10.)

We find also that,

Joshua "built an altar . . . . as Moses the servant of the Lord had commanded, ... and he read all the words of the blessing and the cursing that were written in the book of the law. He left out nothing of those things which Moses had commanded." (Josh. viii.)

Why should he be so particular, now that Moses was dead, and his power need not be feared, unless both he and the nation KNEW by the miracles of Moses which they had witnessed that the latter exercised authority from God?

We might multiply similar proofs, but these will suffice to show that the Mosaic Religion was ordained by God; for we have proved in chapter 13 that Miracles give this testimony to doctrine.

CHAPTER XXXII.

THE TRUTH OF GENESIS.—MOSES NOT DECEIVED, NOR A DECEIVER.—HIS SOURCES OF INFORMATION.

HAVING demonstrated the truth of the last four books of the Pentateuch, it is proper now to show the truth of Genesis.

This book contains a summary of the history of mankind from the Creation to the building of the Tower of Babel and the dispersion of the human race, after which the narrative is confined chiefly to the history of God's chosen race down to the death of Joseph. According to the usually received chronology, the Tower of Babel was built in the year of the world 1800, or 2204 B. C. Abraham was born 1996 B. C., and died 1821 B. C. The Israelites entered Egypt 1708 B. C. Joseph died 1635 B. C.

1. Moses was not deceived in regard to the facts related in Genesis; for we have already seen that the Hebrews preserved carefully their genealogies, and undoubtedly the principal facts of the history of their ancestors, at all events as far back as Abraham; for

they expected that the promises made by God to Abraham would be fulfilled in their nation. Thus the covenant made by God with Abraham is frequently referred to in the later books, as to a fact which is well known to the Hebrews. (See Ex. ii, 24, vi, 3, 8.)

Thus also Moses appeals to God to preserve Israel:

"Remember Abraham, Isaac and Israel, thy servants to whom thou sworest by thy own self saying: I will multiply your seed as the stars of heaven; and this whole land that I have spoken of, I will give to your seed, and you shall possess it for ever." (Ex. xxxii, 13.)

2. There were also means of knowing many of the events related, for example, the history of Joseph, from Egyptian annals, records and monuments; for we have evidence, even to-day, that the Egyptians were very careful to keep such records. There must have been very many extant then which have perished since.

3. Even from the Creation of the world to Abraham, as well as from Abraham to Moses, there were means of knowing the truth, of which Moses could make use, viz., oral tradition, written records, historical songs, monuments, and above all, Revelation from God.

Now, though 2473 years had passed from the Creation to the birth of Moses, the number of generations was but small, on account of the long lives of the first men. Thus Adam was 300 years living with Mathusala, and Mathusala 600 years with Noah, and therefore he must have conversed with Noah's family, and have handed down the tradition of Creation.

Sem saw Isaac, Isaac saw Levi, and Levi lived a

long time with Amram the father of Moses. Thus, as far as the perpetuation of traditions was concerned, Moses was, at most, in the sixth generation after Adam. We cannot say, therefore, that a man like Moses, a historian, skillful in the science of the day, could have been deceived as to the facts which are related of the early history of mankind. The facts he relates are just the salient points of history, just such facts as could be transmitted easily from generation to generation. The details of the ages and genealogies given in Genesis prove that he had to direct him, records which could be relied on, and besides, the long time that one generation lived with the next gave ample opportunity for each generation to acquaint the next succeeding, of all the things which Moses records. If, therefore, the Mosaic history of the period be spurious it must be that Moses was a deceiver, not that he was deceived.

4. In the next place we find that it was the custom in those early days, to record the principal facts of history in song so that they would not be forgotten from generation to generation. The song of Moses which sets forth, in the thirty-second chapter of Deuteronomy, the mercies of God to his people and his vengeance on their oppressors was written for this purpose by command of God. (Deut. xxxi, 19, 21.)

We have, for a similar purpose, the song of Moses in Ex. xv. This song was sung by Mary the sister of Moses, with a choir of the Hebrew women.

From Genesis xxxi, 27, we learn that this was no new custom, but that it prevailed in the days of Jacob, for it is spoken of as a common practice then.

5. It has been proved in chapter 15 that writing was used before the time of Moses. We cannot tell

when writing was first used. There is, therefore, no difficulty in supposing that Moses received information from written records.

6. We have besides examples of the custom of erecting memorial altars, as did Noah, Abraham, Isaac and Jacob in many places. (See Gen. viii, 20; xii, 7;. xxvi, 25; etc.)

Wells were named on account of events which occurred near them, and the tradition of the events was kept up in connection with them. (Gen. xvi, 14; xxiv, 62; xxv, 11; xxi, 31. Compare also the Hebrew in Deut. x, 6, and Num. xxx, 31: *Beeroth Bene-Jaakan*, the *wells of the sons of Jaakan*, etc.)

Stones were also erected as monuments to mark the locality where special events had occurred. (Gen. xxviii, 18, etc.) The knowledge of the events was transmitted in connection with such memorials also.

7. In fine, whatever might be lacking of other means, Moses had Revelation from God. The miracles of Exodus prove this. From God, therefore, he could well have the history of Creation, and all the other facts which he records down to the call of Abraham; and even after, if it were needed. Thus Moses had more than all the means which historians usually have of ascertaining the truth concerning those past ages.

MOSES, THEN, WAS NOT DECEIVED.

8. Neither was Moses a deceiver. This we have already proved in regard to the later books of the Pentateuch. Since he has all the characteristics of sincerity in writing them, he cannot be supposed to have laid them aside in order to concoct a fictitious Genesis. We have proved that it is against his real **character** and divine mission to suppose that he was a

deceiver. These reasons are equally valid as regards Genesis. (See chapters 30 and 31.)

9. An impostor would not have invented such facts as are related in Genesis, for their incongruity would have been detected by his nation, who still held in their minds the traditions of the past concerning the primitive ages, the long lives of antediluvian men, etc. An impostor, therefore, would have omitted the names and genealogies given by Moses, and the dates, for by giving these he would have furnished facilities for the refutation of his history. Besides, we cannot suppose that God would perform miracles to attest the truth of an impostor's story.

10. The exact date of Homer's Iliad and Odyssey is unknown. Herodotus places it at about four hundred years before his own time, which would be about 850 B. C. The siege of Troy, concerning which he writes chiefly, occurred about the year 1184 B. C. Critics agree that, with wonderful acumen, this bard drew from the national ballads of Greece, chiefly, the materials which form the basis of his work, and that if all the details are not strictly accurate, nevertheless they rest upon an honest substratum, and show the real life and manners of their age. Homer is acknowledged to be a correct delineator of the life of mankind in its early stages. In his works we find the state of the arts and sciences in their very beginning. In the writings of Moses we also find the delineation of the manners of men in the very earliest stages of human life. We find the beginnings of the most powerful empires, and the simplicity of manners which must have been characteristic of that early stage of society.

Thus, when Abraham enters Egypt, Pharaoh is at

once informed of the arrival of the stranger. (Gen. xii.) The same happens at Gerar, when Abimelech is king. (xx.) All this meets with its counterpart in our own times. We see the same happen when such men as Livingstone and Stanley enter the territory of the simple monarchs of interior Africa.

Every city has its king in Palestine, and in the neighboring country the largest extent of a kingdom is a small province. (Gen. xiv.) This is in perfect keeping with all that is known of the earliest ages. Thus at the siege of Troy we find a King of Mycenæ, a King of the Myrmidones, a King of the Locri, a King of Ithaca, etc. Thus, also, Abraham with three hundred and eighteen followers, conquers and puts to flight five kings. (Gen. xiv.)·

The wealth of the most prominent men is represented by the number of their servants and of their cattle. (xii, 16; xx, 14; xxiv, 32; etc.)

The heads of wealthy families, the fathers and mothers, and their sons and daughters took part in the ordinary occupations of life, took care of their flocks, received guests, brought water to wash their feet, prepared the meals, etc. (Gen. xxiv.) The food was of the simplest character, even when it was desired to show the greatest respect to honored guests. (Gen. xviii, 2 to 8.) All this is quite natural before the introduction of modern formalities. As we would expect, there is no evidence that there was any great progress made, at that early period, in the arts and sciences, at all events to any much greater extent than would naturally have been transmitted through through the family of Noah from antediluvian times. Thus the building of the tower of Babel, recorded in Genesis xi, and of the cities "Babel, Erech, Accad, and Calnah . . . . and Nineveh . . . . Rehoboth and Calah," etc., shows some progress in architecture, an art which would naturally be one of the first to which the necessities of man would call his attention at a very early date.

If such evidences of the truth of Homer's pictures of ancient times demonstrate the accuracy of his sources of information, why should they not be a proof also that Moses drew his knowledge of early times from accurate sources?

11. The traditions of nations confirm in many particulars the account given by Moses. The proof of this in detail we leave to the next chapter.

CHAPTER XXXIII.

THE TRUTH OF GENESIS.—TESTIMONY OF PAGAN TRADITIONS.

In the traditions of various nations the main facts mentioned by Moses in Genesis are preserved more or less distinctly. Thus we find testimonies to the great chaos which existed before God brought the earth to its present form, the earth being covered with water, the spirit of God vivifying all things, darkness covering the face of the deep, the formation of man from clay, the original innocence and fall of man, the history of Adam and Eve, and of the temptation by the serpent. The Hindoo books relating this history even give the names of our first parents as they are given in Genesis. We find also testimonies to the long lives of the first men, the building of the tower of Babel, the flood, etc.

We already quoted from Colonel Ingersoll the statement that the Egyptian account of Creation bears strong resemblance to the Mosaic, so that he maintains that Moses borrowed his account from them. See chapters 22, 23. Yet he states that the same account substantially was found with the Babylonians and Hindoos. (Pp. 51, 58.)

Did Moses then borrow his account from the Babylonians and Hindoos too? Or did these borrow from the Egyptians? Or did the three nations all borrow from one another? Surely separated as they were from one another, and having very little, if any intercourse with each other, the Colonel's borrowing theory does not appear a very reasonable one. It would certainly seem that their various cosmogonies are distorted from one common source; and if this be the case, then the common source must be that account which existed before the dispersion of the human race, and if this account has been handed down to posterity, to it we must look for the original truth from which the erroneous accounts have been derived. If there is one account, self-consistent, sublime, bearing intrinsic characteristics of truth and originality, whereas the others engraft upon it what is absurd, and evidently a distortion of the original truth, we must conclude that these have copied from one original, but as they have not copied faithfully, they are disfigured by errors which do not occur in the original.

This is precisely the case with the traditions of Pagan nations. Where they resemble the Mosaic narrative, they confirm it as the original, which they attempt to copy: where they vary from it, they have disfigured it with absurdities for which the original is not responsible.

Let us now take a bird's-eye view of the principal events mentioned in the Pagan cosmogonies and histories of the earliest times.

The Egyptian cosmogony is as yet not completely known. However, Ammon-Ra is described as the Supreme principle, uncreated and invisible, distinct from matter, the Creator of all things. Plutarch has preserved the inscription to Isis on the temple of Sais: "I am all that has been, and that will be, and no one has yet lifted my veil."

Apuleius states in Metamorphoses xi, that the sacerdotal hymns thus address Isis:

"By thee seeds are produced, grow and arrive at maturity: thou rulest the order of time, the movements of the heaven: thou givest light to the sun, and all the stars are subject to thee."

Manetho says, as quoted by Eusebius: "The first god of the Egyptians was Vulcan, the principle of fire. From Vulcan was born the Sun, then the benevolent God, then Saturn, Osiris, and Typhon, the brother of Osiris, then Horus, the son of Osiris and Isis."

These notions of Manetho are evidently derived partly from the Greeks and introduced into Egyptian mythology.

In the discourses of Thoth, as found in Hermes Trismegistus, the doctrine of Creation is found:

The judgment of M. Champollion is that the basis of these books is truly Egyptian, but that many of the thoughts interspersed have been introduced from foreign sources.

Mixed with the doctrine of Creation we find in Hermes:

"There are seven agents which contain in circles

the material world, and their action is named destiny."

"The operating Intelligence and the Word, comprising these circles in themselves and turning with great velocity, this machine moves from the beginning to the end, without beginning or end, for it continues always at the point where it begins. And from the totality of these circles, animals without reason have been made from the inferior elements."

Certainly the simple and sublime account in Genesis, which asserts at once the infinite power of God, the Creator, could not be drawn from such absurdities. The notion of Creation in Hermes, must either have been drawn from Genesis, and the nonsense mixed with it, or both were drawn from the common tradition which mankind held before their dispersion through the world.

The idea of the Trinity is also found in the Egyptian Cosmogony. Among the Persians, Zoroaster appeared about 600 B. C. He travelled in many countries to instruct himself in religious knowledge, and the *Zend Avesta* is the result.

According to this book, Ormuzd produced heaven in 40 days, water in 60 days, the earth in 65 days, trees in 30 days, animals in 80 days, man in 65 days, each work being followed by a festival.

Nowhere else than in Zoroaster outside of Genesis, is the division of Creation into six periods found.

Zoroaster visiting Babylon, just when the Jews were in captivity, no doubt became acquainted with the book of Genesis, and some of the difficulties occurred to him which strike modern infidels, such as the creation of light before the sun, and he changed the order of creation to make it seem more likely. Hence he puts the creation of heaven first to include sun, moon, planets and stars, and light. Water is, according to him, created before the earth, and the earth itself is created a considerable time after the whole immense universe, and it takes much longer time. All this to avoid the apparent difficulties of Genesis.

Zoroaster also has a notion of the Trinity.

Among the Hindoos the most ancient sacred book is said to be the book of Manou. Colonel Ingersoll would make the Hindoo books older than the Pentateuch, but M. G. Panthier, a learned Sanscrit scholar, declares that it cannot be older than 1300 years B. C.

According to this book, Manou is supremely powerful. He is alone the first born of beings, knowing all truth.

The visible universe was in darkness incomprehensible and indistinct until the self-existing Great-Power rendered it visible, dissipating darkness.

The Supreme Spirit resolved to make all creatures from his own substance, and produced an egg, brilliant as gold, from which Brahma came forth, the ancestor of all the worlds.

In time the egg became divided and from it were produced heaven, the earth, the atmosphere, the regions of light and the abyss of water.

About 200 years B. C. the Hindoos brought out a new Cosmogony, that of Buddha. This is chiefly remarkable for its difficulties and absurdities.

This system is also founded on the belief in one God Supreme served by hierarchies of Spirits.

The Phœnician Cosmogony is said to have been written by Sanchoniathon, who flourished about the time of the Trojan war, 1184 B. C.

Voltaire pretended that the account in Genesis was borrowed from the Phœnicians, but there is no resemblance whatever between the two: if we except that there is but one Supreme God according to Sanchoniathon: but that God is the Sun. However, as the Phœnician writer, whose existence even is doubtful, is certainly not so ancient as Moses, therefore Moses could not have copied from him.

The Chaldean Cosmogony is known through fragments of Berosus, some few of which have been preserved by Eusebius, who obtained them from Polyhistor.

Berosus lived about 260 B. C. He teaches a primeval chaos. Bel made heaven and earth, formed man's body from clay, but his soul from the divine essence.

The Chinese account of Creation is by Confucius, who lived 500 B. C. He also teaches one Supreme Being the maker of heaven and earth. See the texts of all these systems in Darras' Church History, vol. 1, c. 2.

The formation of man from clay is found in the Latin and Greek fable of Prometheus, and the formation of man's soul by the breath of God.

The Mosaic history of man placed by God in a garden of pleasure finds its counterpart among the Chinese, who say that man obtained happiness after contemplating the tree of life for seven days.

The Hindoo *Rig-Veda* says that the tree of life springs from the throne of Ormuzd, and if man had tasted its fruit he would not have died. Homer and Hesiod also tell of a food of the gods, ambrosia, the eating of which transmits immortality.

Among the Buddhists, the God Buddha discovers

truth and finds his doctrine under the tree of knowledge. (Mr. Schœbel, Buddha and Buddhism. Annals of Christian Phil., 4 series, vol. 15.)

According to the Persian *Zend-Avesta*, Meschia and Meschiané were seduced by *Ahriman* (the Evil Spirit,) under the form of an *adder* who presented to them deceitful fruits. (Vol. 2.)

The Japanese traditions represent the fall of man under figure of a tree around which a dreadful serpent is coiled. Noel's Japanese Cosmogony.

The Mongols say that on the soil where our first parents lived, the plant *schima* grew abundantly, white and sweet like sugar. Its aspect seduced man to eat of it and all things were consumed. (A. Nicholas, Phil. Studies, vol. 2.)

Mexican monuments previous to the discovery of America represented the first man and first woman separated from each other by a tree. The woman is named the *woman of the serpent* and holds in her hand fruits. (De Humboldt, Cordilleras and American Mountains.)

Are all these coincidences merely accidental? The Infidels of Germany are perplexed to explain them. Popular traditions which are extraordinary are always local; but here are traditions which find a place in Theogonies most remote and unconnected. Is there any way to explain them except by a common fountain, the primeval tradition of mankind before their dispersion into different countries? Thus the uniformity of the traditions proves another fact attested by Moses, the original unity of the human species.

Mr. Renan is even obliged to acknowledge that in Genesis we find "the most ancient memorials of the Semitic races. Written at a most ancient epoch, the first chapters of Genesis present to us, if not in detail, at least in substance, the primitive traditions of the Semitic race."

The accord of traditions might be largely extended on this subject, but we have above those which are most clear and decisive. Among the different nations of Asia a primitive paradise is believed, adorned with such circumstances as accord with the tastes of the divers nations. In Thibet degraded spirits tempt men to sin. In Greenland, our first parents are described as having fallen into sin. Their posterity were drowned for their sins and only one man was saved. Under form of a serpent the Scandinavians represented the devil, etc.

From Adam to Noah there are ten patriarchal generations: 1, Adam; 2, Seth; 3, Enos; 4, Cainan; 5, Malaleel; 6, Jared; 7, Enoch; 8, Mathusalem; 9, Lamech; 10, Noah. Berosus gives from the beginning also ten Chaldean kings to Xisuthrus, under whose reign came the deluge.

Sanchoniathon gives ten generations from the father of the human race, down to the present race of mortals.

The Hindoos count ten successive ages or *avatars* down to Manou the Eastern Noah.

The history of the Deluge is also perfectly attested by the traditions and monuments of ancient nations. The proof of this, however, we may leave to chapter 45, where the deluge will be treated of more in detail.

From all these testimonies we draw the inference that the truth of the history delivered by Moses in Genesis is incontestably established by the records and traditions of mankind.

CHAPTER XXXIV.

THE NEW TESTAMENT.—ITS AUTHENTICITY AND TRUTH.—CHRISTIANITY A DIVINE RELIGION.

The proofs of the authenticity, integrity and truth of the books of the New Testament are even stronger than those we have advanced for the Pentateuch. It would, however, swell this book to much larger dimensions than would suit the writer's design, to treat it here at the same length as we have treated the Pentateuch, and it would interfere with the writer's intention to answer *all* Col. Ingersoll's attacks upon the Pentateuch. For this reason, we shall rather indicate the method of proof of the New Testament, than give it in detail. Should this book receive a favorable reception from the public, it is the writer's intention, hereafter, to continue the work here begun, by another volume which will be specially devoted to the consideration of the claims of the New Testament.

The New Testament was written entirely by contemporaries of Christ, and in great part by His Apostles, who were His intimate friends and companions. It is therefore an easy matter, comparatively, to prove that they were not deceived in regard to the facts which they narrate. It was written within a short time of the death of Christ, at a historical period. The evidences of its authenticity and integrity are on this account more numerous and decisive even than the evidences of authenticity and integrity of the Pentateuch. The evidences of the sincerity of the writers of the New Testament, also exceed those which can be adduced in favor of Moses. In every respect, therefore, the historical proofs in favor of the New Testament are complete.

The Catholic Church has a history which goes back for over 1800 years to the very date when the books of the New Testament were written. During that period her testimony has been constant and unvarying that the books of the New Testament are the work of the authors, to whom they are attributed to this day. Even infidels acknowledge that since the third century, this has been the case: but the persuasion could not then have been so universal unless it had originated in the very beginning of the Church's existence. Its universality is attested by a St. Cyprian, a Tertullian, and a Clement in Africa, and by Origen, whose testimony unites both Africa and Asia. The dates of these four writers are respectively A. D. 270, 200, 180, 220.

We have besides in Asia a Theophilus of Antioch, A. D. 168, Theodotus of Byzantium, A. D. 192, Papias of about A. D. 100, Polycarp, a disciple of St. John, martyred about A. D., 164, Irenæus, A. D. 170, who unites by his testimony, his native Asia with France, where he exercised so long his Episcopate.

In Europe we have besides Irenæus, a Clement of Rome, whose name is found as a dear friend of St. Paul, recorded in Philippians iv, 3, a Justin Martyr, who wrote about 140 A. D., Hippolytus A. D. 190, Ignatius, who suffered martyrdom in Rome, A. D. 109, who also thus unites the testimony of the East and West. The list of witnesses might be multiplied to a very great extent. These, however, will suffice to show that the books of the New Testament are certified as authentic by a constant and universal tradition. The heretical sects, the Ebionites, Marcionists,

Montanists, Gnostics, etc., cut off from the early Church, give the same testimony: to say nothing of the innumerable witnesses who give no uncertain sound from the beginning of the fourth century.

The pagans, Celsus and Porphyry, wrote respectively about the years 200 and 260, and Julian the Apostate, about 361. Their works were professedly directed against Christianity and aimed at its overthrow. None of these denied, the authenticity of the books of the New Testament. They on the contrary attribute them to the authors whose names they bear. Thus when Julian forbade Christians to learn literature, he said:

"It will be sufficient for them to explain Matthew and Luke in the Galilean assemblages."

Again: "Neither Paul nor Matthew dared to call Jesus God, nor Luke nor Mark, but that good John . . . ."

The integrity of the New Testament is sufficiently evidenced by the large number of copies which were written of each book, and by the translations which were immediately made into many languages, as Latin, Syriac, etc. It was known in Judea, Syria, Asia Minor, Greece, Rome, Africa, and was received by heretics cut off from the Church, as well as by those who were recognized as members of the Church. It would therefore be impossible to make serious changes without calling down the protests of the many whose care it was to see the text preserved in its purity.

The books of the New Testament were read publicly in the assemblies of the early Christians, as Tertullian, Justin Martyr and others attest. They must, therefore, have been preserved with great care; and indeed when Diocletian ordered all copies to be delivered up to him, very many men and women preferred to die rather than to deliver them, and those who did deliver them were always esteemed as traitors and Apostates. Men and women who so strongly clung to their New Testament cannot be supposed to have been silent if any serious alterations had been made to the text.

Add to this that there has been a constant series of Christian writers who quoted largely from the New Testament. If there had been any corruption of the text it would be necessary also to corrupt in a corresponding way all the sermons and homilies, commentaries and quotations of these Christian fathers, as well as the original itself: and some of them have quoted the text so copiously, that if the New Testament were actually lost, it could be almost entirely reconstructed from a few of them only.

We have already shown that the writers of the New Testament were not deceived. Neither were they deceivers. It would be absurd to attribute to a few obscure, poor and illiterate men, whose morals were so pure that no vice could be attributed to them by such enemies as Celsus, Porphyry and Julian, the design of converting mankind to their doctrines by fraud.

They have all the characteristics of sincerity. They do not aim at rhetorical effect or philosophical sophistry. They state facts simply, without appeal to passion: as when recording the ignominious death of their Master they say, "There they crucified him." Their own faults and cowardice they ingenuously confess, their ambitious bickerings, their incredulity frequently reproved by Christ.

The facts they relate are in most cases public and of great importance where they are said to have occurred. Particularly is this true of the miracles which are related. They do not utter reproaches against those who persecuted them, they make no complaints of injuries received. They relate the time, the places and persons who were concerned in or present at the miracles recorded, so that it would be easy to detect the fraud, if there were any. They name the emperors, kings, proconsuls, governors, and high priests under whom the events occurred, so that no means is concealed by which the fraud would be discovered if there were any in their writings. Impostors do not act in this manner.

In fine they are ready to suffer any punishment in testimony to the truth of their narrative; and as a matter of fact all suffered death in testimony of their sincerity, except St. John, and it is only by a miracle that he did not suffer death also, for he was thrown into a caldron of boiling oil for witnessing the truth of his teaching.

The perfection of their moral teaching is acknowledged. They give rules for the practice of all virtues; and that they themselves practiced those virtues is attested by contemporary evidence. A greater proof of sincerity than this can scarcely be conceived.

They could not have deceived others even if they had wished to do so. Their statements were subjected to the strictest scrutiny. The question at stake was a complete change of religion, the belief in mysteries beyond the reach of reason, the abrogation of Judaism, the overthrow of idols, the belief in prodigies hitherto unheard of, the blind are made to see, the deaf to hear, the dumb to speak, the crippled begin to walk, diseases of all kinds are healed, devils are cast out, the dead are restored to life!

Those who embrace the doctrine are not promised any earthly reward. They must expect affliction, persecution, death and they must practice self-denial, mortifications, fasts and yet both Jews and Pagans embrace this doctrine knowing what they are to expect as believers in it. What else but the notoriety of the miracles wrought by Christ and his Apostles could have induced them to become believers? Certainly, then, the Apostles were not deceivers nor were they deceived regarding the Gospel history which they attest.

In conclusion: as the principal facts mentioned in the Gospels and the Acts of the Apostles, are miracles, we have the divine attestation that Christ and his Apostles established a divine Religion, and therefore CHRISTIANITY IS DIVINE.

In many respects the evidences of Christianity excel those of Judaism. Christ's character surpasses that of Moses. The morals of Christianity bring us nearer to God, because they are more perfect. There is more devotedness in the martyrs, who as witnesses to the truth laid down their lives in attestation of Christianity: the number who did so being estimated at from twelve and a half millions to twenty-five millions in the first three hundred years of the existence of Christ's church. The world was more critical and imposture would be more readily detected in the first ages of Christianity. The writers who attest Christianity are more numerous, and are nearer to the period of its establishment, than are those who attest the Mosaic law. The miracles of Christ and His Apostles are more numerous and splendid than those of Moses. The miracles of Moses are confined chiefly to himself, whereas Christ empowered his Apostles to continue their operation. The modes in which Christ and his Apostles wrought miracles are more varied than those of Moses: they are performed whether the operator be present or absent, by word, by sign, or by a mere act of the will. They are more universal in their character being wrought on creatures of every kind and on the dead as well as the living. Their consequences are more momentous as they have resulted in the conversion of a vast proportion of mankind.

Against the Authenticity and historical truth of the New Testament we often meet the objection made that the genealogy of Christ as given in the first chapter of St. Matthew's gospel in quite different from that given by St. Luke, chapter iii: so that in fact none of the ancestors of Joseph as given by St. Matthew are the same with his ancestors as given by St. Luke.

This objection is also made by Col. Ingersoll, though not in his "Mistakes of Moses." I will therefore reply to it here.

This difficulty was raised by Julian the Apostate, and was answered by St. Augustine in the fourth century of our era. It was really no difficulty to those who knew the Jewish law; and St. Luke certainly could not have considered it as such, for when he wrote his gospel, he knew of St. Matthew's gospel to which he undoubtedly refers in beginning his own. He could therefore have no object in giving a different genealogy, unless both were true. There is no inconsistency whatsoever between them. The genealogy given by St. Matthew is that of Joseph. The genealogy given by St. Luke is that of Mary. This is the usual opinion on the subject.

This being the case how can the genealogy of Joseph as given by St. Matthew prove Christ's descent from David? This will be clear from Num. xxxvi, 8, where it is prescribed that every daughter with an inheritance should be wife to one of the family of her father's tribe. For this reason the daughters of Zelophedad married their father's brothers' sons. (verse 11.) For the same reason Mary married her mother's brother's son. Mary's mother was Anna, the aunt of Joseph, and Mathan, the father of Anna and Jacob, was grandfather to both Joseph and Mary. The genealogy of Joseph was therefore the genealogy of Mary and also of Christ, showing Christ's descent from David through Nathan. The genealogy of Mary given by St. Luke shows His descent from David through Solomon.

We have heard it objected against this: How then can Joseph be called "the son of Heli," as we read in the Protestant Bible in Luke iii? To this I answer that the words "*the son*" are not in the original Greek. It is to show this that they are in Italics in the Protestant Bible. The original reads as in the Catholic Bible, "of Heli." However, by his marriage with Mary, Joseph was adopted into the family of Heli, being his son-in-law.

The facts might have occurred in another way, and some commentators thus explain them.

By Deuteronomy xxv, 5, 6, when a man dies childless, the widow marries his brother in the name of the dead brother, so that she is regarded as rearing children to the dead brother.

Thus Heli died, and his wife married Jacob. Joseph was born of this marriage, and was therefore *by law* the son of Heli, and *by nature* the son of Jacob. Jacob and Heli were brothers by the same mother but by different fathers, viz. Mathan and Mathat. Hence there are two genealogies. Either genealogy was the genealogy of Christ, since, as we have already explained, Mary and Joseph were first cousins.

CHAPTER XXXV.

OBJECTIONS REFUTED.—CREATION.—THE FIRMAMENT.—HEAVEN.

HAVING proved the truth of Revelation, and the Divinity of the Jewish and Christian Religions, it is now proper to examine those of Colonel Ingersoll's objections against our thesis, which we have not already refuted in the course of this work.

We may begin with his chapters on Creation, viz: vi to xv.

Let us here remark that the Colonel starts out with a most egregious blunder, which is carried through his treatise on Creation.

"The Creation of the world commenced, according to the Bible, on Monday morning, about 5,883 years ago." (P. 55.)

Thus, of course, on Monday the Colonel places the Creation of light, on Tuesday was made the firmament and the division of the waters below from the waters above, etc. (Gen. i. See pages 61, 63, etc.) Naturally it follows that he makes Saturday the sixth day of Creation, and Sunday the day of the appointed rest. (Pp. 87, 101.)

Now, to use the Colonel's own expression (p. 99,) "if we know anything we know that" the Jewish day begins at even, and ends the next even. Darkness preceded light, according to the first chapter of Genesis, and the keeping of the day thus is a monument in memory of Creation. (Ex. xii, 18.) Besides, the last day of Creation was Friday, not Saturday; and the day of rest was Saturday, not Sunday. The day of rest began on Friday evening at sunset, and ended on Saturday evening at sunset. (Lev: xxiii, 32.)

Perhaps the Colonel will say this is a mere oversight. Well, one who sets himself up as a public teacher of History, Geography, Astronomy, and all the other sciences (pp. 99, 122, 81, etc.), ought to have some knowledge of a well-known fact whose history extends over nearly six thousand years.

The Colonel says:

"Moses conveys . . . . the idea that the matter of which heaven and earth are composed was created." (P. 56.)

"It is impossible for me to conceive of something being created from nothing. Nothing, regarded in the light of a raw material, is a decided failure." (Ib.)

We proved in chapters 5 and 7 that matter is created. Matter is finite. Whatever is finite is contingent. Whatever is contingent is the effect of an extrinsic cause. The effect of an extrinsic cause is a created being. Therefore, Matter is a created being.

"It is impossible" for you "to conceive of something created from nothing." The operation of Infinite Power can effect that the possible shall become actual or existing. A reasonable being conceives a contingent being as possible, and as matter is a contingent being, a reasonable being can conceive of possible matter becoming actual by the operation of Infinite Power. If you cannot conceive this, you are not a reasonable being.

There is no question of *nothing* being regarded "as raw material." If we can say "the world was made out of nothing," it is not because nothing is the material out of which the world is made, but because ordinary human speech uses this form of expression to signify that a substance previously non-existent began to exist. In the same way, it is only common usage that can justify your use of the word "idea" when you mean "judgment." The primary sense of the word idea, and its philosophical sense, is "the mere mental representation of an object, without affirmation or negation concerning it." Hence, "matter was created" is a judgment expressed in words, and not a mere idea.

Next you assert that before Creation, "An Infinite Intelligence" was "wasting an eternity" doing nothing. (P. 57.)

God in all eternity acts in the exercise of his Infinite Perfections. It is, therefore, not true that he is doing nothing, or wasting eternity. It is not necessary for him to act externally. In creating, he is a free agent. Created beings add nothing to his intrinsic perfections. They are but the external manifestation of his glory and power. You say:

"I do not pretend to tell how all these things really are." (P. 57.)

What right have you, then, to ask that others should explain the mysteries of the Infinite, which you here virtually acknowledge and declare to be inexplicable?

The next assertions, that the account of Creation is imaginative, and that miracles are lies, we dealt with in chapters 13 and 27.

We are next told that the writer of Genesis "believed that darkness was a thing, an entity, etc." We have shown in chapter 26 that Moses spoke of darkness in the current language of the day, and not in the newly invented but useful language of Natural Philosophy. He could do this and still be perfectly correct. By darkness Moses meant the atmosphere itself in such a condition that light could not reach one who had the faculty of vision.

The Colonel has nothing more to say about the work of the first day of Creation.

On the second day, "God made the firmament, and divided the waters which were under the firmament from the waters which were above the firmament." (Gen. i, 7.)

On this text the Colonel says:

"What did the writer mean by the word firmament? Theologians now tell us that he meant an 'expanse.' This will not do. How could an expanse divide the waters from the waters so that the waters above the expanse would not fall into and mingle with the waters below the expanse? The truth is that Moses regarded the firmament as a solid affair. It was where God lived and where water was kept. . . . . They supposed that some angel could with a lever raise a gate and let out the quantity of moisture desired." (P. 63.)

This he illustrates further, by showing that "the world was drowned when the windows of heaven were opened," (Gen. vii, 11,) and that in the *dream* of Jacob the top of a ladder "reached to heaven." (xxviii, 12.)

He goes on to say that God lived on the floor of this firmament, "surrounded by his sons," and that "Moses knew nothing about the laws of evaporation."

"He did not know that the sun wooed with amorous kisses the waves of the sea, and that they, clad in glorified mist, rising to meet their lover, were, by disappointment, changed to tears, and fell as rain." (P. 64.)

Let us analyze this after the Colonel's own fashion. "Colonel Ingersoll is evidently of the opinion that the sun and the water are reasonable beings, moved by their passions. The sun is actually in love, and the water meets with disappointment! Again: He is a believer in enchantment; for the water, from being at first a disappointed lover, in human form, of course (see pages 93, 94), according to his anthropomorphic principles, is metamorphosed into tears! Evidently he knows "nothing of the laws of evaporation."

The Colonel would be likely to answer if we would analyze his sentences in this manner:

"You know nothing of the usages of language, or you would recognize that I have made use of a figure of speech."

In the same way may we answer his commentary on the firmament and the windows of heaven.

The opening of the windows of heaven is evidently a figurative expression for the falling of a large quantity of rain. The ladder whose top reached to heaven is a dream or vision, and the passage of the angels up and down the ladder signifies that the angels minister to God, and execute on earth His will towards men. All this is expressly stated to be a dream, though it is a symbol of what happens in reality. It is dishonest to represent it as literally true.

As regards the firmament, the word is indeed derived from the Latin word which signifies a support or prop, but is Colonel Ingersoll ignorant of the fact that, as it is used to express the sky, the original meaning is modified to make the word express its new signification? There is absolutely nothing in the Bible to justify Colonel Ingersoll's *fanfaronade* on this subject.

Equally futile is the Colonel's conclusion:

"The telescope destroyed the firmament, did away with the heaven of the New Testament, rendered the Ascension of our Lord and the Assumption of his mother infinitely absurd."

Similarly he indulges in ill-timed witticism about Enoch and Elias (Elijah) being taken to heaven. He says, "Enoch and the rest would have been frozen perfectly stiff before the journey could have been completed. Possibly Elijah might have made the voyage, as he was carried to heaven in a chariot of fire 'by a whirlwind.'" (Pp. 65, 66.)

It is the belief of all Christians that there is a place in the universe where God manifests himself to the blessed by a visible display of his glory. Never-ending bliss will be the privilege enjoyed by all who are admitted there. The precise locality we do not pretend to know. God has not revealed this; but we are satisfied with his promise, as we know he is able to fulfil it, though we do not know precisely in what way this will be done. The Bible nowhere pretends that either the firmament or heaven is a solid arch, which is at the same time a home for God and a reservoir of water from which rain is made to fall as it is required. The words of Elihu in Job xxxvii, 18, have been quoted as having this meaning, but God expressly repudiates Elihu's whole speech in xxxviii, 2: "Who is this that wrappeth up sentences in unskilful words?"

On the third day God said:

"Let the waters that are under the heaven be gathered together in one place; and let the dry land appear." (Gen. i, 9.)

Colonel Ingersoll says:

"The writer of this did not have any conception of the real form of the earth. He could not have known anything of the attraction of gravitation. He must have regarded the earth as flat and supposed that it required considerable force and power to induce the water to leave the mountains and collect in the valleys. Just as soon as the water was forced to run down hill the dry land appeared," etc.

It is not necessary to insert the poetic ornaments, the mantles of green, the laughing trees, the trembling hands of Dawn, etc. These add nothing to the argument.

The Rev. Father Lambert has dealt so well with the Colonel's assertion that "water always runs down hill," that I need only, on this subject, give a summary of his remarks.

Water has to get up hill before it can run down. Water rises as vapor or steam. More water rises in the vegetable world through capillary tubes, in a day, than falls at Niagara in a year. The earth being a spheroid, not a sphere, the Equator is thirteen miles higher than the Poles of the Earth, and all rivers running towards the equator run up hill, not down.

Col. Ingersoll, then, shows that it is himself who has "no conception of the shape of the earth." Our Philosopher evidently knows but little of Natural Philosophy.

In what way is the statement of Moses contradictory of the law of gravitation? Col. Ingersoll does not enlighten us on this subject, so we may rest content that Col. Ingersoll is mistaken. There is nothing contrary to gravitation, either in the gathering together of waters, or in the appearance of dry land. To this day waters gather into our rivers, lakes and seas, and dry land appears always when a flood subsides, yet we never hear that the laws of gravitation are disturbed thereby.

CHAPTER XXXVI.

OBJECTIONS REFUTED.—THE CREATION.

The next objection against the truth of Genesis is derived from discoveries in Geology, Astronomy, etc.

Col. Ingersoll says:

The Bible is "false and mistaken in its astronomy, geology, geography, history and philosophy." (P. 243.)

"A few years ago Science endeavored to show that it was not inconsistent with the Bible. The tables have been turned, and now, Religion is endeavoring to prove that the Bible is not inconsistent with science." (P. 242.)

The Colonel does not specify wherein these discrepancies consist. On Astronomy he contents himself with asking a number of questions regarding the extent of Moses' knowledge on this subject. All this has nothing whatever to do with the question, Is the Bible false in its Astronomy? Thus he asks:

"Can we believe that the inspired writer had any idea of the size of the Sun? . . . . Did he know that the sun was (is?) 860,000 miles in diameter? Did he know that the volume of the earth is less than one-millionth of that of the sun? . . . . Did he know of the 104 planets? . . . . Did he know anything about Saturn, his rings and his eight moons?" etc. (Pp. 72, 73.)

The Bible is not a handbook of Astronomy. Its object is to teach Morality and the way to serve God. All this can be attained without the knowledge insisted on by Col. Ingersoll, though it is possible that Moses knew as much about Astronomy as does Col. Ingersoll. This, however, makes not a particle of difference as to the truth of the Pentateuch. No matter, then, even if it were true what the Colonel says:

"Moses supposed the Sun to be about three or four feet in diameter, and the moon about half that size." (P. 74.)

Of this we need only say that the Colonel knows nothing about the extent of Moses' knowledge. His assertion then is simply a piece of impertinence.

As the Colonel does not tell exactly the Geological difficulty, we must look for it elsewhere. As stated by Huxley in his "Lectures on Evolution," by Furniss in his "Anonymous Hypothesis of Creation," and a host of Infidels besides, the difficulty is that:

"The narration of Moses on the formation of the earth is irreconcilable with true science, and especially with Geology."

Does Genesis affirm that the earth was created just five days before the creation of man?

Prof. Huxley says that he will abstain from giving any opinion on this question. "It is not my business to say what the Hebrew text contains and what it does not." (Theory of Evolution: Chickering Hall, 1877.)

He says, however, amid "laughter and applause," that if we give any other interpretation to the words of Genesis than that it does make this statement, that "a person who is not a critic, and is not a Hebrew scholar can only stand up and admire the marvellous flexibility of the language which admits of such diverse interpretations."

The meaning of all this is unmistakable. Prof. Huxley, Col. Ingersoll, and other Infidels assert that the Mosaic record is refuted by Geology.

I maintain, then, that the discoveries of Geology do not clash with the words of Genesis. We read, first:

"In the beginning God created heaven and earth."

"And the earth was void and empty and darkness was upon the face of the deep: And the spirit of God moved over the waters."

"And God said: Be light made. And light was made." Gen. i, 1, 2, 3.

1. Geology teaches that the earth is of very great age. The plants, fishes and beasts embedded in many strata of rocks, which must have been formed by degrees betoken that the earth dates back into most remote antiquity. Now do the above words of Genesis imply that Creation is recent? The first event recorded has no date given: the Creation of heaven and earth: and even then it is not stated that

the second event is closely allied with the first in the matter of time. The Hebrew particle *ve, and*, does not imply immediate sequence. Thus in Chapters vi, xi, xxiv, beginning with the same particle, there is no immediate sequence. A very great time may therefore have elapsed between the events of the first and second verses, and between the second and third verses of Genesis i.

Even fifteen hundred years ago, before Geology was dreamed of as a science, Sts. Augustine, Basil, and Gregory of Nazianzen pointed this out, and Origen and Justin Martyr still earlier. This interpretation, therefore, was not invented for the purpose of meeting the geological difficulty. There is, therefore, so far, no conflict between Genesis and Geology. There is no need of making the Hebrew language so marvellously flexible.

The period which intervened between the original Creation of the Universe, and its preparation for the use of man is not defined. It may therefore have been of very great duration and may have included all the time requisite for the geological effects which have been discovered. There may have been any amount of animal and vegetable life, and undoubtedly Geology seems to require that an immense period of time must have elapsed. There are evidences that the earth passed through many great revolutions and successive acts of Creation, compared with which man's time on earth is but ephemeral. All this, far from clashing with the Mosaic account, confirms it; for every period of change betokens the exercise of Infinite power and wisdom. Every successive period betokens a new Creative Act; for every period has its own Vegetation, its own animal life. Geology demonstrates that these successive Creations are the work of God, for only God could produce these living organisms, different from each other in every geological epoch. Geology demonstrates that the Natural laws were the same in every epoch, as they are now. If animals and plants were the mere result of natural causes like crystallization, operating on inert atoms, animal and vegetable life would have been in those remote ages, the same or nearly the same as it is to-day. If the evolution theory, so favored now by infidels, were true, we would behold the gradual change from one form of life to another till the present stage were reached. But this is not the case. Before man appeared on earth, with the animals and vegetables which are contemporary with him, all life was completely swept away. Such is the teaching of Geology, and the book of Genesis teaches us the same. Previous to the six days' work of Genesis, "the earth was void and empty." i, 2.

Dr. Buckland, by far a more eminent geologist than any of those who have made of this science an engine wherewith to attack the Mosaic Cosmogony, says:

"Moses does not deny the existence of another order of things prior to the preparation of this globe for the reception of the human race, to which he confines the details of his history. There is nothing in the proposition inconsistent with the Mosaic declaration of the Creation."

This explanation of the Mosaic Cosmogony I do not put forward as the interpretation necessarily to be adopted. Other methods of reconciliation have been adopted by men of learning, but perhaps this method has the greatest sanction of authority and evidence in its favor. The late learned and illustrious Cardinal Wiseman also favors this view in his "Science and Revealed Religion." Lecture 5.

"The Scriptural narrative, subjected to the examination of the most different pursuits, defies their power therein to discover any error, forms in the aggregate of various examples, a strong positive proof of its unassailable veracity. Thus, here, had the Scripture allowed no interval between *creation* and *organization*, but declared that they were simultaneous or closely consecutive acts, we should, perhaps have stood perplexed in the reconciliation between its assertions and modern discoveries. But when, instead of this, it leaves an undecided interval between the two, nay, more, informs us that there was a state of confusion and conflict, of waste and darkness, and a want of a proper basin for the sea, which thus would cover first one part of the earth and then another; we may truly say, that the geologist reads in those few lines the history of the earth, such as his monuments have recorded it—a series of disruptions, elevations and dislocations; sudden inroads of the unchained element, entombing successive generations of amphibious animals, etc., ... and the earth remained in that state of sullen and gloomy prostration, from which it was recalled by the *reproduction* of light, and the *subsequent* work of the six days' creation."

But if this be true, how are we to explain that on the first day "God said: Be light made; and light was made," that on the second day the firmament was made, and on the fourth day, the sun, moon and stars? Geology, we are told, teaches us decisively that light existed, and Astronomy proves that the sun and planets existed as far back in the past as did the earth; so that if the earth existed thousands, even millions of years before the days of Genesis, light and the sun must also have existed during that period.

I answer by calling attention to the change in the Sacred Writer's language.

The change is quite perceptible in Hebrew, and is well marked in the English translation. In the Hebrew, *bara* is *created: hasah* is *made*. *Bara, created,* is used in the account of creation, where there is a new being brought into existence. From Gen. i, 1, to ii, 4, *creation* is mentioned seven times. God *created* heaven and earth. He *created* the great whales. He *created* man. Three times in the twenty-seventh verse is the *creation* of man declared:

"And God *created* man to his own image; to the image of God he *created* him: male and female he *created* them."

In ii, 3, we find that "God rested from all his work which he *created* and *made*."

There is a distinction, then, between *creating* and *making*. When God forms a being entirely from substance already existing, he does not *create*, he *makes : hasah*. *Hasah*, to *make*, may be used for *creating*, but not *bara*, to *create*, for *making*. *Hasah*, therefore, does not necessarily imply creating from nothing. It is used much as we use in English the verb *to make*, as when a carpenter *makes* a *door*, or a *table*. He does not *create*, he *makes* it from boards which already exist.

Hence also it is not said that God *created* light on the first day. It is "Be light, and light was." It is not said that he *created* the firmament on the second day, but: "firmament be . . . . and God *made* (*hasah*) the firmament."

Hence it is quite possible that light and the firmament, and the sun, moon and stars had existed from the time when God *created* heaven and earth; but that now they are *fashioned, made,* or, to use Cardinal Wiseman's term, *organized* and *reproduced* so as to be fit for man's use, for whose dwelling place God is now preparing the world.

Thus there is absolutely no contradiction between Genesis and Geology, and there is no distortion of the words of the sacred text. Thus, also, all the difficulties disappear which are brought against the text by Professor Huxley, Col. Ingersoll, Mr. James Furniss and others.

I have already said that I do not give this explanation as the one necessarily to be adopted. Other systems of reconciliation have been maintained by able scholars; and if any *one* of them accounts for the wording of the Mosaic narrative, without being contrary to the *proved* conclusions of Geology, then the Geological objection is of no weight whatever. Now, it is well known that Geology is still very largely speculative as a science, and in some things so is Astronomy. True, in both sciences much has been demonstrated in late years which has confirmed theories that preceded demonstration; but also, many theories which were before almost universally held by those versed in these sciences, have since been exploded, and are now as universally rejected.

In proof of this, I may instance the *corpuscular theory* of light, of which Sir Isaac Newton was the author. The great name of Newton was almost sufficient of itself to cause a theory of Natural Philosophy to be accepted without dispute; but when such a theory was supported by arguments and facts such as he was able to adduce in its favor, it seemed presumptuous to entertain any other opinion than that which he advanced. Nevertheless, the rival *theory of undulations* has at last almost driven Sir Isaac Newton's *corpuscular theory* from the field; and the more it has been studied, the stronger has become the evidence in its favor. Yet even this system can even now only be termed a *theory.*

"Of all sciences," says Cardinal Wiseman, "none has been more given up to the devices of man's heart and imagination than geology; none has afforded ampler scope for ideal theories, and brittle, though brilliant systems, constructed for the most conflicting purposes."

"From the time of Buffon, system rose beside system, like the moving pillars of the desert, advancing in threatening array; but like them, they were fabrics of sand; and though in 1806 the French Institute counted more than eighty such theories hostile to Scripture history, not one of them has stood till now, or deserves to be recorded." (Lecture 5, Science and Religion.)

2. Some have reconciled Genesis with Geology by affirming that the rocks discovered by geology with fossils in them were created as they are, with all the apparent evidences of antiquity. This is certainly possible, and it would be difficult to refute it. The power of God to create the world so must be admitted.

Still it must be acknowledged that this opinion is opposed to the known analogies of nature. If, for instance, we find a fossil animal, whose teeth are worn as they would be by eating, or if we find a fossil animal, with a smaller fossil animal in its crop, as if the latter had been eaten by the former, are we not inevitably led to the conclusion that these animals have lived, and eaten, and died just as such animals do at this day?

This theory, then, is not admitted generally by scientific men; though it would be difficult to prove absolutely that it is false.

3. Another theory is that the fossils brought to light by geology were deposited by the deluge. To this also there are many objections which are, probably, insuperable. Can we suppose that numerous strata thousands of feet thick, have been deposited in regular groups, and for the most part petrified, and with their most delicate parts uninjured, and that distinct races of plants and animals were deposited according to fixed laws, by a sudden and violent inundation? and that in one year all this should occur, whereas according to the universal operation of nature's laws, ages upon ages are required to bring about these effects?

4. Others have thought that the days of Genesis are not ordinary days, but long periods of time during which the processes were going on which geology demands. This theory may possibly be correct, still there are serious objections to it which we need not enumerate here. Suffice it to say that if we accept the theory favored by such great names as Dr. Buckland and Cardinal Wiseman, as well as being suggested by a St. Augustine, a St. Basil, an Origen, there is no need of departing from the ordinary acceptation of the term "day" as a period of 24 hours. It is on

this last hypothesis that I will answer the remaining objections of Col. Ingersoll and others against the Mosaic narrative.

I must not omit to mention two other systems of reconciliation, either of which, if accepted, would seem to reconcile the Mosaic narrative with the discoveries of modern research.

5. Some suppose that Moses is shown the work of Creation in a vision, and that by direction of God he describes the vision as it would appear to one beholding it from the earth. In this case an absolute accordance with facts discovered in the bowels of the earth would not be required. It would be sufficient that the vision be described according to appearances.

6. In the other hypothesis, the first chapter of Genesis, and seven verses of the second chapter constitute a liturgical hymn in which the praises of God as our Creator are celebrated. The week is divided into seven days, on each of which God is to be honored as having performed that portion of the work of Creation which is attributed to that day.

According to this theory, we are not to look to Geology at all for an explanation of the words of Genesis. We are simply to regard God as the Creator of all things, and to devote each day to His honor, under the special aspect recorded in the Mosaic narrative as the work of that day.

7. Many other theories have been devised on this subject. It is sufficient for us to know that there are many modes of reconcilation; and if any one of them can be defended, the whole attack of Infidelity against this portion of the Pentateuch will be repelled.

CHAPTER XXXVII.

OBJECTIONS REFUTED.—THE CREATION OF PLANTS AND ANIMALS.—THE SUN STANDING STILL.—CHINESE ASTRONOMY.

The first section of the preceding chapter shows us how we may answer nearly all the remaining objections against the Mosaic Cosmogony. Thus Col. Ingersoll says:

"Moses says that God said on the third day, 'Let the earth bring forth grass, etc. . . . . And the earth brought forth grass and herb yielding seed after his kind, and the tree yielding fruit, whose seed was in itself after his kind; and God saw that it was good, and the evening and morning were the third day.'"

"There was nothing to eat this fruit; not an insect with painted wings sought the honey of the flowers; not a single living breathing thing upon the earth. Plenty of grass, etc. . . . . but not a mouth in all the world. If Moses is right, this state of things lasted only two days: but if the modern theologians are correct, it continued for millions of ages." (Pp. 68, 69.)

"There is in Nature an even balance forever kept between the total amounts of animal and vegetable life. In her wonderful economy she must form and bountifully nourish her vegetable progeny—twin brother life to her, with that of animals. The perfect balance between plant existences and animal existences must always be maintained." Ib.

Under the caption, "Friday" on pages 84, 85, we

have the same thought repeated, with the addition that:

"Not a scientist of high standing will say that in his judgment the earth was covered with fruit-bearing trees before the moners, the ancestors, it *may be* of the human race, felt in Laurentian seas the first throb of life."

If the book of Genesis is to be impugned, let us have positive proofs against it. We have given positive proofs of its truth, *maybes* cannot be accepted as demonstration against it.

Why the balance should be maintained between plants and animals, if there is no Supreme Intelligence directing all, we are not informed. If Nature is but the operation of blind forces, as Col. Ingersoll maintains, the above is simply nonsense; and if Nature is the Supreme Intelligent Being that directs all things, then Nature must be God.

In any case, whether blind force, or an Infinite and Free God directs all things, there is no reason why plants at least should not be created independently of animals. Hence Col. Ingersoll gives no reason. We are to accept his word as the infallible dictum which must not be disputed.

However he acknowledges that if Moses is right, only two days would elapse while plants existed without animals to eat them. Surely the plants could survive that long without being eaten. In the hypothesis we are assuming, millions of years are altogether beside the question. We take the days of Genesis to be natural days.

The next objection is founded on Joshua x, 13: "So the sun stood still in the midst of heaven, and hasted not to go down about a whole day."

In connection with this the Colonel also objects to the miracle recorded in Isaias xxviii, 8. A Jewish King, Ezechias, "was sick, 'and God to convince him that he would ultimately recover offered to make the shadow on the dial go forward or backward ten degrees. The king thought it was too easy a thing to make the shadow go forward, and asked that it be turned back.' Thereupon 'Isaias the prophet cried unto the Lord, and he brought the shadow ten degrees backward by which it had gone down in the dial of Achaz.'" See also 4 Kings xx, 1, 11. (Prot. Bible, 2 Kings.)

These miracles are not related by Moses. They do not belong to the Pentateuch history: however, as they are constantly in the mouths of Infidels, I will treat of them here. What has the Colonel to object regarding them? He says:

"It is impossible to conceive of a more absurd story than this about the stopping of the sun and moon; and yet nothing so excites the malice of the orthodox preacher as to call its truth in question." (P. 75.)

The miracle regarding King Ezechias he considers more wonderful still, and of course equally or more absurd. (P. 78.)

We might ask how the latter can be more wonderful or absurd, if it be impossible to conceive anything more absurd than the former? We suppose, however, that Col. Ingersoll is to be allowed to contradict himself with impunity. If not, then the "Mistakes of Moses" ought not to have been written.

There is no other reason for calling these two events absurd than because they are miracles. Now we have proved that miracles are not absurd. Therefore Col. Ingersoll has no reason for calling these events absurd.

He says: "If he (Joshua) had known that the earth turned upon its axis at the rate of a thousand miles an hour, and swept in its course about the sun at the rate of sixty-eight thousand miles an hour, he would have . . . . allowed the sun and moon to rise and set in the usual way." (P. 74.)

ANSWER. Since a miracle is in question, it makes little difference whether the rate of the earth's motion be one thousand or one million miles per hour. God is equally powerful in one case as in the other.

He says: "Some endeavor to account for the phenomenon by natural causes."

Yes. There are infidels in disguise who pretend that there are really no miracles in the Bible. The two events are recorded as miracles, and as miracles true Christians believe them.

He adds: "Others attempt to show that God could, by the refraction of light have made the sun visible, although actually shining on the opposite side of the earth." Thus: "The Rev. Henry M. Morey, of South Bend, Indiana, says that the phenomenon was simply optical. The rotary motion of the earth was not disturbed."

Possibly, the Rev. H. M. Morey is right. There is no need to suppose that the motion of the earth on its axis was stayed, when we know that the same effect would be produced by the bending or refraction of the rays of light. Even in working miracles, God usually works with a simplicity resembling the simplicity of nature. We may be satisfied that God wrought the miracles on the two occasions mentioned in holy Scripture, because they are attested by truthful historians. Our only source of information on the subject is the Bible, and as it does not state in what manner the miracle was effected, I do not pretend to decide whether the "phenomenon was simply optical," or that "the rotary motion was stopped." God could have effected it in either way, and in either way there is no absurdity, because God's power is infinite.

It is useless to object that the stoppage of the earth's rotary motion would have produced an immense amount of heat. The miracle may not have been effected in that way. At all events, God undertook to work the miracle, to manifest to Jews and Gentiles His Infinite power, and a physical difficulty could not prevent him from executing his will.

The Colonel objects that the occasion was not, in either case, important enough to justify so great a prodigy. The miracle of Joshua was done, he says:

"That one barbarian might defeat another." (P. 77.)

The miracle in the case of Ezechias is said to be "a useless display of power." (P. 79.)

ANSWER. Is it then for man to fix the limits within which God's wisdom and power are to operate? The Israelites were fighting a defensive battle. The Gibeonites were the allies of Joshua, and on this account five kings joined in league to annihilate them. Joshua could not but regard the confederation as unjust, and even God's honor was interested in the preservation of the allies of his chosen people, as the alliance of the Israelites with them had been ratified by the high-priest of God in his name. God, therefore, to manifest to the Canaanites his greatness, wrought this miracle. If the victory had been attained solely by the sword of Israel, it would have been attributed to the superior valor of the nation. As it was, the vanity of the Canaanite Gods was shown by the superior power of the God of Israel.

In the case of Ezechias, we must bear in mind that the Jewish kingdom was under God's direction and protection in a manner more marked than are even the most religious kingdoms, ordinarily speaking. The kings ruled, even in their temporal sovereignty as God's viceroys; and God had always promised special marks of his favor when the kings and people were faithful to him.

Ezechias had been a faithful King. He had abolished idolatry, and the character given of him is that either before or after him, "there was none like him among the Kings of Juda." (4 Ki. xviii, 5; Prot. Bible, 2 Kings.) Is it a matter, then, of great surprise, that God should by an extraordinary sign from heaven show his approval of the king's conduct? He extended his life for fifteen years, and ratified His promise to this effect, certainly by an astonishing manifestation of His Power.

But Col. Ingersoll wishes to make it appear that Ezechias was already healed, and therefore he needed not the testimony of the new miracle that he would be healed.

In answer to this I would point out that God's promise was not yet entirely fulfilled. Ezechias was healed of his ulcer or boil by the application of the figs, but he was not yet healed of his sickness, completely. His disease appears to have been a complicated one, and he would not be in full health for three days, when he would be able to go to the temple. (xx, 5, 8.) Besides fifteen years were to be added to his life.

The miracle was God's testimony that these promises would be fulfilled.

The treatment of this subject would be incomplete were I to omit an objection which is constantly advanced by Infidels, though not directly insisted on by Col. Ingersoll.

Voltaire in his "Bible explained," puts the difficulty thus:

"Natural Philosophers find it troublesome to explain how the sun, which does not move, stood still" at Joshua's command.

We may allow Col. Ingersoll to answer this difficulty.

"We are told that the sacred writer wrote in common speech as we do when we talk about the rising and setting of the sun, and that all he intended to say was that the earth ceased to turn on its axis 'for about a whole day.'" (P. 74.)

Exactly; and it would have been absurd and unintelligible to have spoken otherwise than in the general language of mankind. The compilers of our almanacs are aware that it is the revolution of the earth on its axis which causes the sun, *apparently*, to rise and set. Yet the phenomenon is always described by them as sunrise and sunset.

Voltaire says "the sun does not move." Astronomers teach differently. The sun moves, 1, around its own axis; 2, around the centre of gravity of the solar system; 3, around the centre of gravity of the Universe.

These consequences follow from the law of the attraction of Gravitation. Voltaire was mistaken.

Now according to those who would have Joshua speak in scientific language, he should have explained all these motions of the sun, and the influence that each motion had on the effect which was visible. There was no other course possible if he were bound to speak in modern scientific language. Joshua had common sense enough to speak in a language which would be intelligible, the language of his nation, and in a certain sense, the language of all mankind.

As we use the word motion in regard to the heavenly bodies, it is always used *relatively*, not *absolutely;* for we do not know the *absolute* motion of any celestial orb. Why then should Joshua be required to speak of *absolute* motion? Why should he alone of all men be compelled at the beck of modern Infidels, to speak a language which no mortal would understand?

Col. Ingersoll's next difficulty is:

"The view of Moses (that the heavenly bodies were as nothing compared with the earth) was acquiesced in by the Jewish people and by the Christian world."

Considering that Moses says absolutely nothing about the relative sizes of the earth and the heavenly bodies, the Colonel's assertion is simply arrant nonsense. He adds:

"The ancient Chinese knew not only the motions of the planets, but they could calculate eclipses. . . . . Is it not strange that a Chinaman should find out (one thousand years before Moses,) by his own exertions more about the material Universe than Moses could when assisted by his Creator?" (P. 78.)

If the Chinese annalists are to be believed the nation has, indeed, a very great antiquity. Their annals reach to the reign of Yao, two thousand five hundred and fifty-seven years before Christ, and they assert that the emperors before Yao go back to three million two hundred and seventy-six thousand years before Christ. Now it is well known that the annals of Confucius did not exist till five hundred years before Christ: for this was the time when Confucius wrote. His writings were destroyed by order of Chi-Hoang-Ti about three hundred years before Christ, and were only written by memory in their present shape at the dictation of an old man, who during the next dynasty pretended to know them by heart. The Chinese have no other authority for their annals, than this. It will be evident to all that there is no reliance to be placed on the fabulous histories related by Col. Ingersoll as if they were gospel truths. Klaproth affirms confidently that no reliance whatever is to be placed on the statements of the Chinese annals which go back further than seven hundred and thirty-two years before Christ.

CHAPTER XXXVIII.

OBJECTIONS REFUTED.—ASTRONOMY.—GOD NOT RESPONSIBLE FOR THE SINS AND ERRORS OF MEN.

THE 10th chapter of Col. Ingersoll's book treats of the stars. Here again he asks a number of questions which have no reference to the truth or falsity of Revelation.

"'He made the stars also.' Moses .... only gave five words to all the hosts of heaven." (P. 81.)

In fact Moses did not use five words to describe the Creation of the stars. He only said "*Ve-eth*

Hakkokabim," also the stars: four words, at most, if we divide the above into its distinct parts. These four words were quite sufficient to convey all the information he intended to give on the subject, viz., that God also made the stars. The Colonel then asks:

"Did he know that the nearest star .... is twenty-one billion of miles away? .... that Sirius is a sun two thousand six hundred and eighty-eight times larger than our own?" etc. (P. 81.)

"It may be replied that it was not the intention of God to teach geology and astronomy. Then why did he say anything upon these subjects?" (P. 82.)

It is true: the object of God in the Pentateuch, is not to teach geology and astronomy. He has, however, a moral and dogmatic end in view in teaching us that the sun, moon and stars, and all things, are His work.

In chapter 37 we have answered the Colonel's onslaught, found on pages 84 and 85 of his book, regarding the co-existence of plants and animals, and of the moner ancestry of man.

He next maintains that:

"A belief in the great truths of science are fully as essential to Salvation as the creed of any Church." (P. 86.)

The main difference between the truths of Science and those of Religion is this: the former do not affect our morals and the latter do. By means of the truths of Religion, we are furnished with motives for fulfilling duties towards God, our neighbors, and ourselves. It is by the fulfillment of these duties that Salvation is deserved. Thus it is that the creed which teaches Religious truth is more essential to Salvation than is merely Scientific truth.

For the third time the Colonel asks, on page 87, whether it is possible that plants, etc., should have existed before animals. We need not repeat the answer already given in the last chapter. The Moner theory, and that of natural antecedents, promulgated on page 88, we will deal with in chapter 40.

We next find the following extraordinary theory propounded by the Colonel:

"If (the Bible) was inspired, of course God must have known just how it would be understood, and consequently must have intended that it should be understood just as he knew it would be." (P. 88.)

"If a being of infinite wisdom wrote the Bible, or caused it to be written, he must have known exactly how his words would be interpreted by all the world, and he must have intended to convey the very meaning that was conveyed." (P. 89.)

Then he infers that all the erroneous views of mankind in regard to the meaning of the Bible were intended by God: the errors of men as to the shape and antiquity and size of this world: the support of slavery and polygamy: the persecutions which men have carried on against each other on the plea of religion; even unbelief itself. (P. 89.)

This is all so preposterous that Colonel Ingersoll might have suspected that some error must pervade his whole theory; and this is, indeed, the case.

We have shown in chapter 1 that God has made man free. In the exercise of his freedom, perverse man disobeys God. His evil acts are attributable, not to God but to himself. In a similar way we are to reason in respect to God's foreknowledge. God's foreknowledge does not force man's actions. The power remains in man to act otherwise, though God foresees his action, or rather sees how he will act. God's prescience does not destroy liberty; it supposes liberty in man. The foreknowledge of God far from destroying liberty, assures it: for God foresees that we, exercising our freedom, will act in such a way. Now God cannot be deceived. Therefore, it is certain that our act will be a free act.

The absurdity of Colonel Ingersoll's reasoning may be illustrated by innumerable examples. Thus the sluggard might reason in a similar way: "God foresees whether or not my crops will be good this year. Whether I labor or not, God's foresight cannot be belied. If, therefore, he foresees that the crops will be good, I need not sow grain. The crop will be good without my doing so. If, however, he foresees that the crops will fail, the sowing of grain will involve useless labor and expense. Therefore, in any case, it is useless for me to labor." The utter absurdity of such reasoning is evident. It is therefore evident that God does not intend that his Revelations shall be turned to ill use, though he foresees that they will be so turned.

Colonel Ingersoll's sophistry is an example of the hallucinations to which a man may become a victim when he is not guided by the light of Divine teaching. The true philosophy of this matter is clearly laid down in Holy Writ.

"Because I knew that thou art stubborn, and thy neck is an iron sinew, and thy forehead of brass. I foretold thee of old: before they came to pass I told thee . . . . for I know that transgressing thou wilt transgress." (Is. xlviii, 4 to 8.)

Colonel Ingersoll's vagaries are another proof of the necessity of the divine light of Revelation to preserve us from becoming the victims of such foolish fancies as he propounds.

But, it will be said, many who err, do so not maliciously but through weakness of understanding. God is at least accountable for their errors.

I answer that God in His wisdom has formed and carried out a great plan. In the carrying out of this plan, some individuals may endure certain hardships; nevertheless the plan itself is beneficial. The hardships, real or apparent, are not to be attributed to the designer; and in the works of God He has even taken care that these hardships shall be turned to the advantage of him who endures them with proper submission to His will. Thus, in the case in point, the errors which are made in the interpretation of God's Revelation are not attributed as sins to those who fall into them through ignorance, unless their ignorance be culpable. Errors concerning the antiquity, shape, and size of the world do not affect morality. Errors concerning our duties to God, our neighbors, and ourselves do affect our moral conduct: but God has even left on earth a guide by whose direction we shall be certainly led to know what is right and what is wrong. If we follow the directions of this guide, evil effects will not follow: that is, moral evil: for merely physical evils and misfortunes are not evils properly so called.

Very frequently also what we consider evils, in a physical sense, turn to the general good. Col. Ingersoll himself acknowledges this when he says in his "Lecture on Skulls":

"If man's eyes had not failed, he would never have made any spectacles, he would never have had the telescope, and he would never have been able to read the leaves of heaven."

Thus the wisdom of God in his disposition of all things, and especially in the giving of Revelation, is completely vindicated. Errors of malice are to be attributed only to those who have by their own fault fallen into them, while errors of inculpable weakness, are not really sins which cast any blot upon the perfection of God's work.

CHAPTER XXXIX.

COLONEL INGERSOLL'S ANTHROPOMORPHISM. — ANTIQUITY OF MAN.—KING CEPHREN'S DATE.—THE CAVE-MEN.

COLONEL Ingersoll, like the Mormons, is an Anthropomorphist. That is, he declares that God must have a human form: of course, he leaves it to be understood that this is subject to the condition, "if there be a God at all." The reasoning by which he arrives at this conclusion is a curiosity.

First, he maintains that Moses represents God as having human form. He says:

"Moses, while he speaks of man as having been made in the image of God, never speaks of God except as having the form of a man."

"The God of Moses was a God with hands, with feet, with the organs of speech. A God of passion, of hatred, of revenge, of affection, of repentance, a God who made mistakes: in other words, an immense and powerful man." (Pp. 92, 93.)

It is humiliating to the intelligence of the 19th century, that a so-called philosopher, reared under Christian tutelage, should give utterance to such an opinion, whereas a Pagan poet, Ovid, understood better in what sense man is said to be created after God's own image:

> "Sanctius his animal, mentisque capacius altæ,
> Deerat adhuc, et quod dominari in cœtera posset:
> Natus homo est." Metam. i, 4.

"A more sacred animal, and more capable of deep thought, was still wanting, which could rule over the rest of creation: then man was made."

It is, therefore, in his power of ruling, in his intellect, in his soul, that man is like to God: not as Col. Ingersoll says: in his "physical image." (P. 92.)

Tacitus, also a Pagan, knows more of the Jewish belief than does Colonel Ingersoll.

"The Jews conceive *in mind only*, of one only God, supreme and eternal, neither changeable nor perishable." Hist. l. i, 5.

If the Colonel had opened the little Catholic Catechism, he would have found that Man is created after God's image " in his soul," and that Man's soul is like to God, in being a "spirit and immortal, and capable of knowing and loving God."

That the Jews believed God to be a Spirit is clear from these and other passages of Holy Writ:

"Keep, therefore, your souls carefully. You saw not any similitude in the day that the Lord God spoke to you in Horeb, from the midst of the fire. Lest, perhaps, being deceived, you might make you a graven similitude or image of male or female: The similitude of any beast, etc., and being deceived by error thou adore and serve them, which the Lord thy God created for the service of all the nations that are under the heaven." Deut. iv, 15, 19.

"Shall a man be hid in secret places, and I not see

him? saith the Lord. Do not I fill heaven and earth? saith the Lord." Jer. xxiii, 24.

"O, Israel, how great is the house of God, and how vast is the place of his possession! It is great and hath no end: it is high and immense." Baruch iii, 24, 25.

"God is not as a man, that he should lie, nor as the son of man, that he should be changed." Num. xxiii, 19.

The Jews, then, did not consider God merely as a powerful man.

This gross idea belongs to Colonel Ingersoll—well, not to Colonel Ingersoll precisely, for he has borrowed it from the half Pagan sources of exploded heresies; but surely it is a poor commentary on Rational Religion that it has substituted for the Eternal, Immutable, Infinite, Self-existing, Omnipotent, Spiritual Being adored by Christians and Jews, a huge and powerful Man. The worst Paganisms of India, Egypt, and Africa have scarcely gone lower. The Colonel says, as his own opinion:

"It is impossible for a man to conceive of a personal God, other than as a being having the human form." (P. 94.)

On the contrary, it is impossible to conceive of God, a being infinitely perfect, eternal, self-existing, and necessary, except as a Spirit, a being above the whole material Creation, and differing essentially from matter in every form.

The Colonel asks, "How did God make man?" (P. 95.) "How were Adam and Eve created?" (P. 97.)

Does he not say, "I do not pretend to tell HOW all these things (Creation) really are? (P. 57.)

How, then, can he have the effrontery to ask, "How did God create man?"

We know that God created man. It is not necessary we should know exactly how he did it.

The Colonel next makes it a great wonder that since the flood up to 1879, the Mosaic account makes only 4,227 years. "Since that event all the ancient kingdoms of the earth were founded, and their inhabitants passed through all the stages of savage, nomadic, barbaric, and semi-civilized life: through the epochs of stone, bronze, and iron; established commerce, cultivated the arts, built cities, filled them with palaces and temples, invented writing, produced a literature, and slowly fell to shapeless ruin. We must believe that all this happened within a period of 4,000 years." (Pp. 97, 98)

Here is certainly a formidable array of events happening within "4,000 years:" but the time is acknowledged a little before to be 4,227 years, 227 years make a considerable time in human progress. And they had to begin by being savages! What? Were the eight parents of the human race, Noah and his sons and their wives, all savages? They were the surviving remnants of the antediluvian age: and surely the antediluvians had time to get out of savagery in 1,656 years, even if Adam and Eve had been savages, which does not seem to have been the case. Well, then, does it not look as if the savage state were a stage of deterioration purely local instead of the starting point of the post-diluvian men?

And "they cultivated the arts, built cities," etc., since.

Well, did not Noah know something about the arts, when he built his ship 547 feet long by 91 in breadth? Remember, you have put forward pompously your intention of finding inconsistencies in the Mosaic record. If the inconsistency is only in your own brain, you will fail egregiously in your undertaking. It does not appear, then, that Noah's descendants were quite so backward incivilization as you would have us believe. And had they not some skill in architecture when they built Babel, Nineveh, and other cities mentioned in Genesis x, 10, etc.?

"They had to pass through the epochs of Stone, Bronze, and Iron."

Are these epochs then so very distinct? Geikie's Geological Text Book tells us:

"In many European countries where metal has been known for many centuries, there are districts where stone implements are still employed, or where they were in use till quite recently. It is obvious also that, as there are still barbarous tribes unacquainted with the fabrication of metal, the Stone Age is not yet extinct in some parts of the world. In this instance we again see how geological periods *run into each other*. The nature or shape of the implement cannot, therefore, be always a very satisfactory proof of antiquity." (P. 902.)

Indeed, from Genesis iv, 21, 22, it appears not only that the "Iron Epoch" was before the deluge, but that even music was already cultivated. Real geologists do not seem to agree very well with the amateur Colonel. It has been well said:

"The writers against Religion have been, for the most part, men of great pride and audacity, but in learning little better than sciolists."

The Colonel's remarks on the antiquity of the Negro race will be treated of in their proper place, chapter

40. Let us now see what he has to say of king Cephren.

"If we know anything, we know that magnificent statues were made in Egypt four thousand years before our era—that is to say, six thousand years ago. There was at the World's Exposition, in the Egyptian department, a statue of king Cephren, *known* to have been chiselled *more* than six thousand years ago. In other words, if the Mosaic account must be believed, this statue was made before the world."

"We also know, if we know anything, that men lived in Europe with the hairy mammoth, the cave bear, the rhinoceros and the hyena. Among the bones of these animals have been found the stone hatchets and flint arrows of our ancestors. In the caves where they lived have been discovered the remains of these animals that had been conquered, killed and devoured as food hundreds of thousands of years ago. If these facts are true, Moses was mistaken." (Pp. 99, 100.)

In the first place, it must be borne in mind that the usually accepted Chronology which fixes the Exodus to the year 1491 B. C., and the entry of the Israelites into Egypt to the year 1706 B. C., is not pretended to be absolutely certain. There are periods both in sacred and profane history, the length of which is not known with certainty. Hence the overthrow of the generally received chronology would not affect the veracity of the Pentateuch, unless the discrepancy were very great indeed. It would only overthrow the received chronology. However, let us examine the matter of King Cephren.

When did king Cephren reign? It is conceded that when Abraham came into Egypt it was during the twelfth dynasty of Egypt. Cephren or Khafren was the builder of the second Pyramid, and he belonged to the fourth dynasty of Manetho. Now, of all the periods of Egyptian history, there is none more fanciful and uncertain than this intervening period between the fourth and twelfth dynasties. Colonel Ingersoll makes Cephren's statue to have been carved *more than* 4121 years B. C.

Manetho is the only ancient authority who gives anything approaching the Colonel's figures. Now, according to Manetho we find the following:

From first year of Menes to Manetho,	3,555 years.
Year of Manetho, B. C.,	350
First year of Menes, B. C.,	3,905
First year of Menes to fifth dynasty,	1,034 years.
First year of fifth dynasty B. C.,	2,871
Allow for reigns of last two kings of fourth dynasty, say,	40 years.
Estimated date B. C. of Cephren's death,	2,911 B. C.

This makes a difference of 1,210 years between Manetho's date and that given by Colonel Ingersoll: no small amount. The Colonel's talk about King Cephren's statue being older than the world, is, therefore, nonsense.

The above figures may be found in the American Cyclopædia, art. Egypt, with the exception of 1,034, which number will be found from Chambers' Cyclopædia, and 40 years' allowance for two kings. The sum 1,034 is thus made up:

Duration of	1st dynasty	250	years.
"	2d "	300	"
"	3d "	200	"
"	4th "	284	"
Total,		1034	"

But are Manetho's dates reliable in this instance? A papyrus in the Turin museum belonging to the period of the 19th dynasty records that between the 6th and 12th dynasties twenty-three kings reigned instead of eighty-six as stated by Manetho: while the monuments only record six kings instead of six dynasties, covering a period of nearly one thousand years. This last fact would certainly bring the period eight hundred years at least, nearer to the birth of Christ, which would give about 2111 B. C. as the date of Cephren's death.

Sir John Herschell and Professor Piazzi Smith endeavored to ascertain, astronomically, the age of the Pyramid of Cheops, which is before the age of Cephren, and thus they fixed the date between 2171 and 2123 B. C., and Sir Charles Lyell says "the exact date of these (Egyptian temples, obelisks, pyramids, etc.,) after they have been studied with so much patience and sagacity for centuries, remains uncertain and obscure." Let us further bear in mind Mr. Champollion's deliberate judgment that not one of all these monuments dates further back than 2200 B. C., and we may judge of the value of Col. Ingersoll's pretended knowledge on this subject. It is a sham.

Are such uncertainties to be taken as a refutation of the proved records of Holy Writ?

Next, as regards the finding of human implements such as the stone hatchets and flint arrows of pre-historic man, mixed with the bones of animals in caves, we must again remember that the term pre-historic does not necessarily mean that the men thus described existed before any history was written. The historic and the pre-historic ages necessarily run into one another, as do the Stone, Bronze and Iron Ages. The same period may have been historic in Egypt and prehistoric in England, Germany and Switzerland: and as far as we are aware, this is actually the case. Geologists acknowledge that the traces of man hitherto found in caves with bones of the mammoth, hyena, bear, rhinoceros, etc., afford very uncertain data for deciding the age when the deposits were made. One of the most recent geological works published in 1882 by the Director-General of the Geological Survey of Great Britain and Ireland, Archibald Geikie of Edinburgh University, says:

"A satisfactory chronological classification of the deposits containing the first relics of man is perhaps unattainable, for these deposits occur in detached areas with no means of determining their physical sequences." (P. 904.)

These deposits may sometimes have been formed of the bones of animals, as hyenas, that made their homes in the caves: in which case it is not likely that men were dwelling there at the same time. The bones of the carnivora must frequently belong to a very different period from that when the caves were tenanted by men. Sometimes these deposits were made by land animals falling into the pits accidentally. At other times, no doubt, men brought the animals there for food, but there is no proof in all this that man is of higher antiquity than is stated in the book of Genesis.

CHAPTER XL.

EVOLUTION.—FABULOUS CHRONOLOGY.—ANTIQUITY OF MAN.—SAVAGERY AND CIVILIZATION.

Col. Ingersoll maintains that the antiquity of man on earth is to be measured by "millions of years." Here is his theory:

"One can hardly compute in his imagination the time necessary for man to emerge from the barbarous state, naked and helpless, surrounded by animals far more powerful than he, to progress and finally create the civilizations of India, Egypt and Athens. The distance from savagery to Shakespeare must be measured not by hundreds, but by millions of years." (P. 100.)

In fact we have seen already that he makes man to have progressed gradually from monad to moner, from moner to higher stages of life, a tadpole, for example, then a monkey, till at last he emerged a man: and now we find that he comes out first a savage, till at last he is evolved into a Philosopher—a Col. Ingersoll in fact.

Now is this theory proved? The Colonel gives no proof of it any better than his absurd statement about king Cephren. The Holy Scripture, on the contrary, plainly declares that the first parents of mankind were created, not slowly developed from lower forms. Here is a statement proved to be part of a divine Religion: a direct Revelation from God. Are we to accept in the face of this a purely imaginative theory, advanced on speculation, without proof of any kind?

for even the most ardent and learned of the evolutionists concede that Evolution is no more than a theory; and it is a theory invented apparently for the purpose of getting rid of the necessity of acknowledging God's existence. It is based, not on fact but conjecture and assumption.

1. It has never been known that one animal species has been developed from another. This Professor Huxley admits:

"There is no instance in which a group of animals having all the characters exhibited by species in nature, has ever been originated by selection, whether natural or artificial." (Lay Sermons, 12.)

2. Nature herself or rather the God of nature has placed an obstacle to the production of new species. Animals of the same species, male and female produce offspring like themselves: animals of different species are sterile. There are a few cases where a hybrid is produced, but the hybrid is always sterile. This is exemplified in the mule.

Col. Ingersoll boasts of the discoveries of man. "The brave prow of discovery has visited every sea; the traveller has pressed with weary feet the soil of every clime." (P. 122.)

He might have added that man has penetrated the recesses of the earth, he has examined critically the traces of life which existed on earth for millions of years: He has found animal and vegetable organizations of high development, without any trace of natural ancestors from which they were developed. Man himself has no discoverable ancestors: for surely it will not be seriously maintained that man has for ancestors any series of animals at present existing, or that ever existed. The Gorilla, the Chimpanzee, the

Orang-Outang all differ essentially from man in all physical features, to say nothing of his soul, which is created after God's image and likeness. Professor Huxley himself admits that:

"Every bone of the Gorilla bears marks by which it might be distinguished from the corresponding bone of a man, and in the present creation, at any rate, there are no intermediate links, between *Homo* (*Man*) and *Troglodytes*." (Man's Place in Nature.)

4. Lastly: If the theory of Evolution were true, the varieties of living creatures would be fortuitous, and there would be no plan, no order in nature, for plan and order cannot spring from mere accident or chance.

But there is order; and Col. Ingersoll himself admits this, for we have seen that he insists on the necessity of order and plan in his argument against the Mosaic account of Creation. It is true that when he argues for the existence of animals simultaneously with that of plants (pp. 69, 85, 87,) he reasons on a false assumption, as far as Creation is concerned, nevertheless, he admits that there is a plan through Nature, and he assumes that this plan is a necessity. Yet he adopts the theory of Evolution, which is inconsistent with plan in the general design of Nature.

5. The history of the human race on earth confirms the account given in Genesis of Man's Creation. There are no evidences of Man's existence on earth till long after the time named by Moses for his Creation. No evidences of antediluvian Man have yet been discovered: though possibly they may be in the future. All history begins at a period after the time indicated by Moses for the beginning of our race, anything earlier being mere fables, as we have shown

in the cases of Egypt and China. (Chapters 37 and 39.)

The same is to be said of the Chaldeans, Hindoos and other nations that had an early civilization. Some have pretended that the Chaldeans have a history of four hundred thousand years; but Berosus the first historian of Chaldea lived only in the time of Alexander the Great, about 334 B. C., and according to Pliny he only gave a regular history of four hundred and eighty years. Only fragments of it are now extant, and where evident fables are eliminated it agrees very well with the facts contained in the Biblical narrative. The history of the deluge, and of the ark by which Noah was saved, and his account of the fall of man and of the long lives of the patriarchs, all agree with Genesis to a remarkable extent. (Duclot, Bible Vindicated, vol. 1.)

Besides the statue of King Cephren, whose claims to immense antiquity, we examined in chapter 39, the only monument which Col. Ingersoll can adduce to prove the fabulous antiquity of man is "a representation upon Egyptian granite made more than three thousand years ago," wherein "the negro is as black, his lips as full, his hair as closely curled as now."

These figures must be very perfect likenesses, if we can attach to them so much faith. Now, it is well known that the Egyptian figures are always grotesque, and that as representations of the human form, they are mere caricatures. A peep into any museum, or into any book on Egyptian antiquities will convince the reader of this. Yet such are the pictures which Col. Ingersoll would try to pass upon us as perfect representations of men three thousand years ago.

Charles Darwin will not be suspected of partiality to the Christian cause, yet in his "Descent of Man," he says, "Mr. Pouchet was far from finding recognizable representations of the dozen or more nations which some authors believe they can recognize. Even some of the *most strongly marked races* cannot be identified with that degree of unanimity which might have been expected." (Vol. i, p. 209.)

It is very possible that the negroes have retained the same physical type for so long a period, for they are in the same social condition that they occupied three thousand years ago: but it is fully established that under the influence of changes of climate, soil, education and mode of life, the physical forms of races change, and sometimes very rapidly.

The Turks of Europe are known to be of Mongolian origin, yet even in the form of their crania they have approximated to the Caucasian type, and they now differ widely from their Eastern Mongol brethren.

Many other examples of like import might be given, but I have said enough to show that the imperfect pictures of Egypt do not avail, against the positive testimony of Moses, to establish an existence of millions of years for that monarchy.

To the Hindoos, modern infidels have also assigned a stupendous antiquity, an existence of four million three hundred and twenty thousand years being claimed in some of their books. Bailly, in his *History of Ancient Astronomy*, states that they were, in his opinion, a fully established nation three thousand five hundred and fifty-three years before Christ, and that the Brahmins had astronomical tables five or six thousand years old.

Mr. Bentley travelled in India purposely in order to ascertain the truth of the Hindoo claims to great antiquity, and found that the earliest astronomical data so much relied on by Bailly could not mark an earlier period than 1528 B. C. (Historical View of Hindoo Astronomy.)

Infidels have also pretended that the history of Christ was borrowed from that of Krishna, who in Hindoo legends is represented as an Incarnation of the Divinity, at whose birth spirits sung hymns of praise, while shepherds surrounded his cradle. The tyrant Cansa endeavored to destroy him, so that it was necessary to conceal his birth, and the child was taken by his parents beyond the coast of Yamouna. He afterwards lived in obscurity, then commenced a public life, preached a perfect doctrine and protected the poor, but was finally nailed to a tree, and before dying foretold the evils which would take place in the wicked age of the world thirty-six years after his death. (Paulinus, "The Brahman System; Rome, 1802.",

The very great similarity of many events in the legend of Krishna with those of Christ's life, and even the likeness of the name were truly perplexing, and gave plausibility to the Infidel pretence that the life of Christ was borrowed from the Hindoo story.

The established authenticity of the life of Christ was not allowed to weigh anything in the scale when confronted by this legend of Krishna, which was pronounced by Sir Wm. Jones as anterior to the Christian era, and at least as old as Homer. The learning of Sir Wm. Jones was indisputable, especially in Hindoo literature, and on his expression of this opinion modern infidels laid great stress, as if it proved that

Christianity is itself a mere legend; though Mr. Jones drew no such inference. It was his opinion that some of the facts of Christianity had been engrafted on the original story of Krishna.

Mr. Bentley, however, applied his mathematical skill to the case, and was fortunate enough to find the Horoscope of Krishna which gives the position of the planets at his birth. By astronomical calculation, he found that the planets could occupy the positions thereon depicted, only on the seventh of August, A. D., 600.

The coincidence of the life of Krishna with events recorded in the Gospels could not be merely accidental, so Mr. Bentley's discovery settled the matter that the Hindoo story is merely a distorted version of Christ's life as recorded in the Gospels.

Mr. Bentley is of opinion that it was concocted by the Brahmans for the express purpose of preventing the people from embracing Christianity.

In other countries there is still less difficulty than with those we have enumerated. All history is of comparatively modern date, though, from its very beginning it is evident that some species of civilization existed. Thus human history is a strong confirmation of the facts stated and implied in Genesis, that at the time of the dispersion of mankind, our race was not in the state of savagery as infidels pretend: and that man's beginning on earth is to be placed at about the date recorded by Moses. History, when properly understood is irreconcilable with the fabulous antiquity which Infidels attribute to man on earth.

Other evidences of these truths might be added There are proofs that a civilization existed in former times over the whole continent of North America

There have been found works of art which betoken a high state of civilization, but we all know that this high state of civilization had disappeared, so that on the discovery of America the continent was almost entirely peopled by savages. On this fact Mr. Mott points out that the present state of savagery has arisen "by degradation, not by progress . . . . but if this be the case over an entire continent, what becomes of the idea that savage life in general is an example of arrested progress and not an example of retrogression?" (Mivart's Lessons.)

Of course I do not mean to deny that man in many cases has progressed. I do not mean to deny that in the nineteenth century the arts have in every department progressed wonderfully, but when we read of the high civilizations of former days, and behold how they have degenerated into savagery, it is unreasonable to assume, as if it were a demonstrated fact, that man's life on earth began with savagery. Due respect should be paid to the testimony of history on this subject, and surely the Sacred History whose authenticity and truth are so well attested is not to be thrown aside as if its testimony were of no weight. This testimony is to the effect that man did not make his appearance on earth as a savage, but at least as a moderately civilized being. This is certainly far more consistent with the records of humanity, than that he has existed for millions of years, and that he has developed himself into the highly civilized being of the present century.

Another consideration must not be omitted, as it throws great light on the Scriptural account of the peopling of the earth. It is founded on the mathematical calculation of the ordinary increase of population. In different countries the ordinary increase of population varies very much. In England it has been much more rapid than in France during the present century. Thus the population of France was in 1801, 27,349,003, according to official statistics. In 1861 it had increased to 37,382,225. (Chambers' Cyclopædia.) The exponential equation, whereby the number of years required to double the population will be found, is, therefore:

$$\left(\frac{37382225}{27349003}\right)^{\frac{m}{60}} = 2.$$

The value of $m = 133.08$, = the number of years required to double the population in France, or nearly 133 years 1 month.

If, now, we assume as correct the generally accepted chronology which places the deluge as having taken place 2348 B. C., we shall have 4,232 years down to the present year (1884). The present population of the globe is estimated to be 1,400,000,000. If, then, on account of their *extreme* old age, we leave out Noah and his wife from the estimate, we shall have 1,400,000,000 descended from 6 persons in 4,232 years. To find the number of years during which the population of the earth must have doubled during this period, we must solve this equation:

$$\left(\frac{1,400,000,000}{6}\right)^{\frac{n}{4232}} = 2.$$

n is found to be = 152.24. That is, since the deluge the population of the earth doubled every $152\frac{6}{25}$ years, very nearly: a very reasonable result. If the Infidel theory were correct, a much longer time must have been required to double the population. Mathematical calculation, therefore, renders the Infidel theory of man's indefinite occupation of the earth very unlikely, while it renders highly probable the Scriptural account that the beginning is to be dated from very nearly the time indicated by Moses.

CHAPTER XLI.

THE SABBATH.—ACCOUNT OF CREATION CONSISTENT.—ORIGIN OF MAN.—CHRISTIAN MORALITY.

God "blessed the Seventh day, and sanctified it: because in it he had rested from all His work which God created and made." (Gen. ii, 3.)

St. Augustine explains these words: "The Omnipotence of the Creator is the cause of subsistence to every creature, and if this virtue were withdrawn from things created, nature and beings of all kinds would cease to exist. Therefore, when the Lord says 'My Father worketh even till now' (St. John v, 17), he shows a perseverance of his work by which he governs and regulates all things. . . . . Wherefore God is to be understood as resting from all his works in this sense that he is not creating as at first, not that he ceases to govern and regulate his Creation." (Sententiæ, num. 277.)

It is thus seen how futile are Colonel Ingersoll's queries and commentaries:

"There ought to be some account of what he did the following Monday. Did he rest on that day? What did he do after he got rested? Has he done anything in the way of Creation since Saturday evening of the first week?" (Pp. 101, 102.)

There is an account of God's work "even till now." He rests in the sense that He has ceased from the great work recorded in the first chapter of Genesis. Moses speaks according to human intelligence.

The Colonel says next:

"If they (theologians) take the ground that the days were periods of twenty-four hours, then Geology will force them to throw away the whole account. If, on the other hand, they admit that the days were vast 'periods,' then the sacredness of the Sabbath must be given up." (P. 103.)

We have seen in chapter 36 that geology does not force us to give up the Mosaic Cosmogony. How the Colonel can infer that the sacredness of the Sabbath must be given up under either interpretation it is hard to see. The Sabbath was instituted to recall to man the memory of God's work, and how He ceased from His work or rested on the seventh day. It makes little difference whether the days were long or short periods; it was in God's power to institute a day on which thanksgiving should be specially offered to Him for our indebtedness to Him in Creation. It is proper that part of our time should be set apart for this purpose, lest in the midst of our secular concerns we should forget God. It is therefore "possible to sanctify a space of time," though the Colonel thinks it is not. (P. 103.)

He wishes to know how we can please God "by staying in some dark and sombre room, instead of walking in the perfumed fields." I am not aware that God has commanded at all any such mode of celebrating the Sabbath as that imagined by the Colonel. The Sunday is to be kept "holy" by serving God more particularly on it, and by abstaining from servile work, the ordinary secular occupation of men.

"Why should that day be filled with gloom instead of joy?" (P. 104.)

There is no reason for being gloomy, and there is no precept of the kind. It should be a pleasure to serve God. "Christ's yoke is sweet and his burden light." (St. Matt. xi, 30.)

"Every Freethinker, as a matter of duty, should violate this day." (P. 104.)

Freethinkers do, as a rule, violate this and other days; for without responsibility to God, man will naturally be governed by his passions, and restrained only by the fear of force which others can bring to bear upon him.

"They should do so as a duty."

How can there be a duty when there is no Being to whom we are responsible?

The Colonel then asks:

"Why should we care for the superstition of men who began the Sabbath by paring their nails, beginning at the fourth finger, then going to the second, then to the fifth, then to the third, and ending with the thumb?"

"The Jews were very careful of these nail parings. They who threw them upon the ground were wicked, because Satan used them to work evil upon the earth. They believed that upon the Sabbath souls were allowed to leave purgatory, and cool their burning souls in water, ... and "if a Jew on a journey was overtaken by the sacred day . . . . he must sit down and there remain until the day was gone. If he fell in the dirt he was compelled to stay until the day was done." (Pp. 105, 106.)

All this is not in the Bible. Col. Ingersoll will gain no credit for honesty by his attempt to make the public believe that these things are to be found in the Pentateuch. If any Jews observe such rules, Moses is not responsible for them. They are not "mistakes of Moses." In the time of Christ, even, Our Lord condemned the numerous superstitions which the Pharisees had engrafted on the law.

"You have made void the commandment of God for your tradition .... and in vain do they worship me, teaching doctrines and commandments of men." St. Matthew xv, 6, 9.

The Apostles "understood that .... they should beware .... of the doctrine of the Pharisees and Sadducees." xvi, 12.

Unnecessary labor was forbidden; and of course the performance of unnecessary labor was punished by the law. The law, of course, endured as long as it was the will of God that such should be the case. But God appeared on earth and left the law of the New Testament. The same authority that appointed freely the Saturday to be kept holy could reverse the law: and this Christ did. (Col. ii, 16.) The Christian church therefore appointed the Sunday to take the position of the Sabbath under the New Law. Thus we see where Christians got the right "to labor on the day" which God "sanctified, and to keep as sacred" a day which previously to the establishment of the Christian law, was devoted to labor.

Col. Ingersoll makes of this a mountain of a difficulty. He says "if any day is to be kept holy" Saturday is the day, "and not the Sunday of the Christian." The mountain becomes but a mole-hill when it is examined. (Mistakes of Moses, pp. 106, 107.)

The Colonel adds: "the Christian Sabbath or the 'Lord's day' was legally established by the murderer Constantine, because on that day Christ was supposed to have risen from the dead." (P. 106.)

The Colonel is astray in his history. The day was established long before Constantine's time. Eusebius, the cotemporary of Constantine says.

"The Logos (Christ) by the new convenant translated and transferred the feast of the Sabbath to the morning light, and gave us the symbol of true rest, the saving *Lord's day*, the first day of the week, etc."

St. Athanasius gives similar testimony, so also do Sts. Barnabas, Ignatius and Justin Martyr, who flourished two centuries before Constantine.

Constantine is called by Col. Ingersoll "the murderer." It is true that the death which he inflicted on his son Crispus is regarded as a great stain upon his otherwise illustrious reign, but a Sovereign is sometimes placed in difficult positions. Crispus was charged with treason, and it seems to have been proved against him. Be the crime of Constantine as great as Colonel Ingersoll represents it to be, surely the crime of a Pagan, as Constantine was at the time, is not a reproach against Christianity.

We are next told that:

"There are two accounts of the Creation in Genesis . . . . These accounts are materially different, and both cannot be true." (P. 108.)

The first account begins with Genesis i, 1, and ends with Genesis ii, 3. "The second account begins with the fourth verse of the second chapter." (P. 108.)

There is no contradiction between these so called different accounts. Two men may describe the same event without mentioning precisely the same circumstances, yet both accounts may be perfectly true.

The two accounts in Genesis are both true. They do not contradict each other in the least.

The Colonel says:

"In the second account man was made before the beasts and fowls. If this is true, the first account is false." (P. 112.)

Answer: but this is *not true*. The so-called second account does not give, nor profess to give the *order* of Creation. It relates merely certain facts in such order as the exigencies of the second narrative demand. The like is done every day by historians. The object of Moses in the second chapter was to show the dominion of man over beasts. The natural order then was to state first the privileges of man. This he does by repeating the manner of man's creation with a living soul, and adding that the garden in Eden was placed under his care. Then the beasts were brought to him to be named. Previously to this episode we are told that God formed beasts and fowl; but there was no necessity here for preserving the order of Creation between man and beasts, for this order had been already narrated a few lines previously. We were already informed in detail that the fowl were formed on the fifth day, the beasts, and finally man on the sixth day. Hence also the following assertions are unfounded and false.

"According to the second account, Adam existed millions of years before Eve was formed. He must have lived one Mosaic day before there were any trees, and another Mosaic day before the beasts and fowls were created. Will some kind clergyman tell us upon what kind of food Adam subsisted during these immense periods?" (P. 112.)

As Adam was created on the sixth day, after both fowls and beasts and plants, there was no difficulty about his getting food. "The millions of years" difficulty we disposed of in chapter 36. Eve was created on the sixth day after Adam.

The Colonel next says that to furnish "a helpmeet for Adam," God, instead of proceeding at once to make a woman, "tried to induce Adam to take one of them (the beasts) for 'an helpmeet.'" (P. 113.)

To prove this he quotes:

"And Adam gave names to all cattle, and to the fowl of the air, and to every beast of the field; but for Adam there was not found an helpmeet for him." (P. 113.)

There is no statement here that can be even plausibly distorted into meaning that God "tried to induce Adam to take a beast for a helpmeet." We are told that God brought the beasts "to Adam to see what he would call them," and not for him to choose a helpmeet from among them. The Colonel asks:

"Unless the Lord God was looking for an helpmeet for Adam, why did he cause the animals to pass before him?"

There was no need to ask so nonsensical a question. The text itself gives the reason: They were brought to be named by Adam. Another reason may, probably, have been to show that there was no beast suitable to be man's companion. This is implied by the context. Colonel Ingersoll's pathetic thanksgiving is out of place:

"Let us rejoice that this was so. Had he (Adam) fallen in love then, there would never have been a Freethinker in the world?"

Why? Are we not told by the Colonel that it is

exactly from the lowest form of beasts, moners yclept, that Freethinkers are descended? (P. 96.) From the "Moners" must you not trace your ancestry through the Gorilla or some such beast? Ah! Colonel, it is not creditable to you to be ashamed of your ancestry. And do you not, in your lecture on skulls, even state positively that you can trace your ancestry "to the Duke Orang-Outang or to the Princess Chimpanzee"? Christians have quite a different genealogy, and can prove it by their records.

To confirm his gross ribaldry, the Colonel quotes Dr. Adam Clark and Dr. Scott. As both of these merely repeat that "among all the animals . . . . there was not a helpmeet for Adam," it is difficult to see how they confirm the Colonel's view.

Dr. Matthew Henry is also quoted with the same purpose. Even if Dr. Henry were of this opinion, the absurdity is not to be attributed to Moses. But Dr. Henry seems only to imply that the animals were brought to convince Adam that he could not be matched among them. He has perhaps awkwardly expressed his meaning, but I am convinced that this was what he intended to express. If, however, he wished to convey what the Colonel pretends, they are mistaken together.

The Colonel next ridicules the creation of Eve out of "one of Adam's ribs." (P. 116.)

As God's power is necessarily infinite, there can be no more difficulty about His creating Eve out of matter already existing than about His creation of the world from nothing. The fact that this was done we already proved in chapters 6 and 7.

We have next the supposed cross-examination of two applicants for admission into heaven. The first was an infidel. He loved his family, paid his debts, but did not belong to any church, for churches were "too narrow" for him. He did not believe that the wicked are punished for ever, nor did he believe that God created Eve as described in the Bible.

"Away with him to hell." (P. 118.) Well: this infidel refuses to believe what God has taught. There is a positive act of rebellion against God. Can a natural love for wife and children be an offset for high treason against God's Supreme Authority? Would it be a sufficient excuse for high treason against the State? Surely not. Now it must be remembered that there is no sin where there is not wilfulness. We have therefore one who wilfully refuses to honor God by acknowledging His veracity, and to pay to Him the homage of his understanding. Can such a one be guiltless?

The Colonel says, however, that belief is not voluntary:

"For my part, I cannot admit that belief is a voluntary thing. It seems to me that evidence, even in spite of ourselves, will have its weight, and that, whatever our wish may be, we are compelled to stand with fairness by the scales, and give the exact result." (P. 42.)

Does it not sometimes happen that fraudulent weights and balances are used? We read that the invader *Brennus*, by means of such weights, endeavored once to impose upon the Romans, and that when the latter remonstrated he threw his sword and belt into the scale, saying that "it is the lot of the vanquished to suffer."

Man has liberty to use his intellect or not. The will moves the intellect as far as the exercise of the intellect is concerned, and therefore that exercise of the intellect is voluntary. Thus we may refuse to examine the motives of credibility of Religion. Our refusal is voluntary. Unbelief is the consequence of this refusal, therefore such unbelief is voluntary. Regularly, therefore, Unbelief in God's Revelation is criminal, and sinful. If, however, the case should occur that the means of knowing God's Revelation are not within reach, there will be no sin, because God obliges no one to an impossibility.

The Colonel's second example is the cross-examination of a Bank Cashier, a member of a "Young Men's Christian Association" who stole from his bank a hundred thousand dollars and deserted his wife and family, committing other crimes also; but because he believed with "all his heart" the Scriptural history of Eve's Creation, profanely called by the Colonel "the rib story," he was admitted to heaven. (Pp. 119, 120.)

This is a slander on Christianity. Christianity does not teach that they who are guilty of such crimes as the Colonel has enumerated, are saved merely by *believing* what God has taught. There are, I believe, some sectaries that teach that God does not impute to the Christian the sins which he may commit after his conversion, but I repudiate this doctrine on behalf of the vast bulk of Christendom: it is not the doctrine of either the Old or the New Testament. The Catholic church known to number nearly two hundred and fifty millions of Christians repudiates it. So do the Greek churches numbering probably ninety-five millions, and I believe the great bulk of Protestants of to-day also repudiate it strongly. I will merely quote a passage from the Old Testament and another from the New, which will prove what I have stated.

"But if the just man turn himself away from his justice, and do iniquity etc., shall he live? All his justice which he had done shall not be remembered . . . . and in his sin . . . . he shall die." (Ez. xviii, 24.)

"Not every one that saith to me Lord, Lord, shall enter into the kingdom of heaven, but he that *doth* the will of my Father who is in heaven, he shall enter into the kingdom of heaven." (St. Matthew vii, 21.)

The Colonel accuses the clergy of slandering him. He deals in generalities. He does not state what the slanders are. I have taken care in this book not to deal in any personalities, even: but I cannot but call attention to the fact that I have proved the Colonel guilty of falsehood in many parts of his book besides this. I may therefore fairly quote his own words against himself, with some necessary verbal changes:

"There is no logic in slander; and falsehood, in the long run defeats itself. People who profess loudly the Religion of Humanity should at least tell the truth about their friends." (See page vi, Preface to Mistakes of Moses.)

The next objection which we find is:

"It is said that from Mount Sinai God gave, amid thunderings and lightnings, ten commandments for the guidance of mankind: and yet among them is not found—'Thou shalt believe the Bible.'" (P. 120.)

And what of that? Is it anywhere claimed that the ten commandments contain *explicitly* all our obligations? The ten commandments are an admirable summary of the law, and contain *implicitly* all our duties, yet there are other commandments which are not found explicitly among the ten. (See Deut. xxvii, etc.) The duty of believing his word is implicitly contained in the first of the ten.

As well might the Colonel assert that murder is lawful, because it is not *explicitly* forbidden in the still shorter summary found in St. Matthew's Gospel, xxii, 37, 39. It is *implicitly* forbidden in the command:

"Thou shalt love thy neighbor as thyself." (St. Matthew xxii, 39.)

Surely the cause which must resort to subterfuges so weak, must itself be very feeble.

The Christian who commits grievous sin at once separates himself from Almighty God, and cannot become God's friend until with his whole heart he returns to God. He must be heartily sorry for his sin: he must be firmly resolved not to sin again, and if he has injured his neighbor in person, property or character, he must repair the injury done. Hence the bank Cashier imagined by Col. Ingersoll would be obliged not only to be sorry for the offenses committed by him, but also to make restitution for his theft, to repair the injury done to his family and neighbor, as far as possible, "otherwise his sin would not be forgiven." (Cath. Catechism.) Is there any resemblance between the true state of the case and Colonel Ingersoll's representation of it?

CHAPTER XLII.

THE GARDEN OF EDEN.—IMMORTALITY OF THE SOUL.

The Colonel is very keen at finding inconsistencies. In Genesis i, 28, we are told that:

"God blessed them, (Adam and Eve,) saying, 'Increase and multiply and replenish the earth and subdue it.'"

In Genesis ii, 15, the Colonel tells us:

Man "is not told to subdue the earth, but to dress and keep a garden." (P. 121.)

It is simply an insult to the intelligence of his readers to assert that keeping of a garden is irreconcilable with dominion over the earth.

We have, however, a more plausible difficulty in the determining of the four rivers of the garden of Eden. The Colonel takes care to make the most of this difficulty. He says:

"There was issuing from this garden a river that was parted into four heads. The first of these, Pison, compassed the whole land of Havilah, the second, Gihon, that compassed the whole land of Ethiopia, the third, Hiddekel, that flowed toward the east of Assyria, and the fourth, the Euphrates. Where are these four rivers now? The brave prow of discovery has visited every sea; the traveller has pressed with weary feet the soil of every clime; and yet there has been found no place from which four rivers sprang. The Euphrates still journeys to the gulf, but where are Pison, Gihon and the mighty Hiddekel? Surely by going to the source of the Euphrates we ought to find either these three rivers or their ancient beds. Will some minister when he answers the 'Mistakes of Moses,' tell us where these rivers are or were? The maps of the world are incomplete without these mighty streams," etc. (Pp. 121, 122.)

Hiddekel does not present the difficulty the Colonel raises. It is known to be the Hebrew name for the Tigris. In fact, philologists tell us that these words are derived by well known philological rules, one from the other. Thus the consonants D, K, L, are respectively allied in the organs of speech with T, G, R, and these letters are frequently interchanged with each other by different nations, as the Chinese call an *American*, a *Melican man*. (See Gesenius' Lexicon, *Hiddekel:* Max Müller's Science of Language, Lecture 5.)

However, without insisting upon this derivation, we have positive testimony that Hiddekel is the Tigris.

Josephus naming these four rivers states that, "Euphrates and Tigris flow into the Red Sea . . . . Tigris or Diglath signifies swift and narrow." (Antiq. Book i, 1.) *Diglath* is the Aramæan name. Daniel speaks of Hiddekel as the "great river" beside which he stood in his captivity, when God gave revelation to him by means of visions. The Septuagint (70) translators say "the great river which is *Tigris Eddekel.*" (Dan. x, 4.) They also translate "*Tigris*" in Genesis.

In Ecclesiasticus xxiv, 35, also, the *Tigris* is the name given to *Hiddekel* in the Greek.

Both in Genesis and in Ecclesiasticus not only is Hiddekel spoken of as a river well known, but Pison and Gihon also. No doubt these terms were, at that time, perfectly well understood by the Hebrews.

The Tigris and Euphrates rise not far from each other, and the ancient writers Quintus Curtius, Procopius, Xenophon and Lucan, state that they rose then from a common source. The Araxes, majestic and slow, is called *Gechon* by the natives, and it waters *Chutha*, Scythia. It is true this country is not *now* called Ethiopia, but being settled by the descendants of Cush, was called Cush, (Ethiopia,) equally with the Cush of Africa. The Araxes has an annual overflow like the Nile, as stated of Gihon in Ecclesiasticus. It empties into the Caspian Sea, and is probably the Gihon of Genesis.

The river called by the Turks *Fasi*, passes through Colchis or Mingrelia, famous for its gold and gums. (Strabo, Book i; Pliny, Book xxxiii, 3.) The country watered by Phison or Pison, is in Genesis called Havilah. This is the name of a son of Cush who settled in that neighborhood. (Gen. x.) The Fasi empties into the Black Sea. It is probably the Pison of Genesis. (Calmet " Terrestial Paradise.")

Cornelius a Lapide, proves that after the Tigris and Euphrates unite at Apamœa, they separate at a city called Asia making a large island, Teredon, and flow into the Persian Gulf. The two lower branches he considers to be the Gihon and Pison of Genesis. This view, also, accords well with what is related in Genesis.

The Euphrates, Tigris, Araxes and Pison rise near each other, and in spite of Turkish misrule, the region at their source is to-day one of the most fertile in the world. This locality, in all probability, is the place of the garden of Eden; though according to Cornelius a Lapide, it would be partly between the junction and subsequent division of the waters of the

Euphrates and Tigris. It appears, then, that these four rivers have not "been obliterated by convulsions of nature within six thousand years;" (Mistakes of Moses, p. 123;) though possibly there has been considerable change in them.

Josephus imagines the Gihon to be the Nile, and Pison the Ganges. He is evidently mistaken in this, as the description given in Genesis is incompatible with his hypothesis. Let us follow the text, and not Josephus.

The Colonel asks: "Can we not account for these contradictions, absurdities and falsehoods by simply saying that although the writer may have done his level best, he failed because he was limited in knowledge, led away by tradition, and depended too implicitly upon the correctness of his imagination?" (P. 123.)

Answer.—No, we cannot. 1st. We have proved that Moses' statements are neither contradictions, absurdities nor falsehoods. 2ndly. "Simply saying" does not "account for" anything: though, indeed, from the frequency with which you "simply say" things, one would imagine that nothing more were required. Proofs are needed, Colonel. Nothing but positive proofs will satisfy us.

The Colonel.—"Is not such a course far more reasonable than to insist that all these things are true, and must stand though every science shall fall to mental dust?" (P. 123.)

Answer.—As the Christian has no desire that science shall become mental dust, your question is verbal balderdash. Again, as your course has been proved to be most unreasonable, it will not become reasonable by comparing it with another unreasonable course.

The Colonel.—" Can any reason be given for not allowing man to eat of the fruit of the tree of knowledge?" (P. 123.)

Answer.—Yes. St. Chrysostom gave a reason fifteen hundred years ago: "God gave the commandment to prove man's obedience. He imposes a law to try man's good will. . . . . God threatens to save, the serpent entices to harass. . . . . With God there is severity which is benignant, with the Devil there is persuasion which is hurtful." (Forbidden Tree, part 1.)

The Colonel.—" Will some minister, some graduate of Andover tell us what this means ?" (P. 124.)

Answer.—Though not a minister of Andover, we have endeavored to answer this. We may add, that if Adam was to merit the heavenly reward for obedience, it was needed that there should be some law which he would have an opportunity to obey.

The Colonel.—" What objection could God have had to the immortality of man ?" (P. 125.)

Answer.—God had no intention of making man infinite. Man's perfections then must be limited, and if limited they must end somewhere. God, being free in His acts may place that limit where He thinks fit: and it is absurd to ask why God has placed the limit in this place rather than in that.

The Colonel.—" You see that after all this sacred record, instead of assuring us of immortality, shows us only how we lost it." (P. 125.)

" Upon the subject of a future state, there is not one word in the Pentateuch." (P. 47.)

Answer.—Even if this were the case, would not

the Revelation of *some* truths be useful to us, even if *all* truths were not revealed? God must be the Judge what truths it is expedient we should know. Besides, it is nowhere asserted that the Pentateuch contains everything that the Jews knew concerning God. In difficult cases, the High Priest and the Sanhedrim were to be consulted. There is no doubt that the Immortality of the soul was known to the Jews. It is taught by their prophets, and the line of prophets, taught directly by God, and to whose directions they were obliged to yield obedience, was constantly kept up. Thus the ancient tradition of the soul's immortality could be constantly kept up among them, even though the doctrine were not explicitly taught in the Pentateuch.

The Pentateuch contains chiefly the history of a nation, the people of God. It deals, for the most part, with the external acts of that nation, as subject to God's Sovereign rule. Thus Josephus explains in his preface to the Antiquities of the Jews:

"Moses deemed it exceeding necessary that he who would conduct his own life well, and give laws to others, in the first place should consider the divine nature; and upon the contemplation of God's operations, should thereby imitate the best of all patterns, so far as it is possible for human nature to do, ... nor would anything he should write tend to the promotion of virtue in his readers; I mean unless they be taught first of all that God is the Father and Lord of all things, and sees all things; and that thence he bestows a happy life upon those that follow him, but plunges such as do not walk in the paths of virtue into inevitable miseries. . . . . But as for our legislator, when he had once demonstrated that God was possessed of perfect virtue, he supposed that men also ought to strive after the participation of it."

Many passages of the Pentateuch manifest the Jewish belief in the Immortality of the soul.

"If thou dost well shalt thou not receive? but if ill, shall not sin forthwith be present at the door?" (Gen. iv, 7.)

Abel received no reward of virtue on earth, since he was cut off by a violent and premature death. These words, therefore, refer to future rewards and punishments, and they were so believed.

"Fear not, Abram, I am thy protector, and thy reward exceeding great." (xv, 1.)

Certainly Abraham did not expect this promise, to be kept, merely by the blessings which would be conferred on his posterity. He had certainly the expectation of a future reward to be enjoyed in the company of his fathers. This consciousness alone could be the cause why Abraham, Jacob and Joseph should be anxious to be interred with their fathers. (xxiii, 16, 20; xlvii, 30; xlix, 29, etc.) This belief is further attested in Job xiii, 15:

"Although he should kill me, I will trust in him."

"In the last day I shall rise out of the earth, and I shall be clothed again with my skin, and in my flesh I shall see my God: whom I myself shall see and not another: this my hope is laid up in my bosom." (xix, 25, 27.)

Other practices of the Jews sufficiently attest their belief in a future life. Saul invoked the dead (1 Ki. xxviii, 11; Prot. Bible, 1 Sam.); though the practice was strictly forbidden. (Deut. xviii, 11.) See also xiv, 1, etc.) We need not quote other texts of both the Pentateuch and the later sacred Scriptures, as these sufficiently evince that in the time of Moses the Jews held the Immortality of the soul as part of their religious belief.

CHAPTER XLIII.

THE FALL OF MAN.

Colonel Ingersoll denies the Fall of Man. He says: "Is it true that man was once perfectly pure and innocent, and that he became degenerate by disobedience? No; the real truth is, and the history of man shows that he has advanced." (P. 126.)

Where, then, are we to find these historical documents that prove man's advance? Profane authentic history in its modern shape, carries us but a small way backwards. It goes but little, if any, further back than the Christian era. Since that time, undoubtedly, man has advanced both intellectually and morally. But is it not undeniable that the influence of Christianity has been very great in producing this result? Even intellectual progress has been in great measure due to her influence; though, indeed, it must be said, moral advancement was her chief object. Before Christianity there were civilizations purely material, but nowhere, except among the Jews, was there the least notion of moral progress. We have already stated the facts which substantiate this.

It is not true, then, that without religion man has made substantial progress. Education purely intellectual cannot elevate mankind. A few scholars may, indeed, without religion, under the influence of the Christian atmosphere which they have breathed all their lives, shape their outward conduct in accordance with the current principles of morality, but a moral nation, without religion, is an impossibility, whatever may be their intellectual training. A Robespierre or or a Danton will not become better by a more extended knowledge. They will only acquire additional facilities to work out their evil designs.

According to Ecclesiastes vii, 4, "God made man right." As a history, even, the account given in the Pentateuch, of his fall, merits all respect. It is a miraculous history; but we have shown that this is no valid reason for rejecting it, for the question relates to the early life of man on earth, whereon he had just been placed by God, who had already employed His infinite power in creating him. Surely there can be no absurdity in His further intervention, either in His placing him in the garden of pleasure, or in His imposing a law for his observance.

Colonel Ingersoll asks, " Why did God not defend his children " against the snares of the serpent? (P. 133.)

We have already answered that God wisely required man's free service, so that the reward he had promised should be merited. Thus it was necessary man should have the liberty of obedience or disobedience, in order that God's design should be accomplished.

We are asked also:

"Is it possible that God would make a successful rival?" (P. 133.)

God did not make the devil as he is. He made him an angel of light; but by his pride and disobedience, he by his own act became a devil. Even as a devil he is not God's successful rival. It is true, his wiles prevail over many men, but the grace which God

affords to all His children will enable them to resi
the devil's wiles successfully. Man cannot be force
to sin against his own will. If, therefore, he choos
the way of death, it is his own act, not that of Go
It was, therefore, by man's own act that he fell in tl
garden of Eden.

Infidels are fond of saying that it was an injusti
in God to make the sin of Adam pass to his posterit

This is the natural condition of humanity. A fathe
by his evil conduct, brings many miseries upon l
ch ldren, even from the moment of their birth. Ev
from this dispensation good results follow. The fa
is a motive which inspires parents with greater horr
for crimes and vices which they know will ent:
misfortunes on their children. Children also have :
additional reason for gratitude to parents who l
their wisdom and good morals have preserved the
from many evils.

Of course Christians do not deny the power
God to have created man in a social condition diffe
ent from his present state. Man might have be
created with such aids of grace as would have effe
tually prevented him from committing sin. Howeve
in the event of creation, God is not obliged to gra
to creatures the greatest possible gifts or benefi
The lesser gift, even, does not become an evil, l
cause a greater can be conceived. Now, undoubtedl
the gift of liberty of choice between good and ev
given to man, is a good gift. God, therefore, m
give it, as He actually does, and it is no valid arg
ment against His justice that He has not given in
stead another gift which we may imagine to be p
ferable. It is very possible, also, that we may
mistaken when we persuade ourselves that the g

we have pictured is the superior one. It may be,
after all, not so desirable as we imagine, in comparison with that which we enjoy. At all events, God is
in no wise bound to adopt our view.

The history of Eve's temptation by the devil, under
the form of a serpent, the conversation between the
two, the statement that the serpent was "more subtle
than any beast," that Eve could be deceived by him,
are altogether a fruitful theme for Colonel Ingersoll's
ridicule. (Pp. 128 to 137.)

Is the Scriptural account, then, so full of absurdities as the Colonel represents? He quotes Dr. Adam
Clark as giving his opinion that "a creature of the
ape or orang-outang kind is here intended." Dr.
Clark is an able scholar, and is frequently very happy
in his line of argument; but he may sometimes fail.
In the present case I see no reason for interpreting
the text otherwise than that the devil clothed himself
with a serpent's body to appear to Eve. The devil
is called "the serpent," and "the old serpent," in
Apocalypse xii, 9, 14, 15 (Prot. Bible, Rev.) Cornelius a Lapide, points out that the subtlety mentioned in Gen. iii, 1, may, according to the Hebrew,
signify the physical aptitude of the serpent to coil
itself in circles, as well as its cunning. Certainly
there is no absurdity in attributing to the serpent
one or both of these qualities, for it possesses them.
Cornelius a Lapide in loco.

There would be some plausibility in denying the
possibility of the devil making use of the body of a
beast for his purposes, if we were not already aware
that spirits can and do make use of material bodies.
The union of soul and body in man is an example of
this, within the experience of all. The possession of

a serpent's body by the devil is not so close or complete a union as the one we know to exist within ourselves. Since, then, the latter is a fact, it cannot be said that the former is impossible.

Assuming, then, that the possession took place, the possibility of the conversation of Eve with the devil, or the serpent, becomes at once established. There is no more difficulty in it than in the use our soul makes of our organs of speech for conversational purposes.

All this being proved, we have only to suppose a moderate degree of astuteness on the devil's part to enable him to deceive Eve; for though her understanding was undoubtedly less dark before her sin, the cunning of the devil is confessedly very great.

Thus all Colonel Ingersoll's difficulties about the Fall of mankind disappear.

We may add here the mature judgment of a wellknown infidel, Bayle, on this very subject:

"From the manner in which the historian relates this sad event it appears evident that his intention was to let us know what actually took place, and this alone ought to persuade any reasonable person that the pen of Moses was under special direction of the Holy Ghost. In fact, if Moses had been the master of his expressions and his thoughts, he would not have enveloped the recital of such an action in such an astounding fashion. He would have spoken in a style more human, and more fitted to instruct posterity. But a greater power, an infinite wisdom directed him that he should write, not according to his own views, but according to the hidden designs of Providence." (*Nouvelles*, 1686, art. 2: quoted by Bergier Dict. Theol. Adam.)

Is there any sense, then, in such questions as the following?

"What and who was this serpent? He was not a man. .... He was not a woman. .... He was not a beast. .... He was neither fish nor fowl nor snake. .... Where did this serpent come from? Why did not the Lord God take him by the tail and snap his head off?" (Pp. 133, 134.)

In fact there is neither head nor tail in the Colonel's whole category of queries.

Equally void of common sense is the slur thrown upon the tradesmen of America by ridiculing "God as a butcher, tanner, and tailor." These trades are by no means dishonorable, though the Colonel's intention is none the less blasphemous, inasmuch as he aims at degrading the Infinite God to the level of Finite Man.

CHAPTER XLIV.

THE DELUGE.—ITS POSSIBILITY.—THE GATHERING OF THE ANIMALS.

THE history of the Deluge is related in the sixth, seventh and eighth chapters of Genesis.

"And God seeing that the wickedness of men was great on the earth .... it repented him that he had made man on the earth. And .... he said: I will destroy man whom I have created from the face of the earth, from man even to beasts, from the creeping thing even to the fowls of the air, for it repenteth me that I have made them."

We cannot conceive a more complete summary of human wickedness than this. I need not again prove that Colonel Ingersoll is mistaken in making God responsible for all man's wickedness. This has been done already.

"But Noah found grace before the Lord."

Noah was commanded to build an ark, and to enter therein with his household, and to take with him of all animals, two of every sort, but of all clean beasts "seven and seven": that is seven of a kind, since the unclean beasts are taken "two and two," vii, 2, which is otherwise expressed in vi, 19, 20, "two of a sort . . . . male and female."

The command of God was obeyed, and thereupon "after the seven days were passed, the waters of the flood overflowed the earth. . . . . All the fountains of the great deep were broken up, and the flood-gates of heaven were opened. And the rain fell upon the earth forty days and forty nights . . . . And the waters prevailed beyond measure upon the earth, and all the high mountains under the whole heaven were covered. The water was fifteen cubits higher than the mountains which it covered . . . . And all things wherein there is the breath of life on the earth died."

"And the waters prevailed upon the earth a hundred and fifty days."

"And God remembered Noah and all the living creatures . . . . which were with him in the ark, and brought a wind upon the earth, and the waters were abated."

"And the ark rested . . . . upon the Mountains of Armenia."

The Hebrew has "mountains of Ararat," this being the Hebrew name for Armenia, as may be seen in 4 Kings xix, 37; Isa. xxxvii, 38.

To use one of Col. Ingersoll's elegant forms of expression "I will remark just here" that the Colonel is rather astray in his Geography. He insists that the mountain on which the ark rested is the one now usually called Mount Ararat.

"It must not be forgotten that the mountain where the ark is supposed to have touched bottom, was about seventeen thousand feet high." (P. 161.)

It is true the Persians call the highest peak of Armenia, which is also the highest of Western Asia, "Koh-i-Nuh," Noah's Mountain. It is true that it is now called Mount Ararat, but it by no means follows that this is the mountain on which the ark rested. Hence the Colonel's sad picture of the animals freezing, and the necessity for "stoves, furnaces, fire-places and steam coils," (P. 161,) is a mere fancy-sketch. The Colonel maintains that the ark must have rested upon "about the highest peak in that country," but there is nothing in Genesis to show this. If you maintain that the account in Genesis is self-contradictory, you must show the contradictions in the text not in your fancy.

The Corydæan mountains of Armenia are of different heights, and when it is stated that "the tops of the mountains appeared" on the first day of the tenth month, this evidently implies that in great measure or for the most part the mountain tops within sight became visible to Noah. It does not at all follow that Noah was on the highest peak.

Let us now take the greatest difficulty which the Colonel can find in the history of the deluge. It is; Whence came the water sufficient to deluge the world? He makes the following catechism on this subject, question and answer.

"How long did it rain?

"Forty days.

"How deep did the water get?

"About five miles and a half.

"How much did it rain a day?

"Enough to cover the whole world to a depth of about 742 feet."

"Some Christians say that the fountains of the great deep were broken up. Will they be kind enough to tell us what the fountains of the great deep are? Others say that God had vast stores of water in the centre of the earth that he used on that occasion. How did these waters happen to run up hill?" (Pp. 150, 151.,

The scriptural account states two sources from which the water was supplied:

"All the *fountains of the great deep* were broken up, and the *flood-gates of heaven* were opened, and the rain fell upon the earth forty days and forty nights." (Genesis vii, 11, 2.)

It is evident that the power of the Almighty was exerted to bring about this prodigy: and when the Almighty wills, all physical difficulties disappear. We will not pretend that this stupendous miracle was brought about by the ordinary operation of the laws of nature: nevertheless it appears that two natural means were used as auxiliaries in producing the deluge, the breaking up of the fountains of the great deep, and a continuous rain for forty days and forty nights.

It is often said by Infidels that all the waters of the earth together would not be enough to cover the land. Yet it has been proved, and all scientific men acknowledge that by subsidence of the land, or by the elevation of the sea bottom, every portion of the earth's surface may be brought beneath the sea. In fact it is acknowledged that every part of the surface has been at some time or other, and repeatedly submerged. On the highest mountains, on the Alps, the Pyrenees, the Andes, the Himalayas, as well as on the vast plains of the Old and New Worlds, there are irrefragable proofs that the waters of the sea have been there. In the bowels of the earth everywhere are found shell-fish, fish-bones and the remains of sea-monsters, and even in the hardest rocks. Probably at the deluge, both the land subsided and the sea bottoms were elevated. This would be very aptly described as the breaking up of the fountains of the deep.

Besides this, possibly, even probably, an accelerated motion would be given to the earth in its daily rotation. This would suffice to bring out from the recesses of the earth the vast stores of water therein contained, and waters would rush from the polar regions towards the equator. Thus would Col. Ingersoll's little problem be solved: "How did these waters happen to run up hill?"

Some remote idea of the vast quantities of water contained in the earth may be attained when it is considered that not only does it exist in fissures and reservoirs in the earth, but that it fills the pores of every rock.

"Gypsum absorbs from 0.50 to 1.50 per cent of water by weight; granite about 0.37; . . . . chalk about 20; plastic clay from 19.5 to 24.5 per cent." (Geikie's Text Book of Geology, p. 299.)

Further: "The Abbé Le Brun made a perfect imitation of the deluge by filling with water a terrestrial globe fitted with valves, and causing it to revolve within a globe of glass. The water rushed from the valves and deluged the terrestrial globe, filling the exterior glass globe, but as soon as the motion was relaxed it re-entered the valves by its own weight." (Duclot, Bible Vindicated, ii, 59.)

If, then, men could find means to make water "run up hill," surely God also could do so.

There is also in the atmosphere a vast amount of water of which undoubtedly God could make use in order to send rain on its mission to punish sinful man.

Science suggests other modes by which the same end could be accomplished; but where there is question of the power of God, it would be a work of supererogation to enumerate them. Thus also disappear the difficulties raised by the Colonel against the possibility of collecting the animals and of supplying them with sufficient food and water, and of preserving them against the effects of an incongenial climate.

However, there are not wanting natural means of explaining most of these points satisfactorily. Where natural means are insufficient, we must suppose divine intervention.

As regards the gathering of the animals, the Colonel takes for granted several propositions which are undoubtedly false. On these his whole argument rests, and with them all his reasonings on this subject crumble into dust.

1. He assumes that before the deluge the continents were very much the same as they are now. Thus he says:

"We know that there are many animals on this continent not found in the old world. These must have been carried from here to the ark and then brought back afterwards. Were the peccary, armadillo, ant-eater, sloth, etc., carried by the Angels from America to Asia? Did the polar bear leave his field of ice and journey toward the tropics? How did he know where the ark was? Did the kangaroo swim or jump from Australia to Asia? . . . . What had these animals to eat while on the journey?" (P. 149.)

One of the foremost Geologists of the world, Cuvier, who was convinced, not only that the deluge was a fact, but that Geology proves that it occurred, says that,

"It engulphed and caused to disappear, countries before inhabited by man, and changed the bottom of the sea into dry land, and formed the countries which are inhabited to-day." (The Revolutions of the Globe.)

Colonel Ingersoll's assumption that the continents were the same as to-day is therefore an absurdity.

2. The Colonel also assumes that the animals must have been distributed before the deluge, in the same way as they are now. Surely this does not accord with common sense, for after the deluge Armenia must have been the centre from which both animals and men dispersed themselves over different parts of the earth.

3. The Colonel assumes that the climate of Armenia was not suited to be the dwelling place of all the animals, even for the space of one year. This assumption is altogether gratuitous; and Col. Ingersoll himself is very loud in his denunciation of those who "believe without evidence or in spite of it." (P. 19.) Let him not expect us, therefore, to believe him in regard to the climate of Armenia. It is to-day a delightful climate. You say "toward the

tropics," to convey, probably, the idea of intense heat. Yes, Armenia was *toward* the tropics in relation to the North Pole; but after all its latitude corresponds to that of the middle part of the Colonel's own State, Illinois. Its climate, then is not quite so intolerable but that the Colonel himself might possibly live in it if he were suddenly transported thither.

It is not at all unlikely that before the flood the climate was very different from what it is to-day, and in all probability pairs of all the animals could be found in Armenia itself or the countries immediately adjacent. At all events, Noah may not have had more trouble about collecting them than had Adam when all created beasts passed before him to be named. Noah is not commanded to *search* for the beasts, as if they were distant and difficult to be found, but to *take* them as the shepherd selects from his flock which is at hand.

CHAPTER XLV.

CAPACITY OF NOAH'S ARK.—PAGAN TRADITIONS OF THE DELUGE.—COL. INGERSOLL'S BLUNDERS.—THE TESTIMONY OF GEOLOGY.

Another objection is put forward by infidels with great persistency, and of course it is not omitted by Col. Ingersoll. They say: "An ark of the dimensions given by Moses could not contain the number of animals requisite for the preservation of existing species."

Col. Ingersoll puts the matter thus:

"The next question, is, how many beasts, fowls

and creeping things did Noah take into the ark?" (P. 148.)

He then says, there are at least twelve thousand five hundred kinds of birds, besides birds of regions yet unexplored, one thousand six hundred and fifty-eight kinds of beasts, about twenty-five being clean, six hundred and fifty species of reptiles, one million species of insects, including creeping things, and probably hundreds of thousands of animalculæ, all of which "Noah had to pick out by pairs." (P. 149.)

Would it not have been more satisfactory if the Colonel had shown how much space each of the animals would require, and to have computed whether the space in the ark was sufficient for them?

The Colonel seems to exaggerate the number of species of birds at all events. Chambers' Encyclopædia gives the number at about five thousand. Many of these live on the water, or are amphibious, and would not need to be brought into the ark, and the same is true of the animals. The reptiles are nearly all amphibious The insects and animalculæ nearly all deposit their eggs where they are secure from the causes of destruction, frost, snow, rain or flood. Hence it is certain that a sufficiency of these would be preserved even from the effects of a general deluge, to propagate their kind after the subsidence of the waters. We have, therefore, only to consider the non-aquatic birds, and the mammals, and even of these all whales live in the water, while many are amphibious, as the hippopotamus, beaver, etc.

"It is certain," says Mr. Glaire, "that nearly all the animals of these two classes are known. The discovery of a new species of bird or mammal is an event in science, and if any one will take the trouble to visit the Paris museum, one of the most complete in the world, he will see that the cells which contain the greater part of the species of mammals and birds of full growth, form scarcely one story of a building which is much smaller than was the ark of Noah."

Chambers' Encyclopædia numbers the mammals at two thousand and sixty-seven. Of the few clean mammals, seven of a kind were brought into the ark: of the rest two of a kind. The total number of individuals could not have exceeded four thousand two hundred. A stall of twelve cubic feet each way would accommodate the largest individual, that is to say, one thousand seven hundred and twenty-eight cubic feet of space, while a very large number would require less than one cubic foot each. Now, the length of the ark is stated to be three hundred cubits, its breadth fifty cubits, and its height thirty cubits: that is to say, omitting fractions, five hundred and forty-seven feet by ninety-one feet, by fifty-four feet =two million six hundred and eighty-seven thousand nine hundred and fifty-eight cubic feet.

The following estimate is liberal in the amount of space allowed to each animal.

APPROXIMATE SPACE OCCUPIED BY MEN AND ANIMALS IN THE ARK.

Space for each individual.	No. of individuals.	Space for each class.
$10 \times 10 \times 10$ ft	8 persons	8,000 ft.
$12 \times 12 \times 12$ "	20 animals	34,560 "
$11 \times 11 \times 11$ "	20 "	26,620 "
$10 \times 10 \times 10$ "	20 "	20,000 "
$9 \times 9 \times 9$ "	40 "	29,160 "
$8 \times 8 \times 8$ "	60 "	30,720 "
$7 \times 7 \times 7$ "	80 "	27,440 "
$6 \times 6 \times 6$ "	120 "	25,920 "

Space for each individual.	No. of individuals.	Space for each class.
5 × 5 × 5 ft.	200 animals	25,000 ft.
4 × 4 × 4 "	400 "	25,000 "
3 × 3 × 3 "	540 "	14,580 "
2 × 2 × 2 "	700 "	5,600 "
1½ × 1½ × 1½ "	800 "	2,700 "
1 × 1 × 1 "	1200 "	1,200 "
	4,208	277,100 ft
Birds: an equal space		277,100 "
Total space occupied by animals		554,200 ft
Total capacity of ark		2,687,958 "
Space for access, provisions and water, and for the few purely land reptiles		2,133,758 ft

Vice Admiral Thevenard of the French Navy, formerly master builder, says "the ark was more than ample to accommodate all the animals with food and water sufficient for their sustenance." (Sea Memoirs, vol. iv.)

I have supposed, hitherto, that the deluge was universal. This was the opinion of nearly all the Ancient Fathers and writers of Christianity. However, many are of opinion that the words of Holy Scripture do not imply absolute universality, but only universality as regards the portion of the earth which was then inhabited by man. It is the known usage of the Orientals to speak of all the earth, or all of anything for a very considerable part; and this usage is frequent even in our more matter of fact Western languages. In the present case, the terms are so strong, so frequently repeated with particular insistence, that it is difficult to believe that a partial deluge is meant. We shall not attempt to decide this dispute here; but the proofs we have advanced show that even the universal deluge is by no means impossible or incredible.

If we ask what testimony Geology gives regarding the deluge, we receive a rather uncertain answer. Geology makes it certain that the earth has been deluged; but many modern scholars are of opinion that the deluges which Geology attests are far more ancient than that recorded in Genesis. Other geologists have arrived at a different conclusion. It will suffice to quote the conclusion of Cuvier, founded on a close observation of innumerable facts.

"I think, therefore, with Messrs. Deluc and Dolomieu, that if there is anything proved in geology, it is that the surface of our globe has been the victim of a great and sudden revolution, which does not date further back than five or six thousand years: that it is since that revolution that the small number of individuals spared from it have been propagated on the earth newly made dry, and consequently that it is since that time only that society has taken up its forward march, formed all its works, raised its monuments, collected its natural facts, and combined its scientific systems." (Revolutions of the Globe.)

The learned geologists Messrs Boué and Pallas are equally positive in their language. This is all in perfect accord with the Mosaic narrative. On the other hand, the geologists who maintain that the Noachian deluge is not proved by geology, do not deny that such a deluge may have occurred. They merely maintain that the revolutions attested by geology are more permanent in consequences, because they were more lasting and more violent than the deluge of Genesis could have been, so that, in comparison, the latter could be expected to leave few if any geological traces.

If the Noachian deluge occurred, we should expect

that the tradition of so great a catastrophe should be handed down among numerous nations, more or less obscured by the omission of some circumstances, and the addition of others; but if it did not occur, it would be absurd to suppose that anything like the history of such an event should be preserved by nations scattered through all parts of the world, and having little and often no communication with each other.

It is so incontestably true that this tradition has been universally preserved, that Boulanger, one of the most incredulous writers of the last century, says:

"That incomprehensible fact, the deluge, which people believe by habit, and philosophers deny by habit, is both most notorious and incontestable. Yes: the naturalist would believe it if there were no traditions to attest it, and any man of good sense would believe it solely on the ground of human traditions. It were necessary to be the most narrow-minded and self-opinionated of men to doubt it, when we consider the united testimonies of physical science and history, and the universal voice of mankind." (Antiquity Unveiled, C. 1.)

The poet Lucian relates the Greek, Scythian, and Syrian traditions, Hieronymus of Tyre, Mnaseas, and others relate those of the Phœnicians, Nicholas of Damascus, and Josephus record those of the Armenians. Similar narratives are found in the ancient sacred books of the Hindoos and Chinese; Humboldt found them among the savages of North America, and Goassin among those of Polynesia, while the most ancient records of the Chaldeans have preserved an account of the great deluge, which, if stripped of its Polytheism, is almost identical with that of Moses, preserving in many places the very words of the Hebrew text: for, as is well known, the Chaldean and Hebrew languages have a great similarity, they being cognate tongues.

Colonel Ingersoll himself acknowledges the universality of these traditions, and he is forced to acknowledge a common origin for them, as they give "the same story in each instance." (P. 168.) He deserves, certainly, the palm for originality of thought, if not for common sense, when he says:

The real origin of them was, in his opinion, "an effort to account for the sun, moon, and stars." (P. 168.)

He is perfectly "assured that they are all equally false." (P. 168.)

Can a man of sense seriously assert that so many different nations could frame so nearly similar narratives of a universal deluge, with no other common data than a knowledge of the existence of sun, moon, and stars?

Colonel Ingersoll says there are two accounts of the deluge, and that according to one, Noah should take "two of all beasts, birds, and creeping things into the ark," while according to the other he should take "seven of each kind" of clean beasts and all birds. (P. 166.)

Commentators agree that where it is said "two of every sort shall go in," the reference is to the beasts only, and the general rule is given, "that they may live," (Gen. vi, 20,) whereas in vii, 2, 3, the special rule is given for birds and clean beasts, for food and sacrifice, since they were to be used for these purposes after the deluge. But if two and seven were to be taken respectively, why does the Colonel insist on counting fourteen birds and clean beasts of each kind when counting the total number of animals in the ark?

He also says that according to the "third verse of the eighth chapter," the flood only lasted one hundred and fifty days, "while the other account fixes the time at three hundred and seventy-seven days." (P. 166.)

How did the Colonel manage to make out three hundred and seventy-seven days?

It must have been *leap year* to make out three hundred and seventy-seven days between Noah's entry into the ark till he came out. How could there be a leap year spoken of by Moses, over fourteen hundred years before the Julian calendar was established? The Jewish calendar was entirely different, even in the length of the years, from either the Julian or the Gregorian calendar. Why, Colonel, in spite of your boast that you could write a better Pentateuch than Moses did, I fear you would have botched it sadly with your anachronisms.

Your assertion is not true, that the third verse of the eighth chapter says that the flood ended with the 150th day. It is said the waters "began to be abated after 150 days." This is very different from what you assert. Where is the contradiction? How do such misrepresentations accord with your professed admiration for "blessed truth?" (P. 30.)

You also lay great stress upon the fact that there is mention in Gen. vi, of only one window.

"Think of a ship larger than the Great Eastern, with only one window, and that but 22 inches square!" (P. 144.)

It is to be remarked that the Hebrew word here translated *window*, viz., *tsohar*, signifies primarily, *light*, and is used undoubtedly for a transparent window. It refers, therefore, merely to the principal transparent window of the ark. There is nothing, therefore, to exclude other windows of less importance, by means of which both light and ventilation could be secured. *Cornelius a Lapide.* Can we think that during the one hundred years that Noah had to build the ark, means of ventilation and of lighting the ark were neglected?

Another difficulty raised by the Colonel, is made a mountain of: after the flood God "said in his heart that he would not any more curse the ground for man's sake. For saying this the Lord gives as a reason. . . . because 'the imagination of man's heart is evil from his youth.' God destroyed man because 'the wickedness of man was great in the earth, and because every imagination of the thoughts of his heart was only evil continually.' And he promised for the same reason not to destroy him again." (P. 163.)

Any child of intelligence could have removed the Colonel's mountain. God punishes man for his persistent evil deeds: but after the punishment has been inflicted, he is moved by his mercy to promise that he will no more send a general punishment on mankind. He will in future deal with sinners individually, and will punish accordingly. He is moved to act thus on account of man's frailty and proneness to evil, "from his youth." This is well expressed in the Catholic translation:

"For the imagination and thought of man's heart are prone to evil from their youth."

The Colonel says:

"For me it is impossible to believe the story of the deluge. It seems so cruel, so barbaric, so crude in detail, so absurd in all its parts, and so contrary to all we know of law, that even credulity itself is shocked."

It is sufficiently vindicated from the charge of cruelty, when we know that it is the punishment of sin. In connection with this the reasons given in chapter 9, for the punishments inflicted on the Canaanites may be read. We have shown that it is neither absurd nor contrary to law. We may add the following evidences that it is a fact.

"On Moel Tryfan, a mountain in North Wales, 1,390 feet above the present level of the sea, there is an immense bed of gravel. This could not have been formed by mere disintegration of the soil, because it is full of sea-shells .... both of the shore and the deep sea. These shells are heaped pell-mell on the gravel, and I believe every geologist admits that this is marine gravel. I take it that it is a sound conclusion that the sea had been up to the top of that mountain in very recent times, or that the mountain had been down to the level of the sea.

I draw a second conclusion from this fact, that the sea was not a permanent sea. It was not the case that the mountain formed the bottom of the ocean for many years, because we should then have had deposits with shells living and dying, as in the case of the sea terraces described by Mr. Smith, of Jordanhill. The sea has been essentially transitory in its operation. The second of the conditions of the deluge is in this way fulfilled. Thirdly, it was tumultuous. It has no marks of quiet bedding. Is it probable that the mountains of Wales alone were 1,400 feet lower than they are now? There might be very local, very partial submergence of volcanic mountains under the sea. But what I have described happened not in a volcanic district, and Moel Tryfan is not a volcanic mountain. But we are not left altogether to presumptive evidence upon this subject. We have similar gravels all over the counties of Lancashire, Cheshire, Staffordshire, and Worcestershire. In Cheshire they are found near the town of Macclesfield, at 1,200 feet above the level of the sea, and very much under the same condition. I think, therefore, that there is fair evidence that the submergence of the land, which, in North Wales amounted to about 1,400 feet, extended over the whole of the British islands." (Summarized from Duke of Argyll in *Good Words*.)

It appears thus that Geological evidences of the deluge are not lacking: and many *more* equally strong might be given.

CHAPTER XLVI.

THE ORIGIN OF LANGUAGE.—BABEL.—EVIDENCES OF ONE ORIGINAL TONGUE.

It is not stated in Holy Scripture that Hebrew was the language spoken by Adam and Eve. Many are of opinion that this was the case, but we have not to defend this, since it is only an opinion. We are assured that Adam and Eve had the gift of speech, and undoubtedly God was as able to give them this gift, as He was to endow them with other faculties.

There can be no absurdity in believing that they were so endowed.

Col. Ingersoll says:

"We know now that it requires a great number of years to form a language." (P. 170.)

No doubt it does as languages are usually formed, that is to say by men. So also it would take a man a great number of years to form a man, or even an oyster, if he had the chemical elements given him, out of which these are made, and even after many years he would not succeed. We are not to judge the power of God in Creation by the standard of man's abilities. From the account given in Genesis we learn that man was created by the act of God's will, and it is certain that he was from the beginning given the use of speech. You ask,

"Does anybody believe that God directly taught a language to Adam and Eve?" (P. 171.)

Yes. Such is the belief of Christians, and there is nothing absurd in this belief. The soundest philosophers have come to the conclusion that man would need to know language before he could invent language.

It is certain that when once man had attained the use of speech, he could extend it by inventing new words for new ideas, or by combining old words so as to form new ones, for daily experience proves that this is constantly done, and thus even entirely new languages are constantly being formed. But could man have invented by himself the first language?

Rousseau himself, well known as an Infidel, acknowledges the difficulty, even the "almost demonstrated impossibility that language should have been originally a human invention." (Encyc. Art. Language.)

Max Müller says:

"We cannot tell as yet what language is. It may be a production of nature, a work of human art, or a divine gift. But to whatever sphere it belongs, it would seem to stand unsurpassed—nay, unequalled in it—by anything else. If it be a production of nature, it is her last and crowning production, which she reserved for man alone. If it be a work of human art, it would seem to lift the human artist almost to the level of a divine creator. If it be the gift of God, it is God's greatest gift; for through it God spoke to man, and man speaks to God in worship, prayer and meditation." (Science of Language, vol. i, p. 3.)

Surely the testimony of this great linguist is more to be relied on than Col. Ingersoll. The first or the third hypothesis of Max Müller is quite according to the account given in Genesis. Col. Ingersoll insists on the second, and by doing so shews that in spite of his boasted superiority over Moses in knowledge of the science of language, he is in woful ignorance on the subject. (See Mistakes of Moses, pp. 170, 175, as quoted in this chapter.)

From all this it follows that the Colonel so far from having proved an absurdity in Genesis, has himself propounded a most improbable theory, which he desires to substitute for the historical statements of Moses, which we have already shown to be the work of a reliable historian.

We must bear in mind that Max Müller's three possible explanations of the origin of language embody his views from a purely scientific point of view. Language could not have had these three origins. It becomes therefore a matter for history to decide which of the three is the correct solution. Moses in his capacity as a historian settles the matter by discarding the second theory, which Colonel Ingersoll adopts. We must therefore confine ourselves to one or other of the other two, either of which accords perfectly with the Mosaic account.

The Colonel next asks:

"How did the serpent learn the same language as Adam and Eve?" (P. 171.)

As we have already seen, the *serpent* here meant is the devil. There is no difficulty in conceiving that the devil was astute enough to learn sufficient for his purpose of conversing with Eve, in a short time. Men have been known to perform feats in language fully as wonderful.

Col. Ingersoll seems to consider that he has found a formidable objection against the truth of the Mosaic history, in the fact that no account is given of the death and burial of Adam or Eve or Noah. (P. 170.)

When we consider that only ten short chapters of Genesis are devoted to the history of eighteen centuries, it will be quite intelligible why only the main facts should be related. In romances in which the writer wishes to work upon the reader's feelings, and his success depends upon his doing this, he would naturally dwell upon subjects which would give an opportunity for pathetic descriptions, but the Mosaic account is a simple record of the main facts which regard the world's history, in its relation to God. It is, therefore, one of the strongest evidences of the truth of the record, that the writer confines himself to those facts which most concern mankind. Genesis is unlike the records of other nations. It is clear, circumstantial and connected. It is not interlarded with the superstitions of idolatry, and it does not invent fabulous thousands, even millions, of years as do the records of other nations. An impostor would have taken the bait and would have invented a fabulous antiquity for his nation, as did the Egyptians and Chinese and others. But no! Genesis gives a plain, unornamented account of facts which perfectly coincide with the manners of the ancient world as far as we know them, and with the probabilities as far as we can form a judgment on them. Still it must not be forgotten that what we have is a record rather than a history of the most ancient period. Even if it were a history, there would be little room for pathetic descriptions. Still less in a mere record of the principal facts. If the simplicity of the narrative had been marred by such descriptions, no one sooner than the Colonel would have pointed this out as a proof that Genesis were but a romance.

In this respect the Colonel resembles the man who was condemned to be lashed. The accommodating wielder of the cat-o-nine-tails desired to strike the culprit in the way he would be best pleased, and as each blow descended, he was told "strike higher" or "strike lower," till at last the executioner in disgust told him he was the hardest man to please he had ever had occasion to whip. The Colonel, also, is not contented with Moses, whether the history in the Pentateuch be detailed, as when Moses led the Israelites out of Egypt, or synoptical, as in the Genesis records.

The same reasoning applies to the Colonel's statement that God made no effort to reform the world before punishing mankind by means of the deluge. He says:

"Nothing in particular seems to have been done.

Not a school was established. There was no written language. There was not a bible in the world. The scheme of salvation was kept a profound secret. The five points of Calvinism had not been taught. Sunday schools had not been opened. In short, nothing had been done for the reformation of the world." (P. 139.)

We know that the Pentateuch, even where it gives details of an event, makes no pretence of giving all the details which occurred. Thus, we know from Psalm 76 (Prot. Bible, 77,) that noise of the waters, storms, thunderings, lightnings and a trembling of the earth accompanied the drowning of the Egyptians in the Red Sea. Yet of all this we would have known nothing from the Pentateuch alone; and in the 17th and 18th chapters of Wisdom many particulars of the plagues of Egypt are related, as also in Josephus, many incidents of the life of Moses, which are not to be found in the Pentateuch. Undoubtedly these authors, sacred and profane, had other sources of information concerning these matters. How, then, can Col. Ingersoll assert so positively that there was nothing done for the reformation of men before the deluge? How does he know there were no schools? How does he know there was no written language? Does not the Colonel assert in his lecture on skulls that written language existed over four thousand years before the Pentateuch was written, as we have shown in chapter 16?

However, it makes little difference whether this was the case or not. We may be sure that God, whose desire is to "save sinners" (1 Tim. i, 15,) did not omit to have penance inculcated on those who perished in the deluge before they were so punished.

Even from 1st Peter iii, 19, 20, we learn that many who had been incredulous while the ark was being built, received the glad tidings of redemption when Christ preached to the spirits in prison. These included, undoubtedly, souls who were converted to God even in the last moment while the waters of the deluge were engulphing them; and thus the deluge, though a temporal evil, was to them a spiritual benefit.

Whether or not there was any John Calvin before the flood, to preach the "five points" is evidently nothing to the purpose. The Calvinists, after all, form a small proportion of professed Christians; but it is certain that the "scheme of salvation" was known, for it was revealed by God to our first parents as we read in Genesis iii; and it may have been otherwise revealed still more clearly. We may very fairly draw this inference from the passage of St. Peter already referred to.

Again, how does Col. Ingersoll know that in the interview with Pharaoh,

"Not one word was said by Moses and Aaron as to the wickedness of depriving a human being of his liberty? that not a word was said in favor of liberty?" (P. 193.)

The laws of Moses condemned slave-stealing as we have shown in chapter 4. Is it not likely, then, that Moses and Aaron made use of argument against Pharaoh, before resorting to the extreme measures which alone brought Pharaoh to terms? In fact from Exodus iv, we may naturally infer that this was the case, and it was for this purpose that Aaron was appointed to accompany Moses, to use his eloquence as the occasion required. (Verse 14.)

The Confusion of tongues at the Tower of Babel is the next subject for Colonel Ingersoll's wit. He says:

"Nothing can be more absurd than to account for the different languages of the world by saying that the original language was confounded at the Tower of Babel. .... How could language be confounded? It could be confounded only by the destruction of memory." (P. 173.)

Yet after this statement he suggests another mode by which the confusion might have been effected, viz: by paralysis "of that portion of the brain presiding over the organs of articulation, so that they could not speak the words although they remembered them clearly." (P. 173.)

Surely some people "should have a good memory," as the Colonel says on page 108.

He adds, page 175:

Moses "knew little of the science of language, and guessed a great deal more than he investigated."

The Colonel himself evidently knows still less of the "science of language." It does not become him to throw stones at Moses on this score.

Why should it be impossible for God to confound language? The only reason which the Colonel implies is that his doing so would be a miracle. We have already proved that this is no valid reason whatsoever.

Others, however, have maintained that the very great diversity of human languages is irreconcilable with the statement that at any time, still less at so late a period as the time of the building of the tower of Babel, "the earth was of one tongue and of the same speech," and Colonel Ingersoll asks, with his usual confidence:

"Is it possible that any one now believes that the whole world would be of one speech had the language not been confounded at Babel?" (P. 174.)

It is nowhere stated that there would or would not have remained only one language, if the confusion had not occurred at Babel. The Colonel's query is, therefore, altogether beside the question, and it is of no consequence whatsoever how it may be answered. Let us, therefore, turn to the consideration of the views of those who maintain that languages cannot have had a common origin.

Until late years most philological scholars took it for granted that any resemblance between two languages must be accounted for by supposing that one must be the child of the other. Modern philologists, however, while not ignoring the filial relationships of languages, recognize that numerous languages are related to each other as sister tongues derived by parallel descent from a common source.

In the sudden sweeping away of many analogies, consequent on the change of views of philologists respecting the origin of languages, the probability of mankind having had originally one tongue seemed at first much less than before. This the late Cardinal Wiseman so ably points out that I cannot do better than quote his remarks on the subject.

"Every new discovery only served to increase this perplexity; and our science must at that time have presented to a religious observer the appearance of a study daily receding from sound doctrine, and giving encouragement to rash speculations and dangerous conjecture. But even at that period a ray of light was penetrating into the chaos of materials thrown together by collectors; and the first great step towards a new organization was even then taken, by the division of those materials into distinct homogeneous masses into continents, as it were, and oceans; the stable and circumscribed, and the movable and varying elements, whereof this science is now composed.

"The affinities which formerly had been but vaguely seen between languages separated in their origin by history and geography, began now to appear definite and certain. It was now found that new and most important connections existed among languages so as to combine in large provinces or groups the idioms of nations whom no other research would have shown to be mutually related." (Science and Religion, Lecture 1.)

It is evident that if languages are derived from a common source, we should find the greatest resemblances between the forms of languages in their earliest stages, and this is precisely what takes place.

Remarkable resemblances have been discovered between the Teutonic and Celtic tongues, Latin and Greek, Russian and other Slavonian languages, and the languages of Persia and India, especially as these languages were spoken over three thousand years ago. So striking are these resemblances, that it is now agreed upon that the ancestors of all the nations we have named must have spoken substantially the same tongue. The differences of language must have arisen in great measure from the different ways in which the various families and tribes pronounced the same words as they became scattered over the different parts of the world, and modern philology has discovered the corresponding sounds which were usually adopted by the different nationalities in their endeavors to pronounce the same original root-word. (See Max Müller, Science of Language, vol. ii, p. 216 and sequel.)

The discoveries of the Sanscrit, the ancient language of India, and of Zend, the ancient language of Persia, have contributed in very great measure to make these results certain, so that now it is fully conceded that, with the exception of the Biscayan and Finnish languages, Hungarian included, all the tongues of Europe, together with those of a large part of Asia, have a common origin. These languages have, on this account, been called by the general name of Indo-European, or Aryan tongues.

Another class of languages, usually called Semitic, quite distinct from the Aryan, includes Hebrew, Syro-Chaldaic, Arabic and Abyssinian. These also are acknowledged to have a common origin.

"The Turanian languages include Tungusic, Mongolic, Turkic, Finnic and Samoyedic, Tamulic, Thibetian, Siamese and Malayic, or the Malay and Polynesian dialects." (Max Müller, ib. vol. i, p. 334.)

These are Nomad languages, and consequently the changes from their original forms were more rapid and complete than in the more settled countries occupied by those who spoke the Aryan and Semitic tongues. There cannot be expected between tongues of this class such resemblances as are found in those already mentioned, nevertheless, Max Müller says:

"These languages share elements in common which they must have borrowed from the same source, and their formal coincidences, though of a different character from those of the Aryan and Semitic families, are such that it would be impossible to ascribe them to mere accident." (Ib. vol. i, p. 334.)

As the various languages become better known, it usually results that they are at last resolved into one or the other of these classes. Thus the primary languages of the world are reduced to a very small number, and we might very well suspect that these few original tongues may have been in turn derived from one common stock. Max Müller is most positive on the possibility of all these distinct classes of languages springing from one original.

"We have examined all possible forms which language can assume, and we have now to ask, can we reconcile with these three distinct forms, the radical, the terminational and the inflectional, the admission of one common origin of human speech? I answer decidedly, Yes." (Vol. i, p. 375.)

There are undoubtedly words of simple meaning, and primary necessity which run through large numbers of languages of the same class, and often there are words which run through not only one class of languages but through both the Aryan and Semitic tongues. I will give a few examples.

Thus the numeral *six*, in Persian *shesh*, in Sanscrit *shash*, in Latin *sex*, in German *sechs*, in Slavonic *schest*, in Greek *hex*, in Zend *qowas*, is found with but slight variation in the Semitic tongues also: in Hebrew *shesh*, in Arabic *shet, sheh*, in Aramæan *sheth*, in Ethiopic *sesu*.

Seven is in Sanscrit *sapta*, in Old German *sibun*, in Gothic *sibum*, in Latin *septem*, in Greek *hepta*, in Zend *hapta*, while the Semitic tongues have, Hebrew *sheva*, Syriac *shebe*, Arabic *sheba't*.

Many other words may be found in Dwight's Philology, Cardinal Wiseman's and Max Müller's Lectures, Sir William Jones' Asiatic Researches, and

Gesenius' Hebrew Lexicon. I may cite a few other examples.

One is in Sanscrit *aika,* in Persian *yak,* in Pehlevi *jek,* in Hebrew *echad,* in Arabic *achad,* in Ethiopic *ahadu.*

Mother is in Sanscrit *ama,* in Biscayan *ama,* in Hebrew *em,* in Arabic *omma,* in Ethiopic *emme.*

Horn is in Latin *cornu,* in Gothic *haurns,* in German *horn,* in French *corne,* in Greek *keras,* in Hebrew, Arabic and Phœnician *keren,* in Syriac *karno.*

Now it becomes a question: what number of words common to two languages will warrant the conclusion that they have a common origin?

Cardinal Wiseman (Lecture 2,) quotes Dr. Young as giving a mathematical formula from which he draws the conclusion that in the comparison of two languages, "the odds would be three to one against the agreement of two words: but if three words appear to be identical it would be more than ten to one that they must be derived in both cases from some parent language or introduced in some other manner; six words would give more than seventeen hundred chances to one, and eight, near one hundred thousand, so that in these cases the evidence would be little short of absolute certainty."

Thus, he adds, in Biscayan "we find, *beria, new; ora, a dog; guchi, little; oguia, bread; otzoa, a wolf;* and *zazpi* or *shashpi, seven.* Now in the ancient Egyptian new is *beri;* a dog, *whor;* little, *kudchi;* bread, *oik;* a wolf, *ounsh;* seven, *shashf;* and if we consider these words as sufficiently identical to admit of our calculating upon them, the chances will be more than a thousand to one that at some very remote period an Egyptian colony established itself in Spain.

I have not at hand the data assumed by Dr. Young in his calculations, but we may arrive at a satisfactory result by the method given in the note. It may be a satisfaction to mathematical readers to find the calculation in detail. *

---

* If we assume the number of primary roots in a language to be five hundred, it will be a fair estimate. Hebrew has five hundred. Chinese four hundred and fifty. Sanscrit is said by grammarians to have one thousand seven hundred and six roots, but Max Müller reduces the number to about five hundred and thirty-five primary roots. Vol. ii, p. 359.

Next, let there be 22 radical letters in the languages compared, and let the roots contain respectively 1, 2 and 3 letters which are permanent. We shall then readily discover the total number of available roots for the formation of the languages.

In the following calculations the symbol $\lfloor\underline{}$ is used to signify the product of the integers 1, 2, 3, etc., to the number placed within the symbol. The processes followed are the ordinary algebraical rules for calculating Combinations, Variations and Permutations.

1. Roots of one permanent letter, $\quad = \quad 22$

Roots with 2 *different* letters $= 2 \times \dfrac{\lfloor 22}{\lfloor 2 \ \lfloor 20} \quad = \quad 462$

Roots with 3 different letters $= \lfloor 3 \ \dfrac{\lfloor 22}{\lfloor 3 \ \lfloor 19} \quad = \quad 9240$

Bi-literal roots with same letter repeated, $\quad = \quad 22$
Tri-literal roots with one repeated letter $= 22 \times 21 \times 3 = 1848$

$\overline{ 11594}$

Thus 10,000 will be a very moderate estimate of the number of available roots, after rejecting such as might not be sufficiently euphonious for use.

2. The total number of languages possible to be formed with 500 primary roots in each will be $\dfrac{\lfloor 10000}{\lfloor 500 \ \lfloor 9500} \quad \dfrac{\lfloor 500}{=} \dfrac{\lfloor 10000}{\lfloor 9500}$

This number, consisting of $9501 \times 9502 \times$ etc. to 500 factors would consist of 1995 figures. Many of the languages, however, would differ from each other only in 1, 2, 3 or more roots.

3. If now we assume one language as fixed, and compare with it another, finding that n roots are identical in both we

From this it is clear that a very small number of identical words, or words that are substantially identical, will suffice to establish an extreme probability, amounting almost to demonstration, that the languages so coinciding have a common origin. We may

---

may find the number of possible cases in which this may occur.

n roots being the same in both languages, the number of ways in which this may occur in 500 fixed roots $= \dfrac{\lfloor 500}{\lfloor n \; \lfloor 500-n}$ this being the number of ways in which n things may be taken at a time out of a total of 500.

4. In each case of the last paragraph (3), there must remain $10000-n$ words from which $500-n$ must be selected, and the number of ways these selections may be made not greater than $\dfrac{\lfloor 10000-n}{\lfloor 500-n \; \lfloor 9500}$, since some of the coincidences will be repeated when these are combined with former result, (3).

5. The selections of the last paragraph (4,) may be applied to the $10000-n$ roots in as many different ways as there are permutations possible of $500-n$ things $= \lfloor 500-n$.

6. Thus the total number of cases in which n roots may be identical in the two given languages not greater than the product of the above three results and not greater than $\dfrac{\lfloor 500}{\lfloor n \; \lfloor 500-n} \; \dfrac{\lfloor 10000-n}{\lfloor 500-n \; \lfloor 9500} \; \lfloor 500-n$.

7. If this quantity in (6) be reduced and divided by the number of possible languages in (2), we shall have the *probability* of two languages having n roots alike, when not derived from a common source. This probability not greater than $\dfrac{\lfloor 500 \; \lfloor 10000-n}{\lfloor n \; \lfloor 500-n \; \lfloor 10000}$

8. It follows that if we give to n various values, we can estimate the probability that two languages have a common origin. If $n=1$, that is if there be 1 common primary root, the probability is not greater than $\frac{1}{20}$ for an independent origin, or is at least 19 to 1 in favor of a common origin.
If $n=2$, probability in favor of a common origin > 800 to 1
If $n=3$,   "   "   "   " > 47903 to 1

And so the probability increases with great rapidity as the number of coinciding roots increases.

therefore very fairly draw the conclusion that even the Aryan and Semitic tongues were originally one language. Thus we see that the discoveries of science far from weakening the authority of Holy Writ, tend in many respects to confirm it.

Could we possibly imagine Moses to have made merely a happy hit in stating so positively the original unity of language, whereas the probabilities then must have appeared so strong against it? Or are we to suppose that his knowledge of the real science of language was the truth as revealed to him by Almighty God? In spite of Col. Ingersoll's sneers, the latter is certainly the most reasonable supposition, even independently of the positive proofs we have advanced.

CHAPTER XLVII.

CHRISTIAN vs. INFIDEL MORALITY: POLYGAMY: DIVORCE: FREE-LOVE.

INFIDELITY is notorious for the inculcation of principles which subvert the morality of nations, as morality is understood wherever the light of Christianity has shone. It is true, there are Christians, or professing Christians, who do not put into practice the sacred and sanctifying principles of Christianity, but in their very neglect they are conscious of their disobedience to the law they should obey. Christianity is not in fault because so many refuse to put her precepts into practice. There are devout souls who do so, and this is enough to show that Christianity is a success, though she does no violence to man's free-will by the use of physical force. Infidelity cannot insist upon these moral precepts, because where there is no responsibility to God, there can be no moral precepts.

Col. Ingersoll says in his lecture on "Skulls:"

"One ounce of restitution is worth a million of repentances anywhere."

This is empty vaporing, inasmuch as restitution is a part of true repentance, and a part of a good thing cannot be worth a million times the whole. Christianity insists upon that practical repentance of the sinner which consists in a complete conversion to God with our whole heart and soul, and which necessarily includes the observance of God's precepts; and restitution of ill-gotten goods is part of God's law. Hence restitution is frequently made by Christians, at all events by Catholics, as I can speak of such from personal knowledge. But can Col. Ingersoll's Infidelity furnish a motive for restitution? If there is no God, there is no moral law and no distinction between right and wrong. Therefore there is no motive for restitution, and Col. Ingersoll's "ounce of restitution" is nowhere. Hence also his declamation about immorality in the Bible is but a bag of wind. (See p. 176.) From Christianity the Infidels have learned whatever they know about morality. The praises of chastity are a constant theme of the Old and New Testaments. These words of the Apostle St. John are a sample of what is to be found throughout the Bible.

The chaste "were purchased from among men, the first fruits to God and to the Lamb." (Apocalypse xiv, 4. Prot. Bible, Rev.)

It is not becoming for an Atheist, then, to accuse Christianity or the Bible of immodesty, as Colonel Ingersoll does:

"If the Bible is not obscene, what book is?" (P. 178.)

First. The charge is false. There is not a passage in the Bible favoring immodesty. The history of Tamar is on page 266 given as an example. Tamar was guilty of a grievous sin, in which Juda the chief of the family was still more guilty than she. The fact is recorded in terms perfectly modest, and the whole narrative relating to Tamar is calculated to show the detestation in which God holds all crimes against chastity. Yet this is Col. Ingersoll's excuse for charging God (of the Bible) with "vulgarity" and "filth." There are in the Bible certain other similar events recorded. There was a good reason why this should be done. The true history of God's people was to be written, that God's merciful dealings with them should be made known, even in their acts of ingratitude and disobedience to His law. Besides, their shortcomings and faults had to be recorded, as well as their virtues, as an evidence of the truthfulness and impartiality of the historian, and to inculcate humility, as a corrective of the supercilious pride of ancestry to which men are so prone. Such narratives also show us how God punishes crime in this world and the next.

2ndly. Such narratives as are modestly repeated in the Bible are usually told by infidels with revolting indecency. It ill becomes Satan to reprove sin. Juvenal says: "We may pardon him that is sound in limb for mocking the cripple, the white man that makes sport of the black, but who can endure to hear without indignation the Gracchi speaking against rebels . . . . or Varres abusing rogues?" (Satire 2, against hypocritical philosophers. Voltaire, Paine and Bennet are examples.)

3dly. It is only from Christian morality that infidels can know the proper relations of modesty to be observed between man and woman. It is from Christian morals that it is known that polygamy is unlawful, that marriage must be held sacred and inviolate, that it must last for life, and that there are relationships within which it cannot be contracted. How, then, can infidels define the limits within which modesty must be observed? Is it not the height of presumption for them to say that the Bible sanctions immodesty, whereas without the Bible itself they would not know what constitutes that vice?

Of course these considerations suffice to show the absurdity of Col. Ingersoll's indignation against Polygamy, of which he says:

"All the languages of the world are not sufficient to express the filth of Polygamy. It makes of man a beast, of woman a trembling slave. It destroys the fireside, makes virtue an outcast, takes from human speech its sweetest words and leaves the heart a den where crawl and hiss the slimy serpents of most loathsome lust. Civilization rests upon the family. The good family is the unit of good government. The virtues grow . . . . where the one man loves the one woman. Lover—husband—wife—mother—father —child—home—without these sacred words the world is but a lair, and men and women merely beasts." (P. 251.)

This is almost the only truth to be found in the book named "Mistakes of Moses." The basis of Society is the marriage tie which unites one man with one woman by a tie which cannot be dissolved but by death, and it is Christianity which has given such a tie to mankind. Why is the marriage tie sacred and inviolate? Because it is the law of God that it should be so. And how do we know that such is God's law? Because Christ has so taught.

"Have ye not read that he who made man from the beginning made them male and female? And he said: "For this cause shall a man leave father and mother and shall cleave to his wife (not wives,) and they *two* shall be in one flesh. What therefore God hath joined together, let no man put asunder .... Moses by reason of the hardness of your hearts permitted you to put away your wives: but from the beginning it was not so. And I say to you that whosoever shall put away his wife, except it be for fornication, and shall marry another committeth adultery,'" etc. (St. Matt. xix, 4 to 9.)

Take away God's revelation, and how will you show that man may not have as many wives as the Grand Turk? In appealing to the Christian sentiment which pervades the United States and Canada against Polygamy, you are stealing Christian arguments under the pretence that they are your property. You are inconsistent in using such arguments while rejecting Christianity. You cannot produce from all the repertories of infidels a solid argument against Polygamy. You seem to be conscious of this, so you do not even make the attempt. All the inconveniences you have enumerated as the result of Polygamy may be its outcome just because the nations where it is practiced have not a perfect code of morality. You attack the Bible as teaching Polygamy. We have seen from the words of Christ that Christianity forbids it. It forbids divorce also. Divorce was allowed, not inculcated, under the Mosaic law, "because of the hardness of men's hearts." The same may be said of

Polygamy, to some extent. Polygamy is nowhere inculcated in the Old Testament, but as Abraham and Jacob were holy men, it is inferred that God permitted Polygamy sometimes at least. Polygamy is certainly now forbidden by Divine law, but the legislator can repeal or suspend his laws. The reasons for the prohibition of Polygamy are the peace of the family, and the proper education of the children which parents are bound to secure. But God can free parents from this obligation, and can provide for the family peace and the education of the children by other means fully as efficient as monogamy provides. God is the master of nature. He can therefore provide for the order of nature as He will. Polygamy, therefore, was not an evil, as far as He may have sanctioned it; and when He did (probably) sanction it in a *very few cases*, it was undoubtedly done for special and good reasons.

And what is really the teaching of Infidelity regarding marriage? It is well known that in America and France, Infidels generally teach that Marriage is a slavery, and that Love must be free. The Oneida Community is one of the fruits of their theory. Judge Black appropriately says in his "Reply to Ingersoll."

"This is the gospel of dirt. I don't say that Mr. Ingersoll swallows it whole. He believes, or at least he practices the Christian doctrine on the subjects of marriage, paternity and property, not because he is bound by the Divine commandment, but because he *feels* like it. Others, rejecting as he does the 'golden metewand of the law,' have an equal right to take their own feelings as the measure of righteousness. So one set of Atheists curses marriage, and another blackguards Polygamy, and they are both right if there be no God above all, and over all."

I need only add, as a testimony to the Infidel theory of marriage, an extract from Eugene Sue's views on this subject. They are the words of his paragon of perfection in his absurd, but too much read "Wandering Jew."

"But this love must yet be consecrated; and in the eyes of the world . . . . marriage is the only consecration, and marriage enchains one's whole life. . . . . Yes, one's whole life! and yet who can answer for the sentiments of a whole life? . . . . Therefore, to accept indissoluble ties, is it not to commit an act of selfish and impious folly? . . . . We ought to pledge ourselves, not . . . . always to belong to one another . . . . for no one can take such a pledge without falsehood or folly . . . . . We ought not to accept indissoluble bonds for . . . . were our love to cease, why should we wear chains that would then be a horrible tyranny?" (Adrienne de Cardoville to Prince Djalma.)

Another instance of the sacredness of marriage from the Infidel point of view is to be found in the "Truth-Seeker" of December 13th, 1884. Under the caption, "Liberal Divorce Laws," the editor rejoices over the fact that the Italian ministry have recommended a law authorizing divorce. He adds:

"This is about as common sense a law as legislators are in the habit of conceiving."

Such are the doctrines on marriage which Infidelity would substitute for the Christian teaching. Under such regulations, what is to become of Col. Ingersoll's "good family, the unit of good government?" What is to become of "husband, wife, mother, father, child, home, without which words the world is but a lair, and men and women merely beasts?" Once let such teachings prevail, imprudent marriages, concubinages rather, will be the rule: under the expectation of future divorce, there will be no restraint on family bickerings and adulteries, families united by the ties of affinity, will be irreconcilably separated in enmity and hate, property will become more than ever a source of discord, and will be dissipated to no good purpose, children will be made orphans, while their parents still live; society will be disorganized, and its very foundations shaken.

Are the women of America prepared to throw aside Christian indissoluble marriage, for Polygamy, Divorce, and Free Love? If so, let them accept Col. Ingersoll's advice, and become Infidels.

CHAPTER XLVIII.

INCREASE OF THE ISRAELITES IN EGYPT.—THE TRIBE OF DAN.—THE NUMBER OF FIRST-BORN MALES.

Colonel Ingersoll takes more than usual pains to prove that from the entry of Jacob and his family, 70 souls, into Egypt till their departure out of Egypt, two hundred and fifteen years only elapsed. It is a question of the interpretation of the fortieth verse of Exodus xii:

"And the abode of the children of Israel that they made in Egypt, was four hundred and thirty years."

From the call of Abraham to the entry of the Israelites, two hundred and fifteen years elapsed. Hence if this is to be counted as part of the time named in Ex. xii, 40, the sojourn of the Israelites from the entry of Jacob till the Exodus will be reduced to two hundred and fifteen years. Some commentators maintain that the period was four hundred and thirty years, others say it was only two hundred and fifteen. It is a question of interpretation. The weight of authority seems to be largely in favor of the shorter period, two hundred and fifteen years, and (St. Paul in Gal. iii, 17) seems also to assert this view. This agrees also with the Septuagint and Samaritan versions of Genesis.

Of course, since it is Col. Ingersoll's wish to show the impossibility of the increase of the Israelites during that period, to the extent mentioned in Holy Scripture, he wishes to make the time as short as possible. The longer period of four hundred and thirty years would present no difficulty whatsoever. I have no hesitation in allowing the shorter period, which is usually taken to be correct.

The Colonel says:

"There were seventy souls when they went down into Egypt, and they remained two hundred and fifteen years, and at the end of that time they had increased to about three million." (P. 185.)

He reasons that as there were six hundred thousand men of war, there must have been a population of at least three million. With immigration, the "United States doubled every twenty-five years," from 1776 to 1876. The same rate of increase among the Hebrews would give in two hundred and fifteen years, thirty-five thousand, eight hundred and forty people at most: He adds "if no deaths occurred." (P. 187.)

Why is this addition made? Are not deaths already taken into account when the comparsion is made with the increase in the United States? Were there no deaths in the United States during the one hundred years between 1776 and 1876? This is evidently added from the suspicion that there is a satisfactory answer to his difficulty, and *so there is.* Nevertheless the Colonel's course is dishonest. He wishes to make his difficulty as formidable as possible, even at the expense of truth.

The Colonel draws the conclusion:

"Every sensible man knows that this (the scriptural) account is not, and cannot be true. We know that seventy people could not increase to three million in two hundred and fifteen years." (P. 187.)

The three million are estimated as the population on the assumption that there must have been at least five times as many persons as there were men of war.

"In every State in this Union there will be to each voter, five other persons at least; and we all know that there are always more voters than men of war." (P. 185.)

This loose way of making statistical statements is very unsatisfactory. Among the voters there are many who reside in neighboring countries, and many naturalized citizens, while there are many residents who have not become naturalized. A good deal depends also on the state of the laws at any particular period, who are the "men of war." Then you do not give the figures for any one State. Now the number of the Israelites in each tribe is very definitely stated, as far as the census was made.

"And the whole number of the children of Israel by their houses and families, from twenty years old and upward, that were able to go to war, were 603,550 men." (Num. i, 45, 46.)

The Levites were not numbered with these. (Verse 47.)

Here then is a clear statement that there were 603,550 men over twenty years of age, descendants of eleven sons of Jacob, and able to go to war. This includes all who were liable to military duty. We shall see soon that it is not necessary to speculate on the total population of the Israelites in order to meet Colonel Ingersoll's argument. However we may follow his line of argument and find its result.

The exact proportion between the men of twenty years of age and upwards, and the rest of the population can be very nearly ascertained. The census of the United States for 1880 gives a total white population of 43,402,970, of whom there were 10,498,717 males between twenty and sixty years of age. The proportion 10,498,717 : 43,402,970 :: 603,550 gives 2,495,149, to which if we add 50,000 for the Levites we shall have 2,545,149 for the population of the Israelites. Now, when we consider that they were blessed especially by God to have the population increase, we may well suppose that the grown up population was larger, so that we may reasonably allow that the "men of war" were one fourth of the population, for they "increased abundantly, and multiplied, and waxed exceeding mighty, and the land was filled with them." (Ex. i, 7, 9, 20.)

There must, under such circumstances, have been a larger proportion than usual, who survived to mature age. We may, therefore, fairly estimate the population of the Israelites to have been 2,414,200, outside of the tribe of Levi, instead of 3,000,000; and probably 2,000,000 would be still nearer the truth. This is Bishop Colenso's estimate, who has issued several books with an object similar to that of the Colonel.

How many ancestors of these entered into Egypt with Jacob? Excluding Levi and his sons, and even Jacob and his wives, sixty-seven are named. To these we must add the wives of those who were married, according to Gen. xlvi, 26. These wives were at least fourteen in number, probably more, since the same chapter speaks of thirteen who are married, besides the Canaanitish wife of Simeon. Hence we have *at least* eighty-one ancestors of the numbered Israelites, instead of seventy, as stated by the Colonel. In what length of time must these double their number in order to reach 2,414,200 in two hundred and fifteen years? A few days over fourteen years, five and a half months. In fact, if we suppose the time needed for doubling to be fourteen years four months, we shall have the population doubled just fifteen times in succession. Eighty-one multiplied by two, fifteen times successively, gives 2,654,208. It is true, the doubling of a population in fourteen years, five and a half months is a rapid increase, still it is neither impossible nor, under favorable circumstances, improbable. The like has often occurred in the past, and will probably occur again. If these facts had been related in profane history, they would have been readily accepted, as indeed similar facts have been unquestioned. Every one is aware that population is very fluctuating in its rate of increase, and under favorable circumstances it is frequently very rapid. Bullet relates in "Reponses Critiques" that an Island in the South Sea "first occupied by a few shipwrecked English in 1589, and discovered by a Dutch vessel in 1667 was peopled after eighty years by twelve thousand souls, all the descendants of four mothers." (See Card. Wiseman's Science and Religion, Lect. 4.)

These doubled their population in less than every seven years and seven months. This is much more rapid than the increase of the Israelites in Egypt.

It will be seen from the answer which I will give to Bishop Colenso's objection specially directed against the account of the increase of the tribe of Dan, that very large families are not required in order to effect a very great increase, in a wonderfully short space of time. It is quite sufficient that the circumstances be favorable to the lives of children, and that marriages be not delayed to a late period of life, to render the actual increase of a people almost incredible, even with ordinary families. Still a few large families will accelerate the increase very much. Now the favorable circumstances existed with the Israelites in Egypt, since they were specially blessed by God to multiply and fill the land.

Very frequently such large families occur, and accounts of them are to be seen in the public journals. Thus a "Mr. Lemay Deloame, at his death in 1849 had a posterity of two hundred and twenty-five children and grand-children . . . . and on the monument of Rev. Dr. Honeywood, Dean of Lincoln, is the following inscription:

"HERE LYETH THE BODY OF MICHAEL HONEYWOOD, D. D.,
WHO WAS GRAND-CHILD AND ONE OF THE
THREE HUNDRED AND SIXTY-SEVEN PERSONS
THAT MARY, THE WIFE OF ROBERT HONEYWOOD, ESQ.,
DID SEE BEFORE SHE DIED
LAWFULLY DESCENDED FROM HER."

(Pettigrew's Chronicles of the Tombs; also Prof. Hirschfelder's reply to Colenso.)

It is therefore clear that this favorite objection of infidels is futile. Many more proofs might be adduced, but every one is aware that such large families frequently occur, and most of my readers will be able to recall instances which have come within their own observation.

Bishop Colenso, and others before him brought the same objection, but applied it also, as having special force, to the tribe of Dan. Only one son of Dan, Hushim, is spoken of in Genesis, yet in the census recorded in Numbers i, it is said he had sixty-two thousand seven hundred descendants of twenty years of age and upwards. This increase is much greater than that of the rest of Israel. Bishop Colenso maintains that as the exodus was said to be in the fourth generation of the sojourn in Egypt:

"Dan's one son, and each of his sons and grandsons must have had about eighty children of both sexes." (Bp. C. on Pentateuch, p. 168.)

Everyone acquainted with the process of computing Compound Interest, knows that a slight increase in the rate per cent, makes a wonderful difference in the amount after a considerable number of years. Precisely the same principle operates here. A slight increase in the average family in the tribe of Dan would make a wonderful difference in the proportion of that tribe to the rest of Israel in the course of two hundred and fifteen years. We have seen that a doubling of Israel every fourteen years, five and a half months would more than produce the population of Israel in two hundred and fifteen years: so the doubling of the tribe of Dan every twelve years eight months would produce more of a population than is attributed to the tribe in the census of Numbers i.

We may arrive at a similar result in another way. Let us suppose that in the family of Hushim there are *four* sons, viz.: one born every second year, commencing with the third year of the sojourn in Egypt.

Next, let each of Hushim's sons have the same number of sons, four; the first in each family being born when the father is 22 years old, and let the same rule continue till the time of the Exodus. On this very reasonable hypothesis, we shall have the result given in the *Appendix to this chapter.*

From the Appendix it will be seen that on this assumption the family of Hushim would increase much more than is stated in the book of Numbers.

The number of men between twenty and fifty years of age would be 98,615, which is 35,915 more than the number given by Moses.

It follows, then, that the increase of the Israelites in Egypt is neither impossible nor improbable, as Bishop Colenso and Colonel Ingersoll pretend; and since the increase of the tribe of Dan is so readily accounted for, which is much greater in proportion than the rest of Israel, of course there remains no difficulty whatever in accounting for the rapid increase of the whole nation. The assumption of three sons in each family of the fifty sons and grandsons of Jacob, (excluding Levi and his sons,) would give 824,000 men between twenty and fifty years of age at the time of the census. This would leave a margin of 220,450 for deaths.

I said above that if a similar fact to the increase of the Israelites had been related in profane history it would have been accepted without difficulty or question. Since writing those words, and while I was in the very act of writing this argument of which they form a part, I noticed a decided confirmation of my whole statement. It is to be found in the Infidel organ, the "Truth-Seeker," of New York, in an editorial commentary on "The Plenary Council" of the Catholic Church, in session at Baltimore. The editor says:

"The wonderful expansion of the Church's power through increase by *immigration* and the birth rate, has made the Romish organization bold and arrogant. In fifty years it has developed from half a million of believers to nearly eight millions." (Truth Seeker, 29th November, 1884.)

Here is a statement which was being read by thousands of Infidels in the United States and Canada while I was writing on this very subject, and probably by Col. Ingersoll himself. With what sentiments did they read that statement? Did they say with the Colonel, "Every one knows that this is not and cannot be true?" Certainly not. They swallowed it *holus-bolus*, because their organ asserted it, and indeed it is *very near the exact truth*, and is rather under than over the correct estimate. Yet this increase in the Catholic body is *much greater* than the increase of the Israelites in Egypt. It exceeds even the increase of the tribe of Dan, which, according to Bishop Colenso, would require 80 children in every family! According to the "Truth Seeker" statement, the Catholics doubled every 12 years six months, while the tribe of Dan required 12 years eight months to double. Yet there are not 80 children in each Catholic family.

I know that it will be answered, "but there was a large Catholic immigration during that period."

I have not overlooked this fact in what I have said.

I appeal to the experience of every resident of every State in the Union for an answer to this question:

Did Catholic immigration in any year since 1834 equal *one-third*, or even *one-fourth* of the natural increase by births?

The answer to this will certainly be, No. Then I infer that if the families of the tribe of Dan were one-fourth larger than those of the Catholics of the United States, their increase would have been much larger than it is stated by Moses to have been. Where, then, is the impossibility? It exists only in the brains of the Infidel objectors.

"And Moses reckoned up .... the first-born of the children of Israel; and the males by their names, from one month and upward, were 22,273." Numb. iii, 42, 43.

On this the Colonel reasons:

"It is reasonable to suppose that there were about as many first-born females. This would make 44,546 first-born children. Now there must have been about as many mothers as there were first-born children. If there were only about 45,000 mothers, and 3,000,000 of people, the mothers must have had on an average about 66 children apiece." (P. 187.)

We have already seen that 3,000,000 is a grossly exaggerated population. If the population were 2,000,000, the disproportion of the first-born would be very greatly reduced. Now there are several circumstances which contributed to diminish the number of first-born males.

First. Those under one month were not enumerated.

Secondly. When Pharaoh issued his decree for the death of the male children, the destruction must have fallen more heavily on the first-born than upon other male children. There is no means of estimating the number who perished in this way.

Thirdly. It is well known that mothers frequently lose the first child in birth, and yet have large families afterwards. Thus the total number of males would be increased, while the number of first-born would remain stationary.

Fourthly. Where polygamy was allowed, there would be children by several mothers, yet only by one father. In such cases there was only one male reckoned as first-born. Thus Reuben was the first-born of Jacob. (Gen. xlix, 3.) Gideon had seventy sons by many wives. (Judg. viii, 30.) Yet he had but one "first-born," Jether. (verse 20.) David had many sons by many wives. (2 Kings iii, 2, 5. Prot. Bible, 2 Sam.) Yet he had only one "first-born," Ammon. (verse 2.) The first-born had rights of primogeniture which were very important. It was, therefore, necessary that the law should define the first-born accurately, and this is done, Deut. xxi, 15, 17.

Fifthly. The first-born, being the oldest, would often be the first to die.

Taking all these circumstances together, it was to be expected that the number of first-born should be much smaller than the number of families, and as the Israelites "multiplied exceedingly," the families were large. It is therefore a proof of the genuineness of the books of Moses, that in such incidental matters his statements accord with all the circumstances of the case.

APPENDIX TO CHAPTER XLVIII.

CHART

Showing the probable increase of the family of Hushim (son of Dan,) during the sojourn in Egypt. (See explanation below.)

Year of Sojourn.	Sons born. 1st Generation.	Year of Sojourn.	Sons born. 4th Generation.	5th Gen.	6th Gen.	7th Gen.
3	1	85	31			
5	1	87	20			
7	1	89	10			
9	1					
—	—	91	4	1		
	2d Gen.	93	1	5		
25	1	95	—	15		
27	2	97		35		
29	3	99		65		
31	4	101		101		
33	3	103		135		
35	2	105		155		
37	1	107		155		
—	—	·109		135		
	3d Gen.	111		101		
47	1				6th Gen.	
49	3	113		65	1	
51	6	115		35	6	
53	10	117		15	21	
55	12	119		5	56	
57	12	121		1	120	
59	10	123		—	216	
61	6	125			336	
63	3	127			456	
65	1	129			546	
—	—	131			580	
	4th Gen.	133			546	
69	1					7th Gen.
71	4					
73	10	135			456	1
75	20	137			336	7
77	31	139			216	28
79	40	141			120	84
81	44	143			56	203
83	40	145			21	413

The sons born in the following years would be between 50 and 20 years old at the time of the Exodus.

Year of Sojourn.	Sons born. 6th Gen.	7th Gen.	8th Gen.	9th Gen.
147	6	728		
149	1	1128		
151		1554		
153		1918		
155		2128		
157		2128	1	
159		1918	8	
161		1554	36	
163		1128	120	
165		728	322	
167		413	728	
169		203	1428	
171		84	2472	
173		28	3823	
175		7	5328	
177		1	6728	
179			7728	1
181			8092	9
183			7728	45
185			6728	165
187			5328	486
189			3823	1206
191			2472	2598
193			1428	4950
195			728	8451
Totals of each generation,	7	15648	65049	17911

Thus the number belonging to each generation, who at the time of the Exodus would be between 20 and 50 years of age, would be:

Of the 6th Generation,   7
 "   " 7th   "   15648
 "   " 8th   "   65049
 "   " 9th   "   17911

        Total,   98615

This leaves a margin of nearly 36,000 for deaths.

EXPLANATION OF THE CHART.

In the above Chart, the assumed four sons of Hushim are placed under the first generation, in the years of the sojourn wherein they are respectively supposed to have been born, viz.: 3, 5, 7, 9. These four sons would have, in the second generation, sixteen sons, the first of whom would be born in the year 25, two would be born in the year 27, three in 29, four in 31, etc. Thus the numbers of the second generation are deduced from those of the first, by taking successively one term of the first, then two, then three, then four, after which at each step a term at the beginning is dropped; also a new term is taken in, as long as there is one to take in, until the end is reached.

The numbers of the third generation are derived from those of the second, precisely as those of the second are found from the first; so that first one term of the second is taken, then two terms, then three, then four, continuously; and at each step a new term is added, whenever a term is dropped, until there are no more new terms to add.

Each succeeding generation is derived from the previous one in the same manner. Then only those terms which fall after the year 145, down to the year 195, are added together, because these terms represent the men who would be between the ages of 50 and 20 years when the census of the Israelites was taken, Num. i. Thus we see that the assumption of four sons in each family of the tribe would give, under the conditions assumed in the text of the chapter, 98,615 men between 20 and 50 years of age in the tribe of Dan, at the time of the census. This is 35,915 more than the number given by Moses. There is therefore an ample margin for deaths.

CHAPTER XLIX.

THE FLIGHT FROM EGYPT.—THE MANNA.—REFUTATION OF MISCELLANEOUS OBJECTIONS.—RELIGIOUS CEREMONIES.

Under the caption "The Flight," Colonel Ingersoll brings forward a great number of objections. Every circumstance which is at all miraculous, and which is related in the Bible, is a subject for his ridicule. Once for all, we must say we proved in chapter 13 the possibility of miracles. We showed that miracles are the means by which God attests Revelation. An objection which takes it for granted that miracles are absurd, is therefore of no weight whatsoever. It is sufficient that, as facts, they be attested by a witness who was not deceived himself, and who was no impostor. Such a witness we proved Moses to be. (See chapters 30, 31.)

Hence the sneering manner in which the Colonel refers to the burning bush, and the change of Moses' rod into a serpent, is of no avail against our positive proofs of the authenticity and truth of the Mosaic narrative. (See "Mistakes of Moses," page 188.) Hence, also, there is no argument in speaking thus of the destruction of Pharaoh and his host in the Red Sea.

"It hardly looks reasonable that God would take the wheels off the chariots. How did he do it? Did he pull out the linch-pins, or did he just take them off by main force? (P. 213.)

An authentic and true history attests that it was done. There is certainly no impossibility for Infinite

Power to effect this. If the fact was done, it is not necessary for us to know the precise manner in which it was done, and it is folly to ask the question "How?"

God sent manna to feed the Israelites in the desert. They needed food, and as they were under God's special protection, He supplied food miraculously. Surely it is not surprising that there should be certain miraculous circumstances connected with it. (Ex. xvi.) Thus it melted away in the sun; nevertheless we learn from Num. xi, 8, that it could be cooked. The amount gathered was "measured by the measure of a gomor, neither had he more that gathered more, nor did he find less that had provided less." (Ex. xvi, 18.) Other circumstances equally miraculous were connected with it.

Is it a refutation to say "it would be a magnificent substance with which to make a currency—shrinking and swelling according to the great laws of supply and demand?" (P. 215.)

The Colonel adds that there are two accounts which disagree and are therefore unreasonable, and he says they are "grossly absurd and infinitely impossible."

God himself gives to Moses the answer to the Colonel's difficulties:

"Is the hand of the Lord unable? Thou shalt presently see whether my word shall come to pass or no." (Num. xi, 23.)

This manna was first furnished to the Israelites in the month succeeding their departure from Egypt (Ex. xvi, 1:) that is to say, in the first year of their abode in the desert. From Numbers xi, we learn that about a year later the people murmured for meat. God sent quails to supply their want. From

Numbers i, 1, it may be seen that this book commences with the second year of the stay in the desert. The account of the manna and of the quails given in Exodus regards, therefore, quite a different event from that which is recorded in Numbers, and there can be no contradiction between them.

The Colonel further objects that the request of the people for a change of food was a very reasonable one, which should not have been punished so severely. (P. 217.)

The occasion of these animadversions is the statement that on account of the murmurs of the people, "speaking against God and Moses . . . . the Lord sent among them fiery serpents, which bit and killed many of them." (Num. xxi, 5. 6.)

It was the covenant of God with His people that he would shew "mercy unto thousands to them that love me and keep my commandments," but that when they were disobedient he would inflict punishment, even "visiting the iniquity of the fathers upon the children." (Ex. xx, 5, 6.) Even when in His justice He inflicts punishment, His mercy is always eminent.

"The Lord God is merciful and gracious, patient and of much compassion and true, who keepest mercy unto thousands, who takest away iniquity and wickedness and sins, and no man of himself is innocent" before him. (Ex. xxxiv, 7.)

We have already shown that, as God is the Supreme Arbiter of life and death, there can be no injustice in the manner in which he may inflict any penalty, even the penalty of death. (See chaps. 9, 27.) On the occasion of his sending the fiery serpents, he punished not the mere demand for a change of diet, but the speaking against Himself and Moses. His authority over them required a public vindication. However, when they had been sufficiently punished, he supplied a remedy by ordering Moses to erect "a brazen serpent . . . . that whosoever . . . . being bitten should look upon it should be healed." (Num. xxi, 8, 9.)

In Ex. xxiii, 28 and Deut. vii, 20, we are told that God will send hornets to drive away the nations whose possessions God had determined to transfer to the Israelites. We are also informed in Deut. xxix, 5, and in 2 Esdras ix, 21 (Nehemiah) that the "garments of the Israelites were not worn out, nor the shoes of their feet consumed with age." In Num. v, 14, etc., the method of punishment of the unfaithful wife is indicated, and God promises, in a miraculous manner to manifest her innocence or guilt.

What God promises he is able to fulfil. Col. Ingersoll's ridicule cannot lessen the power of God, and the fact that he dictatorially pronounces all these events absurd, cannot impede God's Providence over the affairs of men. (See pp. 219, 222, 223.) We have already sufficiently proved God's power of working miracles. We need not repeat the proofs. We need only add to what we have said already, that many of the miraculous events referred to in this chapter do not require miraculous intervention in all their details. God could make use of the ordinary course of nature to effect much, but when miraculous intervention was necessary, it was not wanting.

The same answer is applicable to many other facts grouped together in the last chapter of Colonel Ingersoll's work, and broadly denied. The Colonel denies them merely because they are miracles. Such are:

"Enoch walked with God and was seen no more, because God took him." (Gen. v. 23.)

"The Lord rained upon Sodom and Gomorrha brimstone and fire from the Lord, out of heaven." (xix, 24.)

"Lot's wife looking behind her was turned into a statue of salt." (Verse 26.)

This "statue of salt" is not necessarily the common table salt. In Psalm cvi, 34 (Prot. Bible cvii) and in Jeremias xvii, 6 the Hebrew word *Melach*, salt is used for barrenness or a salt land. The term is also applied to natron, bitumen, volcanic stones, or to minerals of appearance similar to salt, somewhat as it is used also in English. Josephus says:

"Lot's wife was changed into a pillar of salt; for I have seen it and it remains at this day."

Clement of Rome, a contemporary of Josephus attests also that it was then existing, and Irenæus a century later attests that it was then also extant.

The locality is difficult of access, at the southernmost point of the sea of Sodom, in the wild and dangerous deserts of Arabia. It is on this account difficult to ascertain whether or not it still exists. The accounts given by modern travellers are discordant. We may be well satisfied, however, with the truth of the Mosaic record, the record of a faithful witness who wrote what he knew to be true. God's appearance to Moses in the burning bush and the brazen serpent whose sight healed the bite of the fiery serpents are also miraculous events. (Ex. iii, Num. xxi, 9.) So also are the account of Jacob's wrestling with an angel, (Gen. xxii,) the intercourse of Abraham, Jacob and Lot with God and his angels, (xix; xxii; xxxii,) the blossoming of Aaron's rod, and its bringing forth almonds, (Num. xvii, 8,) and similar events. These circumstances are not to be refuted by mere ridicule or denial. They are well attested occurrences, and have all the force of historic facts related by credible witnesses.

In the case of the trial of a wife for infidelity to her marriage vows, Col. Ingersoll maintains that the promise of God to manifest the guilt or innocence of the accused, "has been the foundation of all appeals to God by corsned, battle, water, fire, and lastly by the judicial oath." These must all be equally superstitious in his estimation. The judicial oath is an appeal to the faith of the person who takes the oath, and is certainly not superstitious. The ordeals of battle, water and fire essentially differ from the mode of trial recorded in Num. v. God makes an express promise that he will intervene by making guilt manifest, under circumstances in which the ordinary laws of nature could not produce the same effect. It is evident that in this case only the guilty could suffer. In the ordeal by water, a supposed witch with her limbs so tied that she could not use them, was thrown into the water. If she sank, she was adjudged innocent, if she floated, she was considered guilty and was burned. Here she suffered whether she was innocent or guilty. There is no resemblance between the two cases. Besides, there is no recorded promise of God to intervene in the case of ordeal by water, but there was such a promise in the trial of jealousy. No reasoning, then, can justify the ordeal of water, by means of the trial of jealousy, and the ordeals of battle, fire, etc., are in the same position as that of water.

The drinking of the water of jealousy was a symbolical ceremony, which had its efficacy from God's promise. The Colonel objects to all religious ceremonies. On this plea he objects to the composition of incense for exclusive use in Divine Worship. He objects to the sacred ointment employed in the consecration of priests, (p. 225,) and to the other ceremonies used on the same occasion. (P. 226.) He ridicules the commandment of God that special vestments should be devoted to the use of priests, made after a particular form, and also to the use of certain articles, as a tabernacle, tongs, snuffers and dishes in the service of God. (P. 226.) To this head also must we bring his objection against the ceremonies used by Abraham in offering sacrifice, (p. 182,) and against sacrifice in general. (P. 268.) All are included under the general name of "Superstition." (P. 26.)

Of course there is no means of convincing one who denies, or refuses to believe, the existence of God, and that religious ceremonies are useful in the worship of God. We must begin with such a one by proving that there is a God, whom we are bound to serve and worship. I have done this by means of a synoptical proof. I must here assume that there is a God, and that we must adore Him. The utility of ceremonies in religion follows as a necessary consequence.

Have men the need of manifesting their thoughts and affections by outward signs? Certainly the whole constitution of society proves that they have. Prostration is a recognized mark of respect and submission. The offering of a gift is an acknowledgment of gratitude. A discourse makes a more profound impression when it is delivered with suitable gestures. The use of exterior signs is rooted in the very nature of man. They are necessary for the preservation of good will among men, and they therefore constitute the very essence of etiquette.

This being the case in the social order, ceremonies are necessary in the moral order also to make man religious. Hence in the moral order, sacrifices were offered by all nations, as offerings to the Gods in acknowledgment of their Supreme Dominion. The same ceremony of sacrifice was retained by the Jews in the worship of the true God for the same purpose. It was not a rite borrowed from Paganism. It was from the beginning recognized as the principal act of Religion, and as such was used by Cain and Abel, and after the deluge by Noah. The Pagans therefore retained it by the tradition derived from the original Revelation made by God to man. The Jews had it from the same source, confirmed by the new Revelation made by God through Moses.

The same reasons hold for the institution of other ceremonies than sacrifice. They have a useful effect in making man more devout, because man is impressed through his senses, in spite of all the efforts of so-called Philosophers to throw off their influence, because this influence is part of human nature.

The Jewish ceremonial laws were intended to keep the Jews firm in their belief in one God, the Creator and Conservator of the universe, the Master of Nature, and also to remind them that He was their Legislator, the Father of civil society, the arbiter of all nature who would reward them for doing good, and punish them for doing ill. Many of the rites were also intended to separate the Jews from other nations, and thus preserve them from idolatry. Some ceremonies were also appointed in memory of the marks of God's special protection.

Thus incense was regarded as the symbol of prayer. The ascent of its perfume upward, signified the efficacy of holy prayer ascending to God; and therefore the Royal Prophet prays:

"Let my prayer be directed as incense in thy sight." (Ps. cxl, 2. Prot. Bible, Ps. cxli.)

Oil is strengthening and nourishing. Hence the abundance of corn, wine, and oil implies constantly in Holy Scripture the abundance of all good things. (See Deut. xxviii, 51; xviii, 4, etc.) Oil was therefore appropriately used in the consecration of priests, to signify that they as the depositories of God's authority, strengthened and nourished the people by teaching them sound doctrine. Hence also to secure respect for these sacred symbols, the people were forbidden to use for profane purposes the particular incense and oil which were intended for use only in God's worship. Disobedience to this law was a crime, and was punished accordingly, because of the disrespect involved in despising God's law.

Special vestments or garments were prescribed for the priests "remarkable for glory and beauty" (Ex. xxviii, 40,) to make the public worship of God impressive, and to signify the authority of the priest officiating in God's name. The different parts of these vestments were all calculated to recall some truth revealed, or some mystery of God's mercy to his people.

I need not enter into details of the mystical meaning of each ceremony employed in the old law. Suffice it to say that there was such a meaning for every ceremony, and the Jews were well instructed on this point. There could be no superstition in the use of such ceremonies, for they were also well instructed in the fact that ceremonial worship is of no avail without the homage of the heart and soul. How could there be superstition in the use of ceremonies which were prescribed precisely to prevent the people from becoming victims of superstition? I will merely suggest the symbolical meaning of some ceremonies used in the consecration of priests, to which Col. Ingersoll takes special exception.

The hands of the priest were anointed to signify the richness of divine grace, which, through the sacrifices he offered was conferred on the people. The priests placed their hands on the bullock's head to signify that the bullock became the victim bearing the sins of the people. The slaying of the bullock was the offering made to God in atonement for sin, and in acknowledgment of God's Supreme Dominion over all creatures. The fat, and the caul, and the kidneys were burned on the altar as a sign that our passions are to be restrained and mortified. The blood of the victim was poured about the altar to signify that God received it as an offering of atonement for sin. The hands and feet and ears of the priests consecrated, were touched with the victim's blood to signify that each of these members of the priest was consecrated to God to gain grace for the people by prayer and sacrifice. (*Cornelius a Lapide* on Exodus xxix.)

Similar symbolical significations will be found in the sacrifice of Abraham, and the waters of jealousy.

In the sacrifice of Abraham, the cutting asunder of the victims denotes the afflictions his posterity, the Hebrews, must endure. The birds that hovered round the dead bodies signify the enemies with whom the Israelites had to contend, but whose power was broken by God's Providence, as Abraham drove away the birds.

"And when the sun was set there arose a dark mist, and there appeared a smoking furnace, and a lamp of fire passing between those divisions." Gen. xv, 17.

It shows a great anxiety on Col. Ingersoll's part to make out a case when he casts ridicule on Abraham's dream or vision. This was not a part of the ceremony performed by Abraham. However, from the fact that the vision is recorded we may infer that it came from God for Abraham's instruction, and that its symbolism was revealed to him.

The Septuagint records that this was a vision: *ekstasis*, verse 12. The smoking furnace implied the hardships of the Egyptian bondage, as in Deut. iv, 20. The lamp of fire signifies the power of God, as in Hebrews, xii, 29.

It was the custom when a solemn compact was made, to pass between the divided parts of the victim sacrificed and the contracting parties invoked upon themselves a similar death if they violated their contract. This custom is referred to in Jeremias xxiv, 18.

In the trial for jealousy, God constituted himself the judge, in order to excite horror for the crime of conjugal infidelity. This is another proof of the injustice of Colonel Ingersoll's charge against the Sacred Scripture that it favors obscenity.

It is quite unnecessary to enter into a defence of the use of a tabernacle, tongs, snuffers, and dishes in the ceremonial of the Jews. Everybody can see at a glance that these were articles needed for the decorum and cleanliness of public worship from the very nature of it as we have described it.

CHAPTER L.

MISCELLANEOUS OBJECTIONS REFUTED.—RITUAL LAWS.—FLOCKS AND HERDS IN THE DESERT.

Similar to the objections against the ceremonies mentioned in the last chapter, are Col. Ingersoll's remarks on the treatment of those afflicted with leprosy.

The Colonel represents the leper's treatment as a mere empty form, under pretence of curing the disease. (P. 236.)

The priest was not authorized to cure the leprosy. He was only to pronounce the cure complete. The medical treatment was finished before he was brought to the priest. Hence the Colonel's account of the case is a total misrepresentation. This is evident from the 3d verse of the 14th chapter of Leviticus, the chapter referred to by the Colonel.

"When he (the priest) shall find that the leprosy is cleansed, he shall command him that is to be purified to offer for himself two living sparrows," etc.

The uncleanness here spoken of, from which the leper was cleansed was the legal uncleanness which was imposed partly for the separation of the leper from the people to prevent the contagion from spreading, and partly because the leprosy was regarded as a symbol of sin, the leprosy of the soul. The running water over which the birds that were offered were killed was more fit than stagnant or standing water, because of its purity, to symbolize purification. For a similar reason the earthen vessel was used. This is the answer to the Colonel's questions: "Why should the bird be killed in an *earthen* vessel? . . . Why over *running* water?" (P. 236.)

'All the Jewish ceremonies had their mystical meaning. Of some, this meaning was not at once evident, nevertheless each rite formed part of a grand whole which taken altogether made a magnificent ceremonial well calculated to impress the beholder with that awe and reverence which he ought to feel when brought more immediately into the Divine presence, by his participating in the rites which had been instituted as part of Divine Worship; and it became more impressive still as the symbolical meaning attached to each rite became known. The some remarks apply to the ceremonial of the Catholic Church to-day.

The following from "Jews' letters to Voltaire," will appropriately close my remarks on the Jewish Ritual.

"Our ritual laws, then, which you look upon as whimsical, did not spring from caprice. They were positive laws, but yet founded in reason, and each had a particular motive, although the distance of so many ages prevents us from knowing them all."

"But to these particular motives a general one must be added, which alone would be sufficient to justify the wisdom of these extraordinary institutions. They all tended to one common end worthy of a great legislator. This was to insure the duration of his people, and the purity of their worship against all the revolutions of time. For this purpose it was necessary to attach the Hebrews very strongly to their religion, and this he did most effectually by the multitude of observances which he laid on them. For as the author of the Spirit of Laws judiciously says, 'A religion which is loaded with many rites attaches men more strongly than one that has fewer. The things which we are continually doing become very dear to us. 'Hence,' he observes, 'the tenacious obstinacy of the Jews.' This is a consideration truly philosophical which Moses had before him, and we are much surprised that a man of your sagacity did not catch it." (P. 188.)

It appears that Moses knew more of successful legislation than did Voltaire or Col. Ingersoll.

The next objection we have to encounter is the difficulty the Israelites must have experienced in the desert of Sinai.

"Where were these people going? They were going to the desert of Sinai compared with which Sahara is a garden. Imagine an ocean of lava torn by storm and vexed by tempest, suddenly gazed at by a Gorgon and changed instantly to stone. Such was the desert of Sinai. All of the civilized nations of the world could not feed and support three millions of people on the desert of Sinai for forty years. It would cost more than one hundred thousand millions of dollars and would bankrupt Christendom. They had their flocks and herds, and the sheep were so numerous that the Israelites sacrificed at one time more than one hundred and fifty thousand first-born lambs. How were these flocks supported? What did they eat? There was no grass, no forests. . . . To support these flocks millions of acres of pasture would have been required." (Pp. 210, 211.)

Why this objection is raised, it is hard to say. We can understand that the Colonel should object to the possibility of the manna being furnished by God, for he denies all miracles, but as we have proved that God can perform miracles, and as it is attested that the Israelities were supplied with manna by a miracle, there is no need of bankrupting Christianity by calling upon it to furnish the Hebrews with food. God supplied it.

But the Colonel says "it did not rain baled hay" for the flocks and herds. Where did you learn that the flocks were so very numerous? There is no such statement in the Bible as that over one hundred and fifty thousand first-born lambs were sacrificed at one time. In Numbers ix, it is stated that sacrifice was offered, but there is no reference to the extent of the herds and flocks. It is natural to suppose that due attention would be paid to the extent of their flocks, and that the sacrifices would be in proportion to the ability of the people to make them. This would in the present case make them the more economical.

It is certain that the Israelites had flocks with them: but there is no reason to suppose that they were so extensive that they could not be attended to, or that there were not sufficient pasture for them. Moses had spent forty years in Madian, in the neighborhood of Sinai, feeding the flocks of his father-in-law, Jethro, (Ex. iii, 1,) so that he knew perfectly the resources of the country, and he certainly would not have permitted the Israelites to bring their herds and flocks if there were no food to be obtained for them; and neither Moses, nor any one of a later period, acquainted with the region, as the writer of the Pentateuch evidently was, (see chap. 29,) would have introduced into his history, even if it were a fiction, circumstances which were incredible.

Through the Sinaitic territory vegetation exists to this day. There are shrubs and trees in the valleys, and moisture is supplied by springs or rain, so that there are places lovely in their verdure and fruitfulness, amid the prevailing solitude and desolation: though the country is only inhabited by nomad tribes. The Sinaitic peninsula was, in the time of Moses, inhabited by Amalekites, Midianites, and other pastoral tribes, depending entirely on their flocks for subsistence. Certainly, then, there must have been a sufficiency of pasture. The sweeping away of numerous forests by fire has contributed to make the land more sterile, and the many centuries that have passed since any care was bestowed upon it have left it to the mercy of the drifting sands and the violence of winter torrents. The same causes which have turned Palestine into a bleak desert, though it was a land "flowing with milk and honey," have operated to make the Sinaitic desert more bleak and desolate than it was originally. At all events, "he that turned the rock into a standing water, the flint into a fountain of waters" (Ps. cxiii, 8. Prot. Bible, cxiv,) could also have caused grass to spring from the earth. The manna was accompanied with dew. That dew undoubtedly contributed very much towards fertilizing the earth. (Num. xi, 9.)

Colonel Ingersoll makes a serious mistake when he says the Paschal lamb must be the first-born. The command is that it should be "a lamb without blemish, a male of one year." (Ex. xii, 5.)

Another misrepresentation is made on page 227:

"God commanded the Jews when they were upon the desert of Sinai to plant trees, telling them they must not eat any of the fruit of such trees until after the fourth year. Trees could not have been planted in that desert, and if they had been they could not have lived."

These directions were given for the time "When you shall be come into the (promised) land:" that is into Palestine, not for while they were in the desert. (Lev. xix, 23.)

Then the Colonel asks:

"Why did God tell Moses while in the desert to make curtains of fine linen? Where could he have obtained his flax? There was no land upon which it could have been produced. Why did he tell him to make things of gold and silver and precious stones when they could not have been in possession of these things? There is but one answer, and that is, the Pentateuch was written hundreds of years after the Jews had settled in the Holy Land, and hundreds of years after Moses was dust and ashes." (P. 228.)

There is another and a more solid answer. Does Colonel Ingersoll forget that "the children of Israel asked of the Egyptians vessels of silver and gold, and very much raiment; and . . . . that they lent unto them, and they stripped the Egyptians"? (Ex. xii, 35, 36: xi, 2, 3.)

The Israelites, therefore, had abundance of these things with them. They received but what was due to them for unrequited labor.

The Colonel says:

"When the Jews were upon the desert it was commanded that every mother should bring as a sin offering a couple of doves to the priests, and the priests were compelled to eat these doves in the most holy place. . . . . There were three million people, and only three priests, Aaron, Eleazar, and Ithamar. . . . There would be at least three hundred births a day. Certainly we are not expected to believe that these three priests devoured six hundred pigeons every twenty-four hours." (P. 230.)

This sacrifice and other offerings, like the rite of circumcision, were instituted for the permanent rule of the Jews, but in the desert these rites were suspended. Like the rite of circumcision, they were not practised until they reached the promised land. Thus circumcision, even, was not practised. (Josh. v, 6.) Neither were the ceremonies of the feast of tabernacles, as prescribed in Lev. xxiii, 39, 44. In fact these ceremonies were impossible in the desert. As to the priests eating the doves "in the holy place," this is a pure fabrication of the Colonel, or rather of other infidels before him. The law of purification is given in Lev. xii. The doves "were delivered to the priest," (verses 6, 8), but there is not a word of the priest being obliged to eat them, either in the holy place or elsewhere.

"Why should a mother ask pardon of God for having been a mother? Why should that be considered a crime in Exodus which is commanded in Genesis? . . . . These laws should be regarded simply as the mistakes of savages." (Pp. 230, 231.)

You refer us for this to the twelfth chapter of Leviticus. Have you not a made a sad blunder, Colonel? Leviticus is not Exodus.

You have also quite mistaken the meaning of the law of Purification. There is no crime attributed to the mother for being a mother, nor was the law ever so regarded by the Jews. The law of purification imposed merely a legal uncleanness, founded on physiological grounds, and the small offering was required from the mother as an acknowledgment of God's supreme dominion over all his creatures and of our total dependence on him.

You say "I cannot believe that Moses had in his

hands a couple of tables of stone upon which God had written the ten commandments, and that when he saw the golden calf, and the dancing, that he dashed the tables to the earth and broke them to pieces. Neither do I believe that Moses took a golden calf, burnt it, ground it to powder and made the people drink it with water as related in the thirty-second chapter of Exodus." (P. 232.)

Your refusal to believe does not make the history impossible or incredible. We have proved that it is related by a truthful historian, and your unreasonable incredulity will not render it untruthful or incredible.

Voltaire asserted that "the most learned chemistry could not reduce gold into potable powder." You probably intend the public to believe that this is the case. I cannot otherwise account for your suggestion that there is an absurdity in the statement.

The chemist Mr. Stahl, and others, give a method whereby gold can be reduced to a "hepar," which, taken in water, is of "disagreeable taste, very like that of brimstone powder." His method is:

"Melt in a crucible three parts of salt of tartar and two parts of saltpetre. Throw in one part of gold and it will dissolve perfectly."

This hepar in water being of disagreeable taste, would be an appropriate means of punishing the idolaters. Learned chemists have also shown that *natron*, a mineral found near the Nile, produces a like effect.

The Colonel next states that there is "another account of the giving of the ten commandments" in Exodus, nineteenth and twentieth chapters. (P. 232.) He adds: "Both accounts cannot be true."

This so-called "other account" is merely the beginning of the history of which Exodus xxxii is the conclusion. This is evident from Ex. xxxi, 18.

"When the Lord had ended these words in Mount Sinai, he gave to Moses two stone tables of testimony written with the finger of God." The commandments were first spoken orally by God, as related in Exodus xix, xx: then other ordinances were given, after which occurred the events related in chapters xxxii, xxxiii, xxxiv.

There is evidently no contradiction here.

The Colonel next accuses God of "cruelty and injustice for inflicting penalties for the violation" of his laws, before the laws were published. (P. 233.)

The laws were published (Ex. xix, xx,) and afterwards they were violated. (Ex. xxxii.) Then the punishment was inflicted. The Colonel has therefore invented a grievance where there was none.

Independently of this, the whole tenor of the history shows that the Hebrews had their laws even before the Revelation made through Moses. This is evident from Genesis xxxviii: so that punishment might even have been inflicted under their earlier code.

The Colonel expresses great sympathy with the Jews inasmuch as God was cruel to them, and that he was "always promising but never performing." (Pp. 237 to 239.) He also says that God did not keep His promises made to Abraham. "He solemnly promised to give him a great country, including all the land between the river of Egypt and the Euphrates, but he did not." (P. 183.)

God's promise to Abraham was expressly made to be fulfilled in his posterity, and in them it was strictly fulfilled. "That day God made a covenant with

Abram saying: To THY SEED will I give this land from the river of Egypt even to the great river Euphrates." (Genesis xv, 18.) The promises to the Israelites were made to the nation, and were fulfilled to the nation. His promise, "I am the Lord who will bring you from the work-prison of the Egyptians, and will deliver you from bondage etc.," (Ex. vi. 6,) was fulfilled to the then existing generation, besides other promises made. The promise to lead them into the land of Canaan was fulfilled only to the next generation, but this was because the former generation did not fulfil their part of the covenant. The promises were fulfilled faithfully as they were made. The promises which were conditional were fulfilled when the conditions were observed. It is a misrepresentation therefore to say that God broke his promises.

We are told that "In the world of science, Jehovah was superseded by Copernicus, Galileo and Kepler." (P. 242.)

None more strenuously than the three great astronomers named would repudiate the thought of "superseding Jehovah." They were all believers in God and His Revelation.

"All that God told Moses, admitting the entire account to be true, is dust and ashes compared to the discoveries of Des Cartes, La Place and Humboldt. In matters of fact the bible had ceased to be regarded as a standard. Science had succeeded in breaking the chains of theology." (P. 242.)

Answer. As Natural Science has for its object the knowledge of nature, of which God is the author, Science is certainly good, and Christianity has not a word to say against it. But the truths which Natural Science reveals to us forms but part of the great body of truth requisite for us to know. The most important science is the science which relates to God and to our salvation. The science of the things which relate to God, or Theology, concerns our everlasting welfare, whereas all others concern only this world. Natural science can, therefore, never supersede Theology. One truth cannot be opposed to another. Mathematics cannot refute historical truth. Neither can Natural Science refute Theology.

CHAPTER LI.

MISCELLANEOUS OBJECTIONS REFUTED.—CONCLUSION.

In the last chapter of the so-called "Mistakes of Moses," the author groups together a large number of objections, mere assertions without a particle of proof. Surely Col. Ingersoll is the one whose apothegm is "Believe and obey: if you reason, you will be excluded from the philosopher's paradise." Compare "Mistakes of Moses." (P. 53.)

Many of the objections of that chapter have been answered in the course of this work. We may now proceed to consider the others.

It is first asserted that many doctrines of the Pentateuch were taught among the heathens. (P. 262.) We already proved conclusively that this would not in the least lower the authority of the Pentateuch. It would only show that Pagans preserved parts of the original teachings of God to man: while the Pentateuch alone preserves these doctrines in their entirety.

Besides among Pagan nations such doctrines are but as grains of gold in a mountain of dross.

The superiority of Natural Science over religion is next insisted on. (P. 263.)

We all know that Natural Science has nothing to do with Morality. We have already shown in chapter 9 that it has failed wofully in teaching Morality to man.

The Superiority of Poetic writers is the Colonel's next theme. (P. 264.)

Are the works of Shakespeare, Burns, Byron, Goethe, Schiller, etc. to become the only moral teachers of mankind? Surely but one answer can be given by the good sense of the community: an indignant negative.

He next enumerates evil doctrines which he declares are taught in the Bible. (Pp. 264, 265.) We have already proved that he is a slanderer. (Chapter 47.)

He objects that the Bible teaches that the sons of God married the daughters of men.

It is a Hebrew idiom to qualify that which is strong great and excellent as of God. Thus Psalms lxxix, 11: Prot. Bible Psalms lxxx: Cedars of God; that is the highest cedars: Lexicon of Gesenius *El:* Cornelius a Lapide on Gen. vi, 2, 4. Hence it is the general opinion of theologians that the sons of Seth, of peculiar virtue are here meant and that they married the daughters of Cain.

"The origin of the rainbow is a foolish fancy" according to the Colonel. (P. 265.)

Has the rainbow, then, no origin? Is there no cause for this grand phenomenon?

Perhaps, however, you mean to say that the Bible gives an absurd origin for the rainbow. A writer whose boast it is that you "could write a better book" than Moses did, should be able to tell what you mean. (See Lecture on Skulls.)

God says: "I will set my bow in the clouds, and it shall be the sign of a covenant between me and between the earth." (Gen. ix, 13.)

We must remember that this passage is a translation from another language. The translator gives the sense, retaining as far as possible the original idiom. If a difficulty appears in translation, it will frequently be dissipated if we interpret it by means of the original. We find that one of the meanings of *nathan* is to constitute, and if this sense be given to the word here, we find a beautiful meaning given to the whole passage: God *constitutes* His bow, to be a sign of the covenant between Him and man. It had existed previously, but it is now made the sign of His peace with the human race. Col. Ingersoll's commentary (p. 164) is, therefore, as absurd as it is ridiculous: "Did God put it in the cloud simply to keep his agreement in His memory?"

We are next told: "Methusaleh did not live 969 years."

The great age of the antediluvian patriarchs is attested by a reliable witness, as we have proved in chapter 30. Col. Ingersoll surely has no more reliable source of information. There is, therefore, no credit to be given to his assertion. The long ages of the patriarchs and their ten generations, precisely, are attested also by the Egyptian, Phœnician, Chaldean and Greek traditions. Undoubtedly, also by the Hebrews the same tradition was held before the time of Moses. There is, therefore, sufficient evidence of the historical fact, and Colonel Ingersoll's denial of it is of no weight.

The Colonel objects to belief in Pharaoh's dreams. He does not give a single reason to show that God may not by means of a dream send knowledge of an event. Dreams are not usually to be credited; but when God wishes to make a Revelation by this means, He will undoubtedly also supply means by which it will be certainly known that the Revelation is from Him.

He objects that "widows were commanded to spit in the faces of their brothers-in-law." (Num. xxvi, 9.)

When we consider that this was only done when the brother-in-law refused to give the widow her just due in accordance with the law, it will be acknowledged that the punishment was not excessive.

Some of the Jews, however, maintain that "*in the face*" merely means "*in the presence*" of the brother-in-law.

The next difficulty is that in Lev. xi, 6, the hare is pronounced unclean, "because it cheweth the cud."

Zoology as a science was not studied in the time of Moses as it is to-day, and the scientific classification of animals was not made. Hence the words of Moses "it cheweth the cud," *mahaleh gerah* must be taken in the sense in which they were used in ordinary conversation, not in the modern scientific sense. A certain muscular motion which is habitual with hares was commonly considered as the chewing of the cud, and was so named, and for this reason it is said that the hare "cheweth the cud."

There are, however, some Naturalists who assert still that the hare is a cud-chewing animal. Valmont de Bomare in his "Dictionary of Natural History," says so positively. This author would scarcely have made so positive an assertion if there were not some good reasons for so believing. However, it must be confessed that this is not the opinion of Naturalists generally.

The Colonel says there "are no four-footed birds." (P. 268.)

In Leviticus xi, 20, we read:

"Of things that fly, whatsoever goeth upon four feet shall be abominable to you." Call them birds if you will: the original has things that fly.

The wings of the *bat* are formed by a membrane stretched on the fingers and arms or fore-feet of the bat: so that the bat corresponds perfectly to the unclean animal described in Leviticus. So universal a genius as Col. Ingersoll should have thought of this. The colugo and the flying phalanger may likewise be included under the description given in Leviticus.

We are next told "one who frightens savages with loud noises is unworthy the love of civilized men."

I would say, frighten off the savages the best way you can.

Many of the remaining objections are mere distortions of the text. To evade detection in this, the Colonel takes care to give no references. This will not avail him. He says that according to the Pentateuch, "God was afraid of wild beasts." (P. 267.)

There is certainly no such statement in the Pentateuch. God declares that he will not drive out the Canaanite from the promised land immediately, "lest the beasts multiply against thee" (Ex. xxiii, 29,) but there is nothing like what Col. Ingersoll asserts. How could it be that God should be afraid of the beasts, whereas he says, "All the beasts of the woods are mine." (Ps. xlix, 10; Prot. Bible, Ps. l.)

The Colonel says: "If God objected to dwarfs, people with flat noses, and too many fingers, he ought not to have created such folks. . . . physical deformity is a crime." (P. 269.)

There is no reproach against deformed persons in the Bible; but for the greater outward reverence in the divine worship, those whose deformities are very marked are not admitted to the priesthood. (Lev. xxi, 20.)

He says: God "objected to the raising of horses."

This is another falsification. God merely lays down the law that when, at some future time, there shall be a king in Israel, "he shall not multiply horses to himself" to take a pride therein, and to push his kingdom by unjust conquest. (Deut. xvii, 16.)

We are told that God "was kept from killing the Jews by the fear that the Egyptians would laugh at him."

This is a gloss for which there is no foundation. It is God's will to be moved by prayer. The true reason for this we can only conjecture. It seems to be because our earnestness of desire is commensurate with the earnestness of our supplications. At all events, Moses prays for his people, and averts God's indignation. Moses uses in his prayer the language that if "God should kill in his anger so great a multitude, the Egyptians will say, 'He could not bring the people into the land for which he had sworn: therefore did He kill them in the wilderness.'" (Num. xiv, 15, 16.)

God yields to the prayer of Moses, and modifies the punishment which the people had brought upon themselves by their stiff-neckedness. It is not stated that he was moved especially by the motive that Moses had put forward. This is a pure invention of Col. Ingersoll.

The assertion that God "wants the blood of doves and lambs" and "the smell of burning flesh," is a mere play upon words. We already explained in what way God is pleased with sacrifice. It is because it is the outward expression of our belief that God is the Master of all things, and that we are totally dependent on Him. HE does not need that we should make this acknowledgment, but we need God, and therefore WE need to acknowledge his Supreme Dominion.

The Colonel next finds fault with God for believing "in witches, wizards, spooks and devils." The "spooks" are a fabrication of the Colonel. Undoubtedly the Scripture does insist upon the existence of spirits, and this is quite conformable with reason. The devils are spirits who have abused their free-will, and have therefore brought upon themselves deserved punishment. Once we admit the existence of these evil spirits, there is certainly no absurdity in believing that there are persons who have communication with them. Col. Ingersoll has not attempted to prove that it is absurd. Christians, however, do not believe *in* witches, wizards, spooks and devils. To believe *in* them is to accept their doctrines, and to put one's trust in them. Christians believe that they exist, but it is reserved to infidels to believe *in* them. It seems to be part of the mission of the infidel organ of America, the *Truth-Seeker*, to propagate belief *in* witches and wizards, (spiritual mediums,) and *in* devils.

To answer Col. Ingersoll has not been my main object in this work. It was my chief aim to furnish to the general reader some plain yet conclusive reasons for his belief in Revelation, and especially in Christianity. In establishing Christianity, it came naturally into my plan that I should answer such objections as are usually made against the Holy Scriptures. In doing this I have made free use of the works of Voltaire, Paine and other infidels: and as Col. Ingersoll has of late years made himself conspicuous in the United States and Canada by his attacks upon the Christian Religion, I have thought it advisable to answer especially that one amongst his works which, I believe, has had the greatest circulation. I could not, of course, quote his entire book in a limited work like the present, but I have taken especial care to state his arguments in their full force, and, in nearly every case, in his own words. Sometimes I have been obliged to condense, but in doing so I have taken care not to put forward his arguments in a weaker form than that in which they are put forward by himself.

I flatter myself that I have answered *all* his objections in such a way that their fallacy is evident. If I have failed in anything the defect is in my advocacy, and not in the cause I have sustained.

Notwithstanding the Colonel's gross attacks upon the Christian clergy, I have endeavored to treat my adversary with all courtesy. My desire was to refute his reasoning without personalities against the individual.

The Holy Scriptures, comprising as they do History, Jurisprudence, Prophecy, Dogma and Morals, have many points of contact with the Sciences. If they were the work of impostors, writing, as infidels pretend, hundreds of years after the dates to which they claim to belong, there would be palpable intrinsic evidences of the fraud. They would not be able to stand the rigid scrutiny to which they have been subjected: but they endure every test without scath.

There are, of course, other objections against the Sacred Scriptures, besides those which have been answered here, but we may assure ourselves that if we are unable to refute them, when we hear them proposed, it is because we are not aware of all the circumstances relating to the subject. Sometimes the difficulty we experience may arise from inadequate knowledge of the original language in which they were written, sometimes from our not knowing sufficiently the history of the period to which they relate, sometimes from erroneous notions of morals or doctrine which we may have acquired, or from some similar cause. Our inability to answer such objections should not be allowed to weaken our faith; for we have sufficient evidence to convince us that the Holy Scriptures contain the doctrine which God Himself has delivered to man. In studying the sciences we are ready to accept the observations of men of learning and experience. We must not hesitate, therefore, to accept with implicit confidence the Word of God who cannot deceive nor be deceived. "We know that his testimony is true:" and "If we receive the testimony of men, the testimony of God is greater." (1 Jno. v. 9.)

In conclusion, I desire to express my thankfulness to friends who have given me access to their libraries, or otherwise encouraged me to the writing of this work. Especially I return thanks to the Rev. P. Corcoran, P. P., of Parkhill, Ont., for valuable suggestions and other encouragement given to me during its progress.

www.ingramcontent.com/pod-product-compliance
Lightning Source LLC
Chambersburg PA
CBHW022106290426
44112CB00008B/574